A True Child
of Papua New Guinea

A True Child of Papua New Guinea
Memoir of a Life in Two Worlds

MAGGIE WILSON

Edited and with additions by Rosita Henry

McFarland & Company, Inc., Publishers
Jefferson, North Carolina

LIBRARY OF CONGRESS CATALOGUING-IN-PUBLICATION DATA

Names: Wilson, Maggie, 1953–2009, author. | Henry, Rosita, editor.
Title: A true child of Papua New Guinea : memoir of a life in two worlds / Maggie Wilson ; edited and with additions by Rosita Henry.
Description: Jefferson, North Carolina : McFarland & Company, Inc., Publishers, 2019 | Includes bibliographical references and index.
Identifiers: LCCN 2019009039 | ISBN 9781476677033 (paperback : acid free paper) ∞
Subjects: LCSH: Wilson, Maggie, 1953–2009. | Racially mixed women—Papua New Guinea—Biography. | Papua New Guinea—Biography. | Ethnology—Papua New Guinea.
Classification: LCC DU740.76.W55 A3 2019 | DDC 995.6/5 [B] —dc23
LC record available at https://lccn.loc.gov/2019009039

BRITISH LIBRARY CATALOGUING DATA ARE AVAILABLE

ISBN (print) 978-1-4766-7703-3
ISBN (ebook) 978-1-4766-3542-2

© 2019 Rosita Henry and the Estate of Maggie Wilson. All rights reserved

No part of this book may be reproduced or transmitted in any form or by any means, electronic or mechanical, including photocopying or recording, or by any information storage and retrieval system, without permission in writing from the publisher.

Front cover image: Maggie Wilson, Mount Hagen, circa 2009; *background* Morning view from Maggie's house, Kunguma Village, 2009 (both photographs by Kanawi Danomira)

Printed in the United States of America

McFarland & Company, Inc., Publishers
 Box 611, Jefferson, North Carolina 28640
  www.mcfarlandpub.com

This completion of her memoir is dedicated to the loving memory of Maggie Wilson, who was known as Tilgil ("undo the knot") among her clanspeople, due to the texture of her hair and because they thought she was destined to smooth the way between two worlds.

Table of Contents

Acknowledgments • Rosita Henry ... ix
Prologue • Maggie Wilson ... 1
Editor's Introduction • Rosita Henry ... 3

1. Birth and Belonging ... 9
2. Tribal Threads: The Elti Penambi ... 15
3. Entwined: Law, Life and Land ... 24
4. Kuta Ridge: The White Man's Station ... 32
5. My Village Childhood ... 39
6. Off to School ... 47
7. My First Return ... 54
8. Life with the Leahys ... 60
9. Australia in the 1970s ... 70
10. Picking Up Threads: Back to PNG ... 78
11. Motherhood: Bernadine ... 83
12. Working Woman ... 93
13. Tying the Knot ... 97
14. A Village Baby: Olivia ... 102
15. Here Comes Maki ... 112
16. The Gift of Nadia ... 122
17. Weaving Threads: Women and Politics ... 129
18. Making Pictures ... 142

Table of Contents

19. Friendship Bonds: Haus Poroman • Rosita Henry — 153
20. Mending Breaks: Haus Krai • Rosita Henry — 169
21. Reflections: Tying Up Loose Ends • Rosita Henry — 179

Chapter Notes — 197
References — 204
Index — 207

Acknowledgments

Rosita Henry

It is for me a great privilege—indeed, a joy—to have been able to work on this book with the blessing of Maggie's husband, Keith Wilson, and their children, Bernadine, Olivia, Maki and Nadia. I acknowledge the family's invaluable assistance in helping me conduct the research, for warmly opening their hearts to me and for allowing me to work in the wonderful home that Maggie built in her village above the town of Mount Hagen in the Western Highlands of Papua New Guinea. I can imagine neither a more conducive place to have worked on this book nor a place more strongly infused with her spirit.

The research to complete Maggie's memoir was conducted under the approval of the James Cook University Human Research Ethics Committee (approval number H3460) and all interviews were conducted with informed consent. Maggie's husband and their children all shared their memories in interviews, as did Olivia's husband, Denis Doyle. I am especially grateful to Bernadine and her husband, Kanawi Danomira, for their caring hospitality during my many visits to Mount Hagen. Bernadine spent innumerable hours with me in thoughtful discussion about her mother's life and her own experiences growing up on her beloved mountain at Kuta Ridge, while Kanawi generously contributed his photographic skills.

I am grateful to Father Garrett Roche for his insights and for facilitating access to relevant records held at the Catholic Mission at Rebiamul. Maggie's faithful, long-time friend and business partner in Hotel Poroman, Elizabeth Pora, shared her memories and generously provided support. Lois Logan kindly spent hours with me recollecting life in Mount Hagen and her friendship with Maggie during the 1980s. I also particularly acknowledge Bob Connolly, Thomas Aripe, Barbara Kauga, Arolyn Kawa, Nori Kupal and Pint Kupal for their reminiscences.

Thomas Las, Maggie's younger brother, proved to be an outstanding

Acknowledgments

research assistant and I am especially grateful for his help as translator and cultural mentor. I also thank Maggie's other siblings from the Tugl family—Councilor John Kawa, Kuipa, Pora, Prul, Poning, Tali, Lauie and Rita—, members of her wider Wia Ulgamp Komp lineage and all the residents of the Kunguma and Knep villages, who make up the Penambi Wia clan of Maggie's father Kuan and the Melka people on her mother's side.

I am also deeply grateful to Maggie's many relations on the Leahy side. I especially thank Joe Leahy, Jim Leahy, Gerry Leahy, Bryan Leahy, Margaret Duckworth (nee Leahy), Nancy Leahy, the late Clem Leahy, Rhona Leahy, and George Leahy, who all very warmly and generously gave their time and shared with me their memories of Maggie.

I owe a debt of gratitude to my husband, Bob Henry, and my children, Roselani, Rurik and Rafaela, for their unfailing support and encouragement. I thank my son Rurik for drawing the diagrams, my daughter Rafaela for her editorial work, my nephew Ryan Wirth for his help with a photo, and my sister Rosemarie Rusch for her company during some of the fieldwork and for her help with procuring the maps. I also thank my many anthropology colleagues and friends who, over the past ten years, provided comments on papers that I presented on my research for this book, especially Michael Wood, Barbara Glowczewski, Daniela Vàvrovà, and Shelley Greer. I also thank Alan Rumsey for the contribution of a photograph taken during his fieldwork in the Nebilyer Valley and Simon Beams for, at the last minute, facilitating the creation of the sketch-map of Kunguma Village by Jennifer Vetali, through his company, Terra Search. A special thank you is owed to anthropologist Almut Schneider, who, in 1999, while taking a break from her doctoral fieldwork in the nearby Tambul district of the Western Highlands, stayed with Maggie for a few weeks at her tourist lodge in Kunguma Village. Never one to miss an opportunity, Maggie sought Almut's advice and they spent some time together developing a structure for her book with the help of Almut's friend Isabelle who was holidaying with her. Almut kindly met me in Paris and gave me a copy of the draft of the manuscript that she and Isabelle had begun to edit, which provided a valuable reference point. Finally, I acknowledge with gratitude the kind advice of Layla Milholen and the team at McFarland for their excellent editorial, design and production work—Lisa Camp, Natalie Foreman, Dylan Lightfoot, Sandy Lemly and Robin Bauguess.

Prologue

Maggie Wilson

I have always wanted to write about my life but now that I sit down to do so there doesn't seem much to say. Yet, something urges me to write down what I can. So here I go into the dimmer paths of a wonderful world. I don't recall a single dull moment.

Maii na ul gupa imnga oujepa pilem. Sure, life is full of mysteries and surprises. It's the ups and downs that make living worthwhile and it's amazing that in spite of our many differences, we human beings have only one inevitable destiny: to die. The pressures of life are as real in one culture as in the next, whether it is my tribesmen building a fence to keep the pigs out, or a Western country building a nuclear warhead for defense. All that sweat and pain for an individual existence that rarely exceeds a hundred years. Life is so short. It is a pity that nothing can be done about this even with all the knowledge in the world.

I am tempted at times to pray to the creator for an extension just a while longer to see my way a little more clearly and to understand life a little bit more. Instead, I will not question existence; existing I am, and forever grateful that I have been placed in a unique situation where I have insights into two equally wonderful worlds during only one lifetime. "Why me?" asks one part of me, while another part asks, "Why not?"

This is the story of my life. When I am slightly confused, a part of me asks, "But who isn't?" and when I am down, another part of me rekindles my being. When I cry, a part of me laughs from the distance of my inner self. I simply am. At times life seems worthless. Yet I feel that every moment and every person I have come into contact with is precious. This is why I feel a great need to write it all down. Perhaps in a way I am writing it for myself rather than for you, my reader. I don't know; I haven't written the book yet.

Prologue

Ana mong kai marr oujepa ku pelim. It's true, life is full of good times, and if we didn't have the bad times then we couldn't possibly appreciate the good. Being a tribal and working class woman has its ups and downs but I take it as given. My life is all I have. I am happy and want to share it with you. Be my guest.

Maggie Wilson, Mount Hagen, c. 2009 (photograph by Kanawi Danomira).

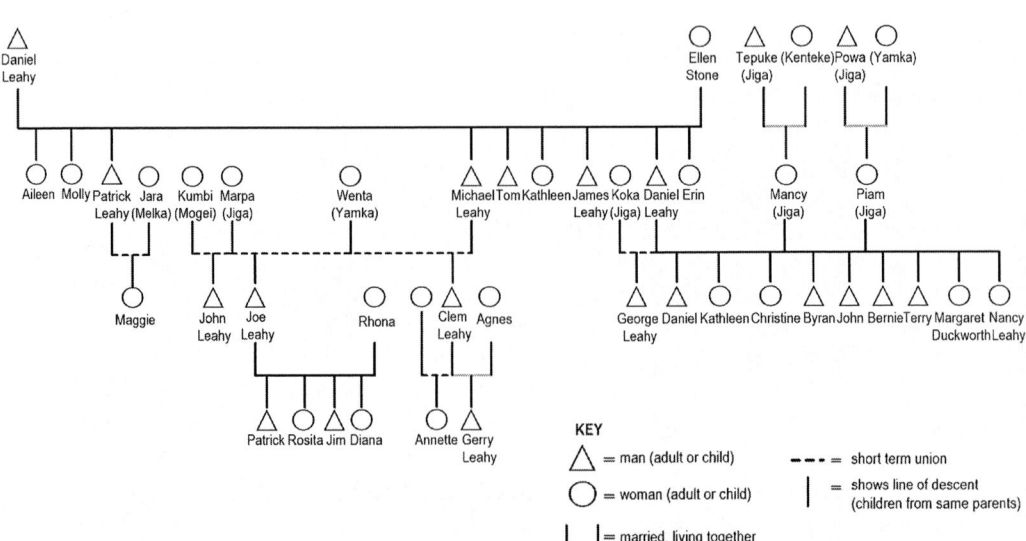

Maggie's family tree—the Leahy side (drafted by cartographer Jennifer Vetali. Reproduced with the permission of Terra Search Pty Ltd, Townsville).

Editor's Introduction

Rosita Henry

Maggie Wilson passed away suddenly in her sleep on 6 April 2009 at her home in Mount Hagen, Western Highlands Province, Papua New Guinea. She started her memoir in 1996, but she was able to work on it only intermittently. Maggie gave me the manuscript to read in January 2000, hoping that I would be able to help her finish it. I deeply regret that I was not able to do this while she was alive.

Maggie and I shared most of our teenage years living at a Catholic boarding school in the far north of Australia (Mount St. Bernard College in Herberton, North Queensland). Maggie and I shared an identity as "PNG girls" at the school and we quickly became fast friends, coping with homesickness by swapping stories of our families back home. I was born in Australia but my parents had moved to Papua New Guinea during the 1960s to live and work; Maggie Leahy was the true child of PNG. While her biological father was Australian, she was born to a Western Highlands woman in a village near Mount Hagen and her stories of growing up in the village fascinated me.

This book consists of Maggie's unfinished manuscript, only lightly edited, with additions based on memories related to me by members of her family, her wide circle of friends and especially her Penambi Wia clanspeople from Kunguma Village near Mount Hagen.

Maggie wanted me to help her with her memoir during the time I stayed with her in 2000 and 2001 while conducting research on the impact and reception of the films *Joe Leahy's Neighbors* and *Black Harvest* but, sadly, we did not get very far. I was preoccupied with my own research project and Maggie lived a life so full that she had little time to write about it! Her memoir was to remain a work-in-progress.

After her funeral, Maggie's daughter, Bernadine, gave me a copy of the manuscript as we sat grieving on the veranda of Maggie's house overlooking Mount

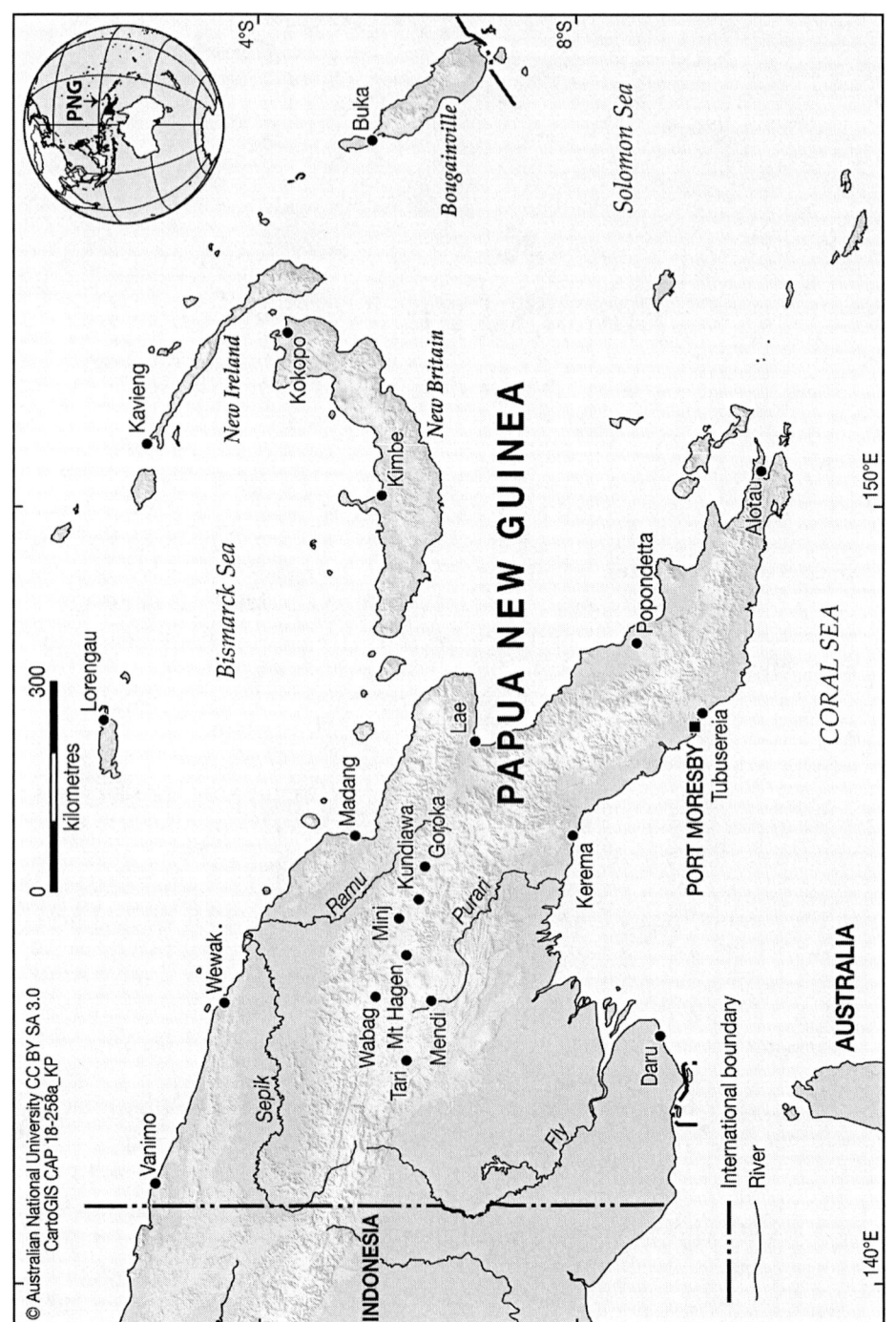

Editor's Introduction

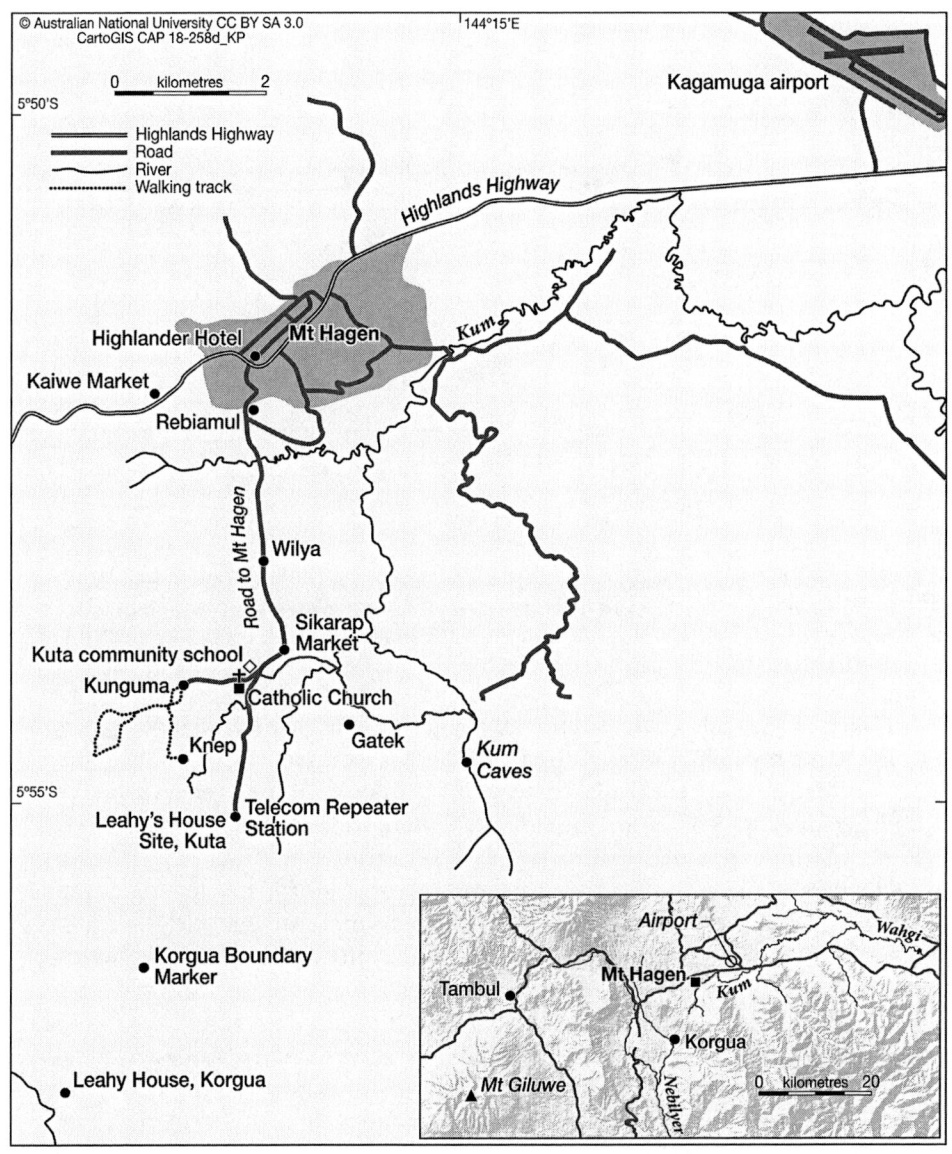

Above: Map showing Mt. Hagen, Kunguma Village, Knep Village, Kuta, Korgua and some other place names mentioned (reproduced with permission of CartoGIS Services, ANU College of Asia and the Pacific, Australian National University).

Opposite: Map of Papua New Guinea (reproduced with permission of CartoGIS Services, ANU College of Asia and the Pacific, Australian National University).

Editor's Introduction

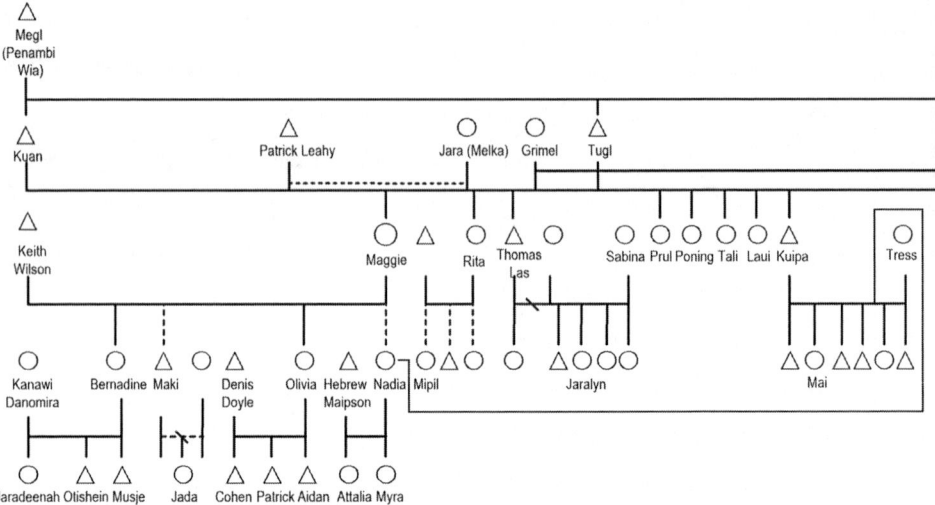

Above and opposite: **Maggie's family tree—the Penambi Wia side. This diagram excludes most of her kin not directly referred to in her memoir (drafted by cartographer Jennifer Vetali. Reproduced with the permission of Terra Search Pty Ltd, Townsville).**

Hagen in the valley below. Remembering that nine years earlier Maggie had asked for my help, I offered then and there to complete it for publication.

Maggie had planned 22 chapters for her book. Of these, she wrote something for only 18 of them. The earlier chapters are quite well polished, revealing the influence of a course she took on creative writing, while the later chapters are much shorter, with some consisting of just a few paragraphs written in a matter of fact style and others no more than a title.

Out of respect for Maggie's voice, I have only lightly edited her writing. I have inserted some footnotes, photographs, maps and genealogical charts to assist readers and have also added a reflective piece to each of her chapters based on my ethnographic research and interviews with her family and friends.

Unfortunately, Maggie never managed to write anything about Haus Poroman, the tourist lodge she built in Kunguma Village, although a chapter title indicated that she had planned to do so. I have constructed this chapter (Chapter 19) mostly from my own memories of visits there and from ethnographic interviews. I have also added two other chapters about events that occurred after Maggie's death. These events reveal the complex web of relationships that Maggie wove during her lifetime, which have continued to have vital significance since her death.

Editor's Introduction

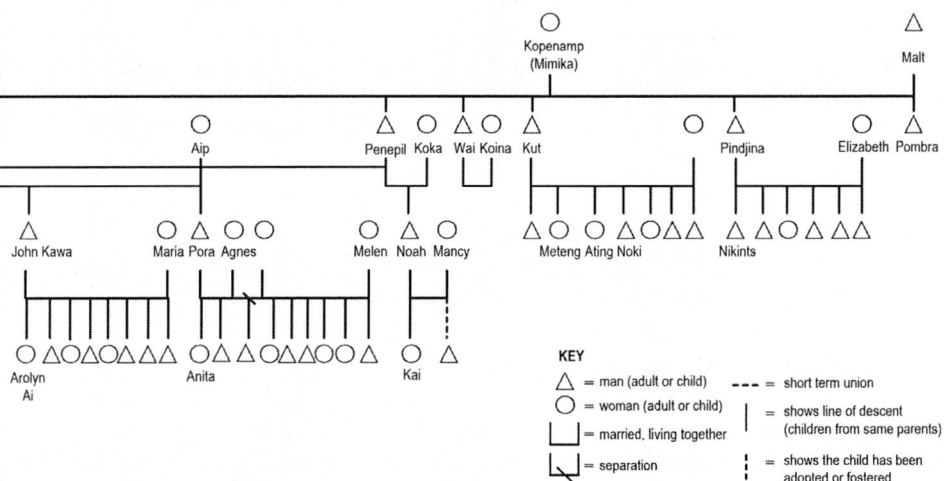

Maggie occasionally includes words, phrases and sentences in her first language (*tok ples* in Tok Pisin). The *tok ples* that Maggie grew up speaking belongs to a single language continuum classified by linguists as Papuan, East New Guinea Highlands Stock, and Chimbu-Wahgi family. Mount Hagen people divide themselves into speakers of Melpa, Temboka and Kowul (A. Strathern 1971: 6). Maggie was a speaker of Temboka, which is spoken in the Nebilyer Valley, on the Kuta Range above the town of Mount Hagen and by groups elsewhere who have migrated from these areas. The orthography that Maggie used to transcribe *tok ples* utterances is her own. I have not edited these but left them exactly as she originally wrote them.

All poems in the book are also Maggie's, published here for the first time.

Maggie's book began as her autobiography, but it is now partly a biography. In the process of writing it, the book has also become my own story in some ways. Nevertheless, while I have effectively become a co-narrator with Maggie, I have tried to avoid becoming the dominant voice.

To honor our abiding friendship, and because it was Maggie who encouraged me to become an anthropologist in the first place, I have completed her manuscript by weaving into the story an anthropological interpretation of cultural matters where it seems appropriate. Thus, in terms of genre, the book might best be identified as an "ethnographic biography." This is what Michael Herzfeld (1997) termed his book about his friend, the Greek novelist Andreas Nenedakis. According to Herzfeld his study is "neither a literary biography nor an ethnography, but fuses elements of both." Unlike most biographies, his book "is less concerned with the personality of the central character

Editor's Introduction

than with the significance of his life and times for the tangle of intersecting social worlds" (Hertzfeld 1997: 1). Similarly, while Maggie's memoir is indeed revealing of her personality, it also concerns the tangle of intersecting social worlds in which she was involved. As Herzfeld (1997: 1) writes, "[t]he tactic of ethnographic biography allows us to move along the trajectory of a life that has bisected many histories and of a person who has dwelt in many communities rather than staying (as most conventional ethnography does) within a single place." Herzfeld's anthropological interests helped him to understand how Andreas negotiated "the engagement of his cultural background, his sense of tradition and value, with the encompassing enormities of his times" (1997: 6). Working on Maggie's memoir has brought me to a similar understanding. As her cousin, Gerry Leahy, put it, "Maggie was interested in people from all over the world and in what they did. She probably never realized that she was herself an interesting concept to other people. Maggie was a unique person, part of the first generation of a historical occasion."[1]

While I was conducting the research for this book, doing fieldwork in Maggie's village, I realized that much of what her kin related to me were tales that Maggie had told them. Their accounts of Maggie's early life not only included stories based on their own memories of events; some were part of a stock of stories that Maggie had shared with them, and that she reproduced in writing for this memoir. Maggie has assembled narratives about her early life that have taken on mythical qualities and these continue to be re-produced and circulated by those who knew her in their "narrative practices" (Gubrium & Holstein 2008).

Maggie's memoir is a collective narrative. It is the product of the narrative practices of all of her family and friends who continue to keep her memory alive through retelling the tales she once told them, interpreting the dreams they have had of her since she passed, and raising her name again and again at public events.

Thus, while on the one hand this book can be read simply as a memoir, it can also be read as a complex "narrative ethnography" involving the interplay of many life stories, not only Maggie's and mine, but the numerous other people "whose lives and worlds are in view" (Gubrium & Holstein 2008: 251). Their reflections about Maggie provide insights into what it means to live and love in Papua New Guinea today.

1
Birth and Belonging

The strap of Jara's *bilum* (net bag) pressed across the top of her head under the weight of her load. She had collected many things during the six months on the white settlement. Patrick Leahy was a hard man but a kind and generous person with his traders. He gave special items to those he liked. He liked Jara and gave her lengths of colorful fabric, mirrors, beads and other items. The best gift he gave her though was not in the hand woven *bilum* she carried on her head but in the *bilum* inside her. The best gift of all was growing in her womb.

Jara smiled to herself, "At last, I will be a mother. At last, Kuan will have his child." She looked at her husband confidently striding ahead of her on the narrow track through the rainforest. She could almost detect a spring in his step. After six years of marriage, she had borne no children and this had come between them. The love of her youth had become poisoned by resentment, particularly after Kuan, assuming Jara was barren, took another wife; but, she was also fruitless.

Kuan brooded over his misfortune for a long time until he arrived at a novel solution. He had heard of boys with red skin and soft hair born to highland women in neighboring tribes. Perhaps he and Jara could also get a son from the white man. Jara was reluctant and fearful at first but Kuan persuaded her with the promise of a child. His scheme worked and now he was triumphantly leading her back home. She would have liked to stay longer but they had to leave before the white man detected the life that was secretly growing inside her.

I don't know if Jara, my mother, smiled. I wasn't here then.

The white men, who had arrived in the highlands twenty years earlier, were the Leahy bothers, Michael and Daniel. Michael left but Daniel established a gold mine and settlement at Kuta Ridge. He hired his brother, Patrick Leahy, as a carpenter to oversee the building of his house. Patrick was a rabble-rousing, hard-drinking man who was already over fifty years old but had never married. He conspired with the highland men working at the mine to find him a woman. Kuan plotted with his clansmen to supply Patrick with Jara. They told Leahy that Jara was an unmarried woman.

Although it was Kuan's idea, it did not sit well with him. The whole time his wife was at the settlement, he stayed there, sick with misery. Yet, he was convinced that his suffering would be worth the reward. A child, touched by the spirit of these powerful white men, would give Kuan power and wealth, but mostly it would give him a much longed-for child.

Some of his clansmen thought that he was just pretending to be ill so he had an excuse to stay at the settlement medical post near Jara. Was he worried she would not return to him? Perhaps he was afraid he would lose the brideprice he had paid to her kin? What was it about the power of the whiteskins' spirit that led him to make such a sacrifice?

I don't know; I wasn't here then. I only know what my elders have told me.

Kuan and his brothers dreamed of having many children to recreate the Penambi Wia clan after the terrible tribal war that had almost destroyed them. Kuan, as the eldest, felt particularly responsible for rebuilding their *haus man* (patriline) but he had remained childless. Now they prayed to their ancestors for Kuan to be blessed with at least one child. What a risk he took to get that one! But his plan had worked and after six months of worries Jara was going to have a baby, a powerful, special baby.

The village elders told me that Kuan had triumphantly announced to everybody, "At last I will have a child. Oh, Ancestors, please let it be a boy. I need a son." They told me that as soon as Kuan knew my mother was pregnant, he set off with her for the village. If the white man discovered that Jara was carrying his child, would he let her go? No sense in taking any chances.

Through the rainforest, they walked surefooted on the wet, slippery track to the village. Above, a bird of paradise gave its piercing morning call. Raindrops on the leaves brushed against their faces and hair. In the peace of the rainforest their thoughts moved to the future and to happiness.

It must have happened like that, I imagine; I was not there.

My mother's co-wife, Grimel, my grandmother (my mother's mother) and Kuan's brother's wife, Koka, attended my birth. My aunty Koka told me that my father had sent for her around 6:00 p.m. after my mother went into labor. When she came to the birthing hut, my grandmother and Grimel were already there. While Grimel and Koka were busy getting ready for my birth, making fire for light and heat, making sure that the baby *bilum* they had woven for me was ready and comfortable, my grandmother gathered leaves

1. Birth and Belonging

from the *kukul* tree. They laid them near the fire, to make them dry, warm and soft for my bed in the *bilum*.

My father was very impatient, shouting for news of my birth. He was waiting to call out to the whole village that my mother had given birth. His edginess made Koka very nervous. Kuan urged his brother, "Tugl, go to the birthing hut and find out what is happening!"

"Go yourself," his brother said, squatting down with him beside his fire.

"I've been there, but the women got annoyed with my calling out and sent me away."

Koka told me that my mother seemed to be in labor for an eternity and that my father had paced back and forth. In the end, the entire village was anxious for the baby to be born so that my father would stop bothering them. Yet, they understood and tolerated his disturbances because it was his first child. They even called on the spirits to ensure a safe delivery.

My father had done all he could to assure that I would be healthy and male. He had even sent *ma* down to the river with the women so they could rub her growing belly with water. Women's hands, wet with the clear river water, had massaged and shaped the baby into correct form, two arms with fingers, two feet with toes and all the parts that make up a well formed baby.[1] Kuan had also insisted that *ma* spend time with Koka, who had borne a son a few months earlier, as it is known that a woman who has given birth to a son can influence the sex of an unborn child to lean towards male. He had done all he could. Now he could only wait and see. Between his pacing, he sat brooding and drawing pictures in the dirt, his mind bouncing between a happy future with a son and the worries of the moment. Jara's groans and cries of pain unnerved him. Many village women had died during delivery, along with their babies.

Koka had only just borne her first child, Noah, and Grimel was completely inexperienced, but my grandmother was older and wiser. She assured Koka and Grimel that everything was fine and urged *ma* to push hard, so the pain would soon be over. Grandmother kept repeating, "Just think, a baby in your hands." *Ma*, groaning and moaning, murmured, "Oh mother, I can't bear this much longer."

Grimel took out a long bamboo container of water and said, "Here Jara, have a drink."

"Sister, you must be crazy, can't you see I'm in no position to drink; I am dying! Drink the water yourself!"

Then Grimel started to mumble to the *bore-kore* spirits, "Oh, all you dead spirits make the mother and baby well. I will convince Kuan to kill the biggest pig in the house for you spirits."

My grandmother remembers that she cut my cord just after nightfall. When Kuan heard the news, he came rushing into to the birth house. Grimel screamed at him, "What do you think you are doing? You men are forbidden to enter this women's house." Kuan replied, "I just want to take a quick look at my baby, I don't mind at all that she is a girl. I thank you *pugwa*, God. Oh how I have longed over the years to hear the sweet cry of a baby." My grandmother said, "Kuan, indeed you have the spirits on your side; it is a strong, healthy baby girl. Just wait until we settle her in the *bilum* and pass her out to you for a look. Grimel, put some more *pitpit* grass in the fire, so that I can see what I am doing!"

I was there but I don't remember this.

Koka bravely held out the crying, struggling baby to Kuan, saying, "I am sorry it's a girl and she has such a funny color." Kuan hesitated for a moment and then took me in his arms. He may have been disappointed but he held me under his armpits, as I wriggled, perhaps unhappy with the cold night air and the need for food. This was my first contact with my *wutta*, my father, as he lovingly brought me into the warmth of his body. "I don't care," he said, tenderly looking at the squirming new member of his clan. "She's a gift. We'll kill pigs to celebrate and honor our ancestors."

I was born on 28 December 1953,[2] the first and only child of Kuan and Jara Megl, and also the only child of Patrick Leahy. I was christened Magdalene Veronica Megl by Father Ross,[3] the priest at the Catholic mission at Rebiamul, but my mother's brother, Kerowa, named me Wakapa after a cute golden-brown tree possum. The name Magdalene is not a traditional name, but then I was not a traditional child.

The women by the river did indeed shape me into a healthy child, but my two strong feet were to be set in two cultures. My two eyes would see through two different lenses, my two hands would work in two eras. I was born to have a life woven from two ways of thinking, two sets of religious beliefs, to wear two hats and play the part of both male and female in my society. I am a mother and I am the only woman in my tribe whose place is beside the men on the *singsing* ground. I fought for this position, which only a few women are privileged to have.

Reflections
Rosita Henry

I sat pouring over Maggie's manuscript at a roughly hewn table in the meetinghouse at Haus Poroman, the tourist lodge that she had built on her clan land in Kunguma Village, on a mountain ridge above Mount Hagen. It was 11 January 2000 and Maggie had invited me to read the autobiography she was writing. Although Maggie had visited me a few times in Australia and we kept in touch through letters and phone calls, 25 years had passed since my last visit to Papua New Guinea. During that trip in 1974, I stayed with Maggie at her Uncle Dan Leahy's coffee plantation in the Nebilyer Valley. I was 18 years old and had just completed my first semester at the Australian National University. Entranced by the lectures of Professor Anthony Forge, who had done fieldwork among the Abelam in the Sepik area of Papua New Guinea, I had eagerly taken the chance to spend the midterm break with Maggie, to experience for myself some of what I learned in his first-year anthropology class. As we hugged goodbye, I naively promised Maggie that I would soon return as a fully-fledged anthropologist. But life was to take us in other directions.

Reading the first chapter of Maggie's manuscript, I felt a warm sense of intimacy with the characters. These people were familiar to me—Maggie had told me stories about them when we were homesick teenagers at boarding school in Australia. She had especially shared her treasured memories of her *wutta*, Kuan. While I listened to her with fascination back then, I had neither understood the web of relationships into which she was born nor fully recognized the cultural differences that Maggie's stories revealed. Informed by the rich ethnographic literature on the highlands of PNG, her stories carried new significance.

Kuan was not Maggie's stepfather, as I had imagined him to be when she first told me of him so many years ago. To appreciate the nature of the relationship between Kuan and Maggie requires knowledge of Western Highland beliefs about conception and parenthood. Conception and the healthy growth of a fetus results from repeated acts of sexual intercourse until about the sixth month of pregnancy, when the child acquires its spirit (*min*). The fetus is a combination of blood from the mother's womb (*mema*) and the father's semen (*kopong*). *Kopong* translates as "grease" or "fat" and its ultimate source lies in the land. After being born, a child grows by ingesting breast milk and food that contains *kopong*, the "fat" of the land. It is the *kopong* from the land on which a woman lives and works—her husband's land—that contributes to the growth of her child and links it through shared bodily substance to its patrikin. In other words, "the *kopong* of the land is transformed through human reproductive and productive labor into human corporeal and social life" (Henry 2013: 275).

Thus, in terms of highlander cosmology, Kuan was not Maggie's stepfather but her father, and she was his legitimate daughter and a member of his clan, the Penambi Wia. As Marilyn Strathern (1972: 43) notes, even if a child is initially conceived of another man, if a woman has a husband "he is undisputed pater, and for all intents and purposes genitor."

Marriage involves an exchange of brideprice[4] between the kin of the groom and the kin of the bride. A young man will generally depend on his father, elder brothers, or his mother's brother, if he is living with him, to help raise the brideprice (which traditionally consists of pigs and shells, rare oils, possum, cassowaries, salt and other valuables). If he can raise the brideprice, a man may marry more than one woman. As Maggie writes, Kuan had two wives, Jara and Grimel. While the relationship between some co-wives is relatively amicable and supportive, Hagen people typically characterize the co-wife relationship as one of jealousy, rivalry and competitiveness (M. Strathern 1972: 52). However, a co-wife will frequently assist at childbirth, as Grimel did at the birth of Maggie.

I continued to read Maggie's manuscript until the gathering storm clouds of the late afternoon sent me scurrying back to the house Maggie had allocated me at the lodge, a roundhouse constructed of bush materials—woven walls and a roof thatched with *kunai* grass. Haus Poroman Lodge consisted of a cluster of such huts with footpaths leading through carefully tended gardens to a large building constructed of the same bush materials and featuring a kitchen, dining room and bar. A big open fire built on a platform in the center of the room, around which guests would gather before and after dinner, warmed the building.

In addition, the lodge complex included a dormitory style building designed for backpackers and the meetinghouse where I read Maggie's manuscript and where she ran Tok Pisin classes for Japanese Volunteers abroad (JICA). By establishing Haus Poroman in her home village, Maggie had created employment for many of her kin, not only from her father's side, the Penambi Wia, but also from her mother's side, her uncles and their offspring, who had settled in Kunguma Village and the nearby hamlet of Knep.

2
Tribal Threads: The Elti Penambi

Na eltika penamb ampael. I am an Elti Penambi woman. We are members of the Penambi Wia sub-clan. I grew up knowing that in the past we were fearsome.

Nanga yambu ing napille kar mourling. You, my ancestors, were great warriors. We were notorious for potent raids on neighboring villages, taking all their possessions. We killed men and took land, women and pigs. Our tribe's continual raids infuriated the other tribes and eventually their combined forces brought about the downfall of our great power as fierce fighters. There are still tribal fights among my people today. A part of me thinks we are wild and primitive.

Yet, we do not always fight. The fights are among some tribes while others continue their daily activities: hunting, making new gardens, building houses, raising pigs and crops, negotiating new ties through marriages and conducting funeral services. Even the fighting tribes have time for peace. After some years of fighting, there is always time for feasting and peacemaking. We do not need some other culture to tell us how to be peaceful.

The missionaries arrived: Bang! "We are right and you are wrong." How dare these strangers tell us that our tribal fighting is wrong when they instigated two world wars in the last fifty years? It's true, I am proud of our warriors, just like the French are proud of Napoleon or the Australians are proud of the convicts.

My people know when to fight and when not to fight. There is nothing wrong with our way of life. It is balanced. *Ulg imma pora kanda kanda mint tep mourll.*

The incident that sparked the final battle for my tribe was when we picked a fight with the Mogeis, our closest neighbors and only friends at the time. According to my father, Tugl,[1]

It happened when some of our tribesmen went to watch a tribal fight between the Jigas and Mogeis, and one of our Elti men was killed accidentally. It was at his funeral feast that one of the Mogei men was spitting.

In our tradition, as you know, it is wrong to spit at something and it is considered to be very offensive. Even today this is for me an unbelievable insult. We had just buried him a few days ago and he hadn't even had time to decay! How dare he do this! *Kolgamp nekem*!

His actions were provocative and surely he must have known what effect this must have on us, the deceased's tribe. "Perhaps he's happy that one of our Elti Penambi men has been killed," everyone at the funeral started to whisper.

As time passed, more and more people heard this and said how disrespectful it was to spit and that he should not get away with such behavior. Some people said he wanted to be insolent. Because of this, and only this, one of our Elti men went and killed a Mogei man. That was it.

After that, every clan wanted to see the end of the Elti Penambi. The Mogei joined forces with the Kopi Nogopurs, Truka Mamikas, Pilga Paragas, Tona Wipakas, Jiga Yamkas and Ulga Oupukas. According to Tugl, the final battle occurred four crop cycles, or years, before the arrival of the white man. This would make it the late 1920s. The combined forces of the six thousand or more warriors did not give our five hundred Elti Penambi men a chance for survival; all our warriors were killed and our women and children were scattered over the Wahgi and Nebilyer valleys, where we are living today.[2]

My father Kuan was the eldest surviving child of our lineage in the Penambi Wia subclan at about thirteen years old; he had four younger brothers, Tugl, Wai, Penapil and Kut, who was the youngest at only two or three years old. Their father, Megl, had died of natural causes two crop cycles before this war but their mother, my grandmother, was killed during the war.

My father, his brothers and other Penambi Wia were taken in by a faraway tribe called the Melkas, which was my grandmother's tribe. The tribe raised my father and his brothers, married them to daughters from several different subclans and sent them back to Kunguma in the 1930s with the hope that they would repopulate the nearly extinct Elti Penambi tribe.

Some of the Melka women did just that. Melka Amp Niranga,[3] who was married to Wia Angimp Mek, had three sons. Melka Amp Mare, also married into the Wia Angimp subclan, had two sons. Melka Amp Arknakumba had three sons. And Jara, my mother, who remarried into the Penambi Wia after Kuan died, had two other children with Kuan's younger brother Tugl—my sister Rita and my brother Thomas Las. These four women took part in regenerating the Penambi Wia clan as it is today. We are now around 500 people.

They also gave birth to some daughters who, apart from me, have given strength to other clans.

Reflections
Rosita Henry

Maggie's brother, Thomas Las, was translating *tok ples* sentences in Maggie's manuscript for me when he offered to tell me a story about how during the tribal war in the 1920s Kuan and his brothers had escaped and found shelter with the Melka people.

> It is more or less a legend about this spiritual guidance being, Mugl Timbil, who lived up at Mt. Bul (Mugl). The story is very well known. He used to live up there and our fathers say he was half human and half spirit, because he had a human face and body from the front and when he turned his back he had trees and ferns growing from his back. If he turned his back, you could not recognize him; he just looked like a rainforest, but when he turned around you could see that he was human.
>
> At times, he would come into house to get the leftover dinner, to eat the *kaukau* [sweet potato] left from the night before for breakfast. Sometimes he would lick men in their private parts while they were asleep and they would get up and feel that there was something and he would just quickly jump out of the house and go away. He would play tricks on people. During the war times, he would help the tribes in many ways.
>
> At one time, I heard a story from my last-born father, Kut, about the time they were chased out and they were about to leave the land at Kuta and go down to Kembia where my grandfather (my mother's father) was. Most of their land had already been taken by the enemy tribes. Everybody moved up to one place, a village right next to Kuta, and all the men met and said, "We have come this far and our land has been taken. What should we do and where are we going to go? Or should we stay and fight?"
>
> All the men brought a pig each and they decided to bring the pigs to the top of Mt. Bul, where Mugl Timbil lived, to look for spiritual guidance. They brought the pigs there and made a *mumu* but they couldn't see anyone. They slaughtered the pigs, got the rocks to get the *mumu* done and made the *mumu* pit and still there was no sign. Then one of the guys got up and said to the rainforest, "We have been chased out. Our land has been taken and we are about to go. We have just come here to make our last decision about where we [are] to go and who is going to be friendly with us and take us in. We are lost and that is why we are here. We think that you are still living here so we have come to you to direct us in any way possible." And still there was no sign.

So one of the guys climbed up to Ku Kitl, a big tall rock up there. The mountain is Mt. Mugl or Bul and the rock is called Ku Kitl. He was sitting there looking around thinking, "Where are we going to go?" Then he saw a little sign from the smoke. The smoke rose and then it went from the south side to Kuta and straight down to Kembia where my grandfather, Kentmel, used to live.

He called out, "Hey, you guys, I think I have just seen something," and all the guys rushed up to the rock and asked, "What is it?"

"Well Aundige Mugl Timbil, the spiritual guide, has not said anything to us but I can see that there is something happening. See the smoke from the cooking of the rocks? It is rising and making a direction towards Kuta and down to Kembia side. I think that is where we should go." Everybody agreed. They said that Mugl Timbil was giving them the direction and if they went there they probably would be saved.

So when the *mumu* was cooked and taken out they left some there for Mugl Timbil and took some back to where the women and children were at the village next to Kuta. They ate the meat and that same night they took the long trip down to Kembia.

The next day, all the Mogei tribe, all the enemy tribes, came up. Every place was empty. There was no one there. They came up to Kuta and when they went to the village, the fire was still hot but there was no one there. So they followed the track[s] and they went right down to the Pelga tribe (the Pelga and the Melka tribes are neighbors).

My tribe had passed the Pelga tribe and they were going towards to [the] Melka tribe, when the Mogei and other enemy tribes caught up with them and killed many people, including my father's mother, my grandmother.

Kut was a little boy. His mother said, "Look the enemy is getting near so you go. Just leave me here and you go," but the kid did not want to leave his mother. He ran a few meters and when he looked back, he could see the enemy killing his mother, so he went ahead. From there my grandfather Kentmel of the Melka tribe took him and his older brothers in as new friends. Kut told us this story and that he saw his own mother killed.[4]

Thomas and I later walked through the drizzling rain to Wia Kut's house, on the road above the village *singsing* ground. Along the way, we gathered three of Kut's sons who were hanging out at the small village trade store and *fun haus* that one of them owned. Their father was the last of the five brothers who had escaped the 1920s tribal war and later returned to Kunguma to reestablish their patriline on their own clan land.[5]

Western Highlanders organize themselves principally in terms of patrilineal descent, tracing their clan membership and ownership and inheritance of land through their fathers. Upon marriage, women customarily move to their husband's clan land. However, a woman can also choose to remain on her own clan land and negotiate with her father and brothers for permission for her husband to live there with her, as Maggie did. In such cases it is common for the offspring of the couple to become assimilated into their mother's clan. Thus, Maggie's children grew up as Penambi Wia and have been assimilated into the clan as agnates, in line with the "well known ability of Highlanders to absorb non-agnates—and even non-'kinsmen' into agnatic groupings" (Merlan and Rumsey 1991: 43). As "co-resident matrifiliates," Maggie's children are recognized as "equivalent to people whose affiliation is based on a paternal tie" (Merlan and Rumsey 1991: 70).

I was eager to meet with Wia Kut to ask if he might share his memories of the tribal war and what he knew of the history of the Penambi Wia people. In particular, I was interested in the way Western Highlanders organized themselves in terms of paired tribes and subclans, so that at the highest level the Elti and Penambi were joined as Elti Penambi. This tendency toward pairing occurs not only in relation to the segmentary group structure but also in many other aspects of social life. It is a "special idiom" which people use to indicate alliance relations (A. Strathern 1972: 223). Hermann Strauss, a Lutheran missionary who worked for many years in the highlands between 1936 and 1971 (Hays 1994), provides insights regarding this concept, which he refers to as "complementation" (Strauss 1990; first published in German in 1962). Each segment of a group is paired with another segment of the same order. Thus, the Elti and the Penambi are referred to as Elti Penambi *ragl* ("the two of them"). As Strauss (1990: 11) notes:

> In my opinion this is not a principle—not even a "male and female principle"—but a vital experience of the need for complementation, of the way in which all things, living and dead, require something else, a complement of fulfilment, without which the individual being is "out of its place" or "out of line," is removed from the center of things and unfulfilled.

Wia Kut was sitting at the fire in the center of his house when Thomas and I entered with Kut's three sons. The frail old man warmly welcomed us into his house and urged us to gather around the fire on the matted floor. I commented on the small cassowary that I had noticed outside in a wooden cage. Kut's sons explained that they were planning to include it in a gift they were accumulating for an upcoming bride price exchange.

Wia Kut did not speak English and very little Tok Pisin, so I asked Thomas to explain the purpose of my visit, after which Kut immediately launched into a narrative that bore no interruption. I noticed that his sons listened with avid interest, but since he was speaking very fast and in Temboka to boot, I couldn't understand a word! There were no pauses to allow Thomas to translate, so all I could do was wait patiently, nodding encouragement until Kut was finished. Thomas then translated from memory as best he could:

Before the big tribal war in the 1920s, the Penambi Wia used to live on land at Wilya,[6] towards Hagen town, and at Kump, near Kugulwe, where Maggie was born. So, the Penambi Wia from Wilya were also known as the Wilya Wia.

The first Wia were two hunter-gatherers travelling together. One stayed at Kump, the neighboring land to Kugulwe. The other left his boar behind at Kump and travelled up to Kugulwe. Kugulwe was a big forest then with big Pandanus trees growing and there were lots of wild cassowaries and possums and birds. So he hunted and he kept all his cassowaries and possums as he moved upwards. Before he moved on he built houses to shelter the cassowaries he had caught, to keep them there so he could come back and collect them later. So we were called *teg turugl apetegl, em pa tegl*.

When he turned up at Kunguma, he did the same. Where Kunguma is now there was a big forest then. He hunted and caught all these cassowaries, possums, and birds. He did the same as he did in Kugulwe and built houses and kept the cassowaries there and then he moved on. He moved up the hill and down towards Wilya and as he reached Wilya he saw it was very fertile land and the forest was very thick. There were big Pandanus trees and there were many cassowaries and possums, so he felt that he would not move any further but would make a camp there and stay for a while.

The Paraka and Wakapa tribes lived at Rebiamul and a Paraka man and his wife and daughter

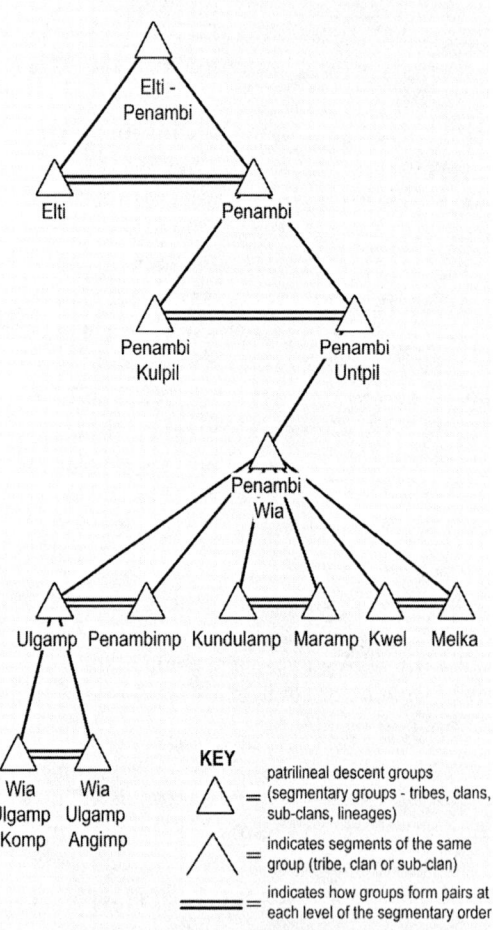

The Elti-Penambi segmentary group structure, illustrating the system of pairing of groups. Maggie was a member of the Wia Ulgamp Komp lineage of the Penambi Wia (drafted by Jennifer Vetali. Reproduced with the permission of Terra Search Pty Ltd, Townsville).

saw that there was smoke coming up at Wilya. The father decided to leave his wife and daughter behind and go to investigate who had made the fire, because they knew that there had never been anybody there before. When he arrived at Wilya the father saw all the possums that had been caught. There were some cooked ones and there were some live ones. He also saw many cassowaries in cages. So he thought, "There must be someone here. I will find out who he is."

The Paraka tribesman saw that this man had made a lot of gardens; cut up the bush and made heaps of gardens and he was making fire to burn down the logs to plant food. Then the Paraka man saw the Wia hunter and asked him if he had any seeds to plant in his garden, but the Wia man said he did not have any seeds.

Wia Kut, Kunguma Village, 13 September 2009 (photograph by Rosita Henry).

So the Paraka man went back to Rebiamul and told his wife and daughter that he had seen this man who had made lots of gardens and had cooked a lot of cassowaries and possums. He brought back cooked cassowaries and possums to his wife and daughter.

The next day he returned with his wife and daughter bringing *kaukau* seeds, *pitpit*, and all the other food seeds for the hunter to plant in his new gardens. When they arrived, more cassowaries and possums had been cooked and there was no one else to eat them, so they were fortunate to have a lot of meat while they helped the Wia man plant the gardens that he had worked on.

Then the Paraka man decided that his daughter should marry the Wia man who was doing gardens there. So Wia Kangelt[7] came back up to Kunguma, got his cassowaries, and went down to Kump and got his cassowaries and his pig and brought them back to give to the girl's father and mother as brideprice.

They got married and the Paraka woman gave birth to three sons. The first son was the Penambimp, the second the Kundulamp, the third the Maramp. These are the small tribes of the Penambi Wia today, the Penambimp, the Kundulamp, the Maramp, and the Ulgamp, who was the originator himself, the father of the sons. That's how the Wia tribe came to be.

When his three sons grew up to become young men the father told the

Penambimp to take the Kantal range; he told the Kundulamp to take the Ketelkemp Klekimp range and he told the Maramp to take the Kikepe range. He told them to take these mountain ranges individually, to form their own tribes.

The father, the originator, put up this little spring for people to go and drink. It is still there. I saw it when I was young. My sons have seen it too. He also cut up a special tree. He brought a cutting to Togoba and planted it there. I saw that growing into a tree, when I was a child.

I don't really know where the father came from before he was at Kump. He probably came down from Tambul hunting and gathering and moved down to the Nebilyer Valley, across to Kump, lived there for a while, moved up to the Kuta range and down to Wilya, lived there for a while, got the girl, and that's how we, the Wia, originated.[8]

After saying farewell to Wia Kut, Thomas and I wandered back to Maggie's house. Kut's narrative had left me with much to muse over. He had related a story of a traveling ancestor, one of two brothers, who had founded the Penambi Wia and allocated them land. According to Kut, the traveling ancestor first settled at Wilya, close to Hagen town, where the Mogei people now live. They were dispersed from there and surrounds, including the mountain ridge at Kuta, during the big tribal war that Maggie describes.

In his account Wia Kut also refers to a particular tree from which the "father originator" took a cutting, planting it at a place called Togoba. I wondered about the significance of this tree. Was Kut perhaps referring to the *mi* (divinatory substance) of the Penambi Wia? Thomas later told me the cutting was from a tree called Pulung, the wood of which they used for making handles for spades and tomahawks. Although I had never heard Thomas or any of Maggie's kin refer to *mi*, I had read about this concept in the ethnography *One Father, One Blood*, where Andrew Strathern (1972: 36–41) provides an exegesis of a myth told to him by Kawelka Ongka. Ongka relates how his people, the Kawelka, settled their territory in the Hagen area. It struck me that Kut's story had very similar elements.

Hagen ideas about *mi* fascinated me and I wondered what the *mi* of Maggie's clan might be. I mentioned the concept to Father Garrett Roche from the Catholic mission at Rebiamul when visiting the mission seeking information on Maggie's life. Father Roche generously lent me his copy of *The Mi-culture of the Mount Hagen People* by Hermann Strauss (1990). Focusing on the Hagen concept of *mi*, which refers not only to a divinatory plant, animal or thing (such as a stone), but also to the hidden ancestral power that resides within it, Strauss presents a brilliantly insightful understanding of social organization among Hagen peoples.

Instead of using the terms "tribes," "clans" and "lineages," Strauss uses Hagener terminology, referring to tribes as "seedlings" (*mbo tenda*) and clans as "part seedlings" (*mbo kats*), thus stressing the significance of their idiom of growth and fertility and the concept that people themselves are seedlings "planted" in particular places. According to Strauss, each tribe or "seedling" is believed to have "another half," its *mi*, which makes it whole, and members of the same "seedling" form a "blood community" with their *mi* and call it "brother" (Strauss 1990: 16–18). Strauss stresses that *mi* has both a protective and a legal function. It is used as a "prohibitory sign"; for example, a *mi* sign might be planted somewhere as "a sign of ownership" to let people know that property has been stolen from a place and that compensation is being demanded. To evoke one's *mi* is "the equivalent of swearing an oath" and to invoke the *mi* while lying "has the same consequences as perjury" (Strauss 1990: 20). In other words, *mi* is a customary law concept about the hidden power that ties people to one another through life and land.

3
Entwined: Law, Life and Land

I was born twenty years after my tribe's first association with the outside world, beyond the hills and valleys of the Western Highlands. The white men, as missionaries, gold prospectors and coffee growers, had begun to show my people a different way of life. The old ways were still strong, but they were now in competition with new ways.

A rapid transformation had taken place among all the tribes and the newcomers, the white men, experienced equally swift changes. My tribe at this time was still fascinated by the Westerners and their sophisticated modern technology. My people wondered, "Are they God's own relatives or are they spirits of our own dead. How are we to know?"

One thing was certain: They were a terrifying force. This was obvious in the weapons they carried—the power of the gun compared to the power of the bow and arrow; the ageless stone axe against the steel axe; the sharp steel knife in contrast to the bamboo knife. My tribesmen were eager to learn from the white men their way of doing things, as it was much faster. You could cut building materials with the steel axe in two days whereas it might take two months with the stone axe.

My first encounter with a steel axe came after my tribe got paid for our land at Kuta with salt, mirrors, knives, kina shells and axes. Only some senior members from the tribe got the axes as they were rare essentials and in great demand. My Uncle Kerowa, my mother's brother, received one of these axes. His son Tep used to be very possessive over this axe. When I asked to use the axe, he would always reply, "This axe is not your father Kuan's axe." All of us children wanted to have a go at cutting something with the axe but he never let us use it. I thought Tep was incredibly mean because he would not even let his older sister Maipang have a go.

One misty morning I heard the axe in use and followed the sound to where Tep was cutting a banana tree. I could not resist the temptation to use it just once so I tried to pull the axe from him. He pulled back, we struggled for a while, and then the axe fell and cut my foot. Blood was spurting everywhere. I screamed in pain and Tep too began to cry because he was so scared. Uncle Kerowa came running out of the house and slapped him. He thought he had cut me on purpose. My uncle carried me into the house, blood dripping everywhere. My *wutta* heard me crying and came running to Kerowa's house. When he saw the blood, he took it and put it all over his face. My *wutta* buried his face in my wound and cried, "Who did this to my girl?"

Kerowa offered to pay compensation for the loss of my blood and killed two pigs for the spirits to ensure that the foot would heal quickly. My *wutta* crushed some plants and placed them on my foot. He covered the wound with big leaves that stick like plaster and each day he changed the dressing. The cut healed within a couple of weeks, but to this day I still have the scar on my foot. Clearly, the goods that my tribe were paid for our land were highly valued at the time.

These first years of European colonization were times of tranquility, of peace, of a mutual fascination between two cultures meeting. Once I saw a photograph of my Uncle Danny Leahy's young, glowing face and breathtaking smile. He was showing mirrors, dolls, and cloth to Hagen women, who, curious and overwhelmed, looked at them with bright eyes. I could not help thinking, "How wonderful it must have been to be a woman at that time." I imagine that my Uncle Danny would have enjoyed all those women running after him at his gold mine at Kuta Ridge.

I remember one morning when I was two, three or four years old, waking at dawn with my head resting peacefully on my *wutta*'s warm arms under the cover of a *pandanus* mat. Gently removing his arm and placing my head on the wooden pillow, he called out to my *ma* and his other wife, Grimel, asking if they were ready to join the other women on their way to work at the white man's station. The household was already up and the fire in our hut was blazing. Still half asleep, I got up and cried, "I want to come with you, *ma*!" My *wutta* made a soothing sound, "Sshh, sshh," and carried me out of the house. I hugged his neck and rested my head on his shoulder, clinging to him in total contentment as he urged me to listen to the singing. Through the canopy, the northeastern sun sent out its golden early morning rays, creating magnificent light strips and dark shadows over the vast mountain country. The birds, flying from tree to tree, seemed to sing and flap their wings in unison with the women's song. Slowly the singing faded away into the distance. The words of the song roll over and over again in my mind:

> *kuk wena pengla*: On the pretty head dress
> *dagl gnukl pengla*: On the long precious bark skirt
> *kona kot monum*: There is a drop of rain

koneri neri: Do not rain
hunta mull¹ kwi pigrotep: Hunta's ageless rock being carried away
wile wamp wia: Whilst doing this Wilya Wamp
kanda rut denam: With a cane put his feet down
hik nui nangi-ha: Don't be cross
kumbol dri neri: Don't fight
wang wang dampoa ialgo wia: Slowly but surely the job shall be done
waipa wia waipa iwaipa ialgo wia: Chorus

What the white men said became gospel, no questions asked. What white people had was what we wanted. If we had to work very hard to get it, that was not a problem. Hard work was nothing new. My people had toiled the land since time began and they were very proud subsistence farmers. Now, however, for the first time, they worked hard for completely different aims. On the one hand, they worked for the obvious material things, axes, salt and kina shells, and on the other hand, the people worked for something that they could not quite comprehend, the law. Who is law? What is law?

Men, women and children went to work building medical centers, roads and bridges and planting coffee alongside the newcomers. Keta, one of my tribeswomen, told me that these times were hard times and when all her pretty and special traditional clothing got spoiled she got mad with these strange men but did not dare say anything. Keta said that all of the women just went on working, wondering why these strangers had come here with their mean ways. Women would hide under trees and behind tall *pitpit* grass to feed their babies since the *bosbois*, the white men's offsiders, would belt them if they caught the women not working. Some *bosbois* even beat women to death and pushed them into the rivers. They made sure that the work the *kiaps* [colonial government officers] wanted done was done. Most women would leave their babies at home, as they had to work in the river carrying rocks all day and never had breaks. Keta said that these were the ways of the *kiaps* and the thing called "law." The women did not even have the time to cook their sweet potatoes properly. They were told repeatedly that something called "law" was coming soon and that other white-skinned people would follow the "law" into our valleys. Our tribes were told to build the roads quickly using their traditional digging sticks. Some of the men would join the women and carry river gravel for the roads. The people even built an airstrip by hand.

For budding young Western entrepreneurs there was no shortage of land. I have an image in my head of these young, ambitious Australians, plodding up the Wahgi valley, eyeing our fertile territories. After all, they could buy all they wanted with their kina shells, salt, mirrors, knives and axes. Land was an all-important item at the time, and still is. Many tribal conflicts had occurred over land, but the colonial administration came and purchased land from the tribes. My people and our neighboring tribes sold a part of their land, known as Kuta Ridge (about 600 hectares), to my uncles Mick and Danny Leahy. The land was vacant after the Elti Penambi tribe was defeated in that great tribal war of the 1920s. Since Kuta Ridge had been sold, my tribe resettled the space in the areas surrounding the Ridge when they returned to their land.

The colonial administration ensured that land bought by the white men was sizable and they often justified the purchase by saying that it was nobody's land, as the tribes had vacated it due to tribal conflicts. Yet, according to our custom, land disputes are settled by exchanges of goods and valuables, so that people eventually return to reclaim their land or come to some agreement as to who should be the new owner of the land. Sometimes this is an occasion for a big *moka* exchange.[2] This process involves the gradual building up of friendships among tribes and individuals over several years. At first, we make friendly gestures by exchanging garden goods and then we exchange pigs and other things of value, such as feathers for body decoration. Today we mainly exchange cash and pigs.

The common land on which tribal fighting took place and which was left vacant until disputes were resolved was seen by the colonial power as nobody's land. This so called nobody's land all over the Highlands of Papua New Guinea became the white man's land and the newcomers busied themselves with planting acres and acres with coffee trees, building their youthful dreams into the plots. Coffee in the highlands today is known as green gold. When the *kiaps* asked the villagers to help plant these coffee trees, they were excited to do so and to see this new wealth grow. They did not know anything about coffee but they took the administrator's word for it, that these trees would bring prosperity. The bright red cherries signified wealth, like the *omak* sticks hanging down a big man's chest.[3] The *omak* is the measurement of a man's wealth displayed for all to see—the longer the *omak*, the richer the wearer. It was an impressive sign. The white men realized this and relied on support from those who wore the longest *omak*. These men became the white men's intermediaries, relaying and ensuring their message got through to the people.

Since Independence, most of the plantations have been sold back to the local people and some of our tribes people have become very rich and successful business people. It is a good thing indeed that the customary landowners who worked to set up the plantations for very little were eventually able to retrieve their land as well as the products of their own labor. Yet, this achievement would have been impossible without the knowledge of the white men—the steel, the investment. What value would coffee have without a plane to export it?

At the time of Independence, roads, medical centers, schools, towns and airports were already established, but now they became our responsibility. Today I cannot switch on the television or the radio without having to listen to problems related to land in this country, be it land for a school, a road, a medical center or a telephone-radio receiver station. The original landowners feel cheated out of their land. Yet, what we received for the land was of high value at the time. Steel by far saves a lot of time and painful labor. Today we pay 69 *toea* for 500 grams of salt but before the white man came we had to get a kind of salt that came from Kawidl, a long distance away, and it passed from hand to hand before any of it finally arrived here.

But where is the money of our land going? Where is the money from our copper, gold, oil and trees? It is certainly not going into education or transport, certainly not into the medical or communication systems. Perhaps this is why customary landowners are increasingly disrespecting the law and the original contracts for the sale of their land, and are trying years later to get more and more money for their land. We used to have our own land laws, a system of compensation, the meaning of which was to stay in a relationship with the new owner for a long time in order to profit mutually from the exchange.

Once in the mid-1980s I had to be the law. It followed an evening of drinking and partying with men in high political and financial positions. A woman was raped while I was asleep in the next room and in the morning asked for my help. What should we do? According to tribal law, we could demand compensation from the man and his clan for the family and the woman's clan. A share of the compensation would then be given to the victim, who would have nothing to say in the negotiations. I had to weigh this up against what I knew of the Western law—the pride and good name of a woman against a man with his political and social power. Even if she could "win" in court, she would still be the loser. A woman is treated as if she is the guilty one, cross-examined to see if she might have "asked for it."

We opted for another solution. I went to see the men personally and called on them to account for their actions. Finally, after three weeks of private meetings and discussions, the men admitted their guilt in front of me and the victim and agreed to compensate her directly. Did we do the right thing? I am still not sure. A few years later, I was invited to talk to a gathering of politicians and others about women and the law, which forced me to reflect seriously about the way that I had responded to this crime against women:

Today I am asked to speak about women and law from a lay person's point of view and as such I find it rather difficult to define law. Therefore, I'd like to start by asking questions. What is law and what do we expect from law? The law is a set of rules to safeguard the welfare of all people and their interests and we women expect the law to protect us, treat us fairly, ensure our equal rights and provide solutions to our problems.

But often women are disillusioned with law, because law doesn't always provide solutions to our problems. I know many of you here have both positive and negative encounters with the law, be it customary, criminal or civil law. Sometimes decisions made by our courts are biased, depending on sex, class and race. Therefore, it is very important for us women to understand that law can help us as well as harm us.

We must also understand that most of the existing laws are made by human beings who are mostly men and these laws are enforced by human beings who are also mostly men and who are insensitive to the needs of women and can make mistakes. It's very important for us women to be involved in the making of laws and in the enforcement of laws. It is also equally important for women to have enough knowledge to challenge assumptions about women on which some laws are based, thus creating awareness and changing people's attitudes towards women.

I'd like to conclude by saying that there are many different ways of looking at the law and working with law. Law can work for us women but at the same time, it can work against us. Therefore, it is very important for us to know the strengths and the limitations of law. The law can empower us women only when we realize what law cannot do for us. By challenging it, we can make it work for us.

Reflections
Rosita Henry

It was not until many years later that Maggie told me about her role in negotiating and mediating a resolution in this rape case. She wondered whether she had done the right thing in trying to resolve the situation privately, outside of both "traditional law" and the "modern" legal system. It weighed heavily on her.

Maggie saw herself as blessed to have been born only twenty years after "first contact" and to be able to bear witness to the rapid social changes that her people were experiencing during the decades before and after Papua New Guinea's independence from Australia. These were heady times for Maggie, full of promise and enchantment about the possibility of a new and perhaps better way of life.

At the same time, Maggie was proud of many of the social and cultural practices of her highlands kin and struggled to reconcile the contradictions she experienced firsthand between tradition and modernity. Maggie felt that she had been born to help disentangle the knots between these two ways of life, "the two of them." She was able to mix with people from all walks of life, from her village kin to important provincial leaders and national politicians. As President of the Western Highlands Women's Council and later as a Board Member of the Mount Hagen Town Authority, she played a key role in encouraging highlanders who were focused on the trappings of modernity to take pride in their own beliefs and practices. During a visit to Hagen from the Governor General, Maggie invited him to her village for a re-enactment of a traditional clan story about Mugl Timbil, who was named in the song she remembers the women singing as they went to work on the Leahy gold mine at Kuta during the early 1950s.

When the Town Authority decided to publish a booklet (c. 1990) featuring people and places of the town, Maggie worked hard to see it completed, contributing much of the material herself. She showed me her copy of the booklet during my field trip in January 2000. In addition to a chapter on the

Performance of a play about Mugl Timbil. Maggie Wilson (front, far left), Joe Leahy (front, far right), c. late 1980s (Wilson family collection).

history of her people immediately before and after the arrival of the Australian explorers, she had also contributed, under the heading "tribal history," a story about Mugl Timbil. With Maggie's permission, I carefully transcribed her story onto the back page of my field notebook (January 2000):

> Once upon a time, there lived a spirit called Mugl Timbil (Man of Heavens) up on the Aundibla range, which adjoins Kuta Ridge, just south of Mt. Hagen. It is believed that he was the giver of life, and joined the tribes as they are known today. One day he built a man's house (Cuitapa). When the house was completed, he held a big feast in honor of all the tribespeople in the Mt. Hagen area. He called over the rivers, across the mountains and down into the valleys and brought the people together.
>
> Once they had gathered, he called the tribes, two by two, to join and gain strength for fighting and making moka ceremonies. This was the beginning of our social structure.
>
> Chanting, he called out the names of the new tribes, Elti Penambes, Tona Waipkas, Ulga Oupukas, Pelga Parkas, Kopi Nokpas, Jiga Yamkas and so on, and each time he would say to himself, who have I left out?
>
> Only the Moki he left alone. He addressed them as Maip Mokis. He felt that they were powerful enough already and so did not need to associate with another clan. Mugl Timbil wasn't wrong. To this day you can see Moki strength around the town. They own the AGC building and the six-story Kamuk Trading, a landmark in Mt. Hagen, and have produced notable leaders such as Sir Wamp Wan, Raphael Doa and many more.
>
> If Mugl Timbil was here he would think twice about putting the Jigas and the Yamkas together because they are both powerful clans in their own right. Today we have a leading national politician from each clan. Paul Pora, National Finance Minister, comes from the Yamka tribe and Paias Wingti, former Prime Minister and current leader of the opposition, comes from the Jiga tribe.
>
> Mugl Timbil would have been proud of his choice of Kopis and Nikpas, because they do well together. Michael Mel, leader of the National Party and clan member of the Nokpas, helped form the Pipilka Corporation, which owns the biggest coffee plantation in the Western Highlands Province.

Mugl Timbil's good judgment has been proven. To this day tribes are known by the names he gave them.[4] People are proud to be associated with their tribes. When a person is addressed, his or her tribal name is spoken first and then his or her given name. Success in business brings a good name not just to the business person but to his or her whole tribe.

4
Kuta Ridge: The White Man's Station

My uncles Mick and Danny Leahy came to Papua New Guinea lured by gold fever, leaving behind them the depression-stricken Australia of the late 1920s. My father, Patrick Leahy, is the eldest of nine children. He had four brothers and four sisters.

I learned from Uncle Dan over the years that both my grandparents were Irish and came to Australia during the nineteenth century. They met and married in Australia. My grandfather was considerably older than my grandmother. He was a womanizer at times and enjoyed his drink. He worked for the Queensland Railway and later held several other casual jobs, which did not pay enough to support his large family. My grandmother bought a small dairy farm near Toowoomba and struggled to raise the children herself. They found it difficult to make ends meet and sometimes some of the children had to skip school to work and help their mother put food on the table. Uncle Dan said that she did very well considering the hard times they had.

As the boys got older, they started to look for advantageous prospects. Uncle Mick heard about the gold rush in Wau and joined thousands of other Australians who came to PNG in hopes of a new start. It was a big step away from the gloomy Australia of those days. The Leahy brothers were among the first white men to reach the highlands.

My mother's father, Melka Kopiamp Kentmel, told me that he was about thirty-six years old, married with four wives and nine children, at the time he heard rumors of some strange people, perhaps spirits, coming into our valley with even stranger belongings. He said he was not afraid. Instead he announced, "Let them come. If they want to make friends with us then we will be happy to do so, and if they want to fight then that is fine too. If they have things we like, then we may have some things they want to have; we can exchange with them. If they are enemy spirits then we will call our own

4. Kuta Ridge

spirits to take care of them. I don't know these strangers and they don't know me. Why would they cause trouble for me? I have not stolen their land, killed their pigs or taken their women."

My grandfather Kentmel told me that he folded his arms across his chest and stood at one end of the *singsing* ground, staring straight at the white men as they made their way down the hill; he could not believe the amount of luggage they carried with them. He thought these strangers were like old women. *Wal tempa tok mak.*

Their dog was the first to approach and, even though this was the biggest dog he had ever seen, he was not afraid of it. The dog started to walk around him, sniffing, and then he licked my grandfather's feet. As the strangers came closer in their clothes, Grandfather Kentmel thought that some parts of their bodies had bird colors and he didn't know quite what to make of it. They tried to get him to pet their dog, but he just stood there dumbfounded. Little did he know that, twenty years later, one of these strangers would be the uncle of his favorite granddaughter.

My uncles Dan and Jim and my father, Patrick Leahy, followed Mick's lead. I have no personal memories of my father since I did not know him, but from what I have heard about him, I like him. In fact, I am the Leahy's greatest fan, not only because of kinship but also because I admire their pioneering spirit. Mick and Danny Leahy came to the highlands of New Guinea in 1933 and shortly afterward Uncle Dan set up alluvial mining at Kuta. My father was working for his brother at Kuta at the time I was conceived.

Kuta Ridge in the 1950s was the gateway to the highlands. It was a vibrant active place and a very busy center for trading. There was a piggery, gold dredging and cattle and sheep grazing. The wool from the sheep was used to produce cozy blankets for the cold misty nights and soft warm floor rugs for comfort and convenience. Women from my village and others nearby were employed to make these blankets.

Many other tribes would come to Kuta from Baiyer River, Ialibu, Chimbu, Mul and other faraway places. They came to trade with the Leahys and would use our village as their stopover. Besides trading with the Leahys, they also traded with my village people; this established new contacts for my tribe. Inter-marriages with these tribes occurred, and when we had feasts it was a mixed crowd, larger than ever before.

Being the nearest tribe to Kuta, my people had closer access to the Leahys and gained more wealth from them by trading with them twice a week, exchanging sweet potatoes, sugar cane, bananas, passion fruit and many other crops for shells, the new salt, mirrors, steel axes and other things that were a novelty to us. Before the arrival of the Leahys, we had only our traditional kina shells, our stone axes and salt made from the ashes of burnt river plants. The new things were rare commodities that everyone was after and because my tribe had privileged access to these items it was considered wealthy. I was a child of one of the most privileged tribes of these times. In earlier times my people had been powerful as fierce fighters, but now they were powerful because of these commodities.

Our society at the time had its own economic structure based on kina shells, pigs, tree oil and *muruks*. I don't remember when I first saw a *muruk*, but I remember the sound of my grandfather's hungry birds. These two giant cassowaries would start to stamp with their strong feet until somebody came to feed them. On their heads, they carried something that reminded, and still reminds me, of a stone axe—they were strong enough to kill a man. I used to give them sweet potatoes but I was always careful to pull back my small hands quickly, keeping my distance. Can you imagine this enormous bird, strong, powerful, with claws as big as a man's forearm, nearly as tall as a man, with a blue, red and yellow neck, and shiny black feathers in which you can see all of the colors reflected?

Did my uncles, Mick and Dan, who brought *kina* shells all the way from the Torres Strait Islands, enhance the economic structure of my people? In the past, the shells were passed from hand to hand through the Southern Highlands and no one really knew their source. No, the Leahys did not enhance the traditional economy; instead they created inflation. The sudden increase in the number of *kina* shells degraded their value. I am laughing as I write this because this morning an old man of my mother's tribe came to the Lodge to sell me a *kina* shell, which he got long ago from the Leahys!

The different tribes were kept busy trading with the white men, and I think that was probably a good thing, because it meant my people had no time for tribal fighting. People were more carefree and respectful of each other. Although language barriers still existed, people managed to overcome them. My people were able to travel to places where they had never been before and suddenly were experiencing a wonderful freedom of movement.

My Uncle Wai once told me a story about his experience of going to new areas. He was keen on travel so he took a job as a carrier for the first Patrol Officers going into Enga Province.[1] One of his jobs was to fetch water from the river for the camp. On one occasion, his bosses decided to set up along the Lai River for what seemed to him a very long time. Wai felt lonely until he met a girl named Tina at the camp. Because he was homesick, he treated Tina and her family as his own family.

One day while Tina was visiting a faraway place for a pig kill, the Patrol Officers talked about returning to Mount Hagen. Uncle Wai thought that perhaps he would have to leave before Tina could return. He did not want to leave without telling Tina that he had to go and that she would have to stay. Heartbroken, he composed a song about her. When I was growing up I used to go to Uncle Wai's house and ask him to sing this plaintive song to me. All of the children from the village would sit very close together on one side of the fire while Wai had the whole floor on the other side to himself. Sitting cross-legged, turning the sweet potatoes over the burning coals, he would hum this song and we would hum with him. It was as if he were looking through the fire and through us children to a faraway place, a secret place of his own. None of us could reach him there. The humming was so soft, so romantic, so heart breaking that I was not sure if the tears in his eyes were caused by smoke or his memories of Tina[2]:

> *Nanga yambu aperentip*: I have forgotten my people
> *Tina lip ma tantip*: Tina is like my mother.
> *Tina nu mint nanga yambilee*: Tina is all I have
> *Ultuk na nen pump moll*: I am leaving tomorrow
> *Tina nu wana kanap pamba*: Tina you have to come, before I go
> *Na nu kanap pamp Tina nu wena na kanap pamp*: I have to see Tina before I go

Tina came back from the pig kill in time to see Wai before he left for Mount Hagen. If Wai could have had it his way, he would have married Tina and brought her back to Hagen with him, but the *kiaps* thought he was too young to marry and that a young wife would be an added burden on their expedition.

Wai never saw Tina again, but he did bring something back with him—the sweet memory of her, which he treasured all his life, although he eventually married Koina.[3] He even named his first daughter after Tina. I never knew her because she died before I was born.

Koina (front) and Tingerr (back), Kunguma Village, 13 September 2009 (photograph by Rosita Henry).

Reflections
Rosita Henry

Maggie's biological father, Patrick Leahy (Paddy), left the highlands when Maggie was still a child. Although she remembered meeting him once, she never really knew him outside family stories. He was born in 1899, so must have been over 50 when his only child, Maggie, was born. Among her personal papers, I found a photocopy of a piece by Christopher Ashton (1978) on the Leahy family that included some information on Paddy's life, but nothing about him fathering Maggie. There is also a good description of Paddy in John Fowke's (1995) biography of Dan Leahy, again with no mention of Maggie. Fowke (1995: 7) notes that the Leahy brothers were all "solidly built" but that:

> Paddy, the eldest, most closely resembled the common conception of a wild Irishman.... Paddy had tremendous shoulders and arms, a big bull of a man who made a name for himself on the football field before a bad knee injury put paid to further play. The only one in the younger generation of Leahys to have a liking for drink, Paddy made up for them all, and in fact binge drinking was to be a problem for him all his life. Equipped with a temperament to match his bull-like build, Paddy was always ready to use his fists to settle an argument.

Due to a falling out over Paddy's drinking habits, his brother Michael Leahy (Mick) did not invite him to accompany him on the famous gold prospecting expedition into the Highlands of New Guinea in the early 1930s that lead to the discovery of a large population the rest of world never knew existed. Instead, Mick took his youngest brother Daniel (Danny). Their adventures during this time have been well documented (Leahy and Crain 1937; Connolly and Anderson 1987; Fowke 1995; Simpson 1962), including in the film *First Contact* by Connolly and Anderson (1983).

Maggie's cousin, Joe Leahy, son of Mick Leahy to a highlands woman, Jiga Amp Marpa, remembers Patrick Leahy well. When I asked Joe to tell me about the Leahys at Kuta, he recalled:

> I think it was 1948 or 1949 when Paddy Leahy came to Kuta. I was on the station but I didn't know I was a Leahy. When my mother was pregnant, I think my father, Mick Leahy, handed my mother over to Towa. Towa was his best *bosboi*, you see, one of the guys from the coast that came up with the Leahys in 1932.
>
> I was born at Kuta and I grew up at Kuta. I didn't know my father was Mick Leahy; I thought that Towa was my father. I was close to this man, old Towa; I was really close. When Mick Leahy found out that there was myself, Clem and John, all born from different mothers, he left Hagen and went to Zenag, on the coast near Lae. When he came to visit Kuta, old Dan's *kukboi*, Aiya, would call out to the compound where we were living and say, "Hum-

4. Kuta Ridge

bug mustn't come up to the house because Mick Leahy is coming with his missus." They called me humbug.

We were all kids playing around and when the *kukboi* called down from the mountain all the kids would go rushing. They were all *hamamas* to see some new things but I was left stranded. I thought to myself, "Why is the *kukboi* saying that?" I knew that I had a different type of hair so I thought that must be it. I asked my mother for a *laplap* to cover my hair but I forgot that my face was sticking out like a sore thumb! I followed them, stood, and just watched from a distance. I didn't dare go closer.

Paddy Leahy came up from Lae, I think. He had a plantation in Wau, in the Morobe Province. When he was at Kuta, he was working for old Dan, building the double story house. At that time, old Dan had about ten or twelve women so I think Paddy was interested in a woman too. Somehow, Kuan himself brought his wife Jara to Paddy, but I didn't know this then.

I was put to work with Paddy. I was only a young kid. Paddy had some Penambi Wias and a few others working for him on the house and I used to do the translating. That's how I got to know Paddy.

He was a really hard man. One morning I didn't go to work so he grabbed me and belted me. He was a big solid bloke with big arms. I tried to run but I couldn't so I bit him on his arm. He let me go and I ran so fast, he couldn't catch me.

He was hard but he had a very, very soft heart. We had never tasted white man's *kaikai*. We had never tasted tea, coffee and things like that, but Paddy, he was a big eater. He'd have his breakfast and then come to work. Later he'd go back to the house, get a few pieces of meat, and give them to me on the side. Then I looked at him and thought, "Oh, he's trying to make friends with me." I thought, "He's a good man," but he probably knew who I was, even though my father never acknowledged me.

Paddy did not complete the house. Dan and Paddy had an argument and Dan chased Paddy out of the place.[4]

Joe did not come across Maggie at Kuta until she was already a grown child of perhaps eight years old. He had no idea at the time that she was a Leahy and his cousin. He did not take much notice of her when he first saw her but remembers being told that she was Wia Kuan's daughter. Later, after he began to work for Danny Leahy on his coffee plantation in the Nebilyer Valley, he met her again:

When I was working down at Korgua on the plantation as a *bosboi* I used to recruit all the Penambi girls. Maggie was one of them. They came and worked on the coffee plantation and I used to have to pay them. I used to look at her and think, "She's a nice girl," but I didn't know she was my cousin. I might have married her or she might have married me, because Mick and Danny Leahy never told us we were cousins! When she came and worked on the

37

plantation, they said she was Penambi Amp Tilgil and I said, "Oh she's a Penambi, ah?" She was already *tanim het* and all that.⁵

Tanim het (turn head) in Tok Pisin, or *amp kanan* in the Temboka language of the Penambi, is the name for a traditional courtship ceremony. Marilyn Strathern (1972) provides a detailed description of the ceremony. *Tanim hets* are typically attended by up to 20 visiting men, who crowd into a large house with members of the host clan. The party sings love songs while some of the visiting men pair up with the girls to "turn heads" with them. Overt sexual advances are not permitted. As Marilyn Strathern (1972: 82) notes, participating in *tanim het* does not necessarily lead to longer lasting relationships and partners can engage in *tanim het* "with no further intentions in mind." Moreover, girls are always chaperoned by older women and "a man who acquires a reputation for being too adventurous in his style of turning head may find himself the object of public ridicule. Any suggestion that a girl is dispensing sexual favors is thought by her kin to prejudice her later chances of a good match; nevertheless, at the time there are romantic hopes that more lasting affairs will come of such encounters."

When I told Joe that Maggie had taken me to a *tanim het* during my visit in 1974, he laughed. *Tanim hets* are of the past, he told me. Perhaps the *tanim het* I went to with Maggie was one of the last such events in this area.

Joe Leahy (middle) with Maggie Wilson (right) and Rosita Henry (left), Kilima Plantation, 13 January 2000 (photograph by Christopher Morgan).

5
My Village Childhood

When I was about six or seven years old, my Aunty Koina decided to change my name from Wakapa to Tilgil which means "untie the knot."[1] From then on people started calling me Wia Tilgil or Kundul Tilgil.[2]

I really treasure the memories I have of my childhood in the village. I remember one drizzly afternoon, returning from the rainforest, dripping wet, cold and hungry. My feet were covered in red clay and the cold mountain mist had settled on my hair. I could not wait to cook the string of mushrooms I had picked. That's why I took a shortcut by trying to climb over my Uncle Wai's back fence. But the timber was rotten and the fence collapsed beneath me, causing me to land flat on my face. I picked myself up and wiped the mud out of my eyes to find Wai standing in front of me. For a moment, I was fear stricken, expecting him to be angry about his broken fence. But Wai's eyes danced as they searched me all over. He said, "And whose pig-kill are you returning from?" I mumbled, "No one's." He took me by the hand and led me to his house by the *marita* tree. He poured rainwater over my head from a bamboo container and made me wash the mud from my body before inviting me inside to warm my hands over the hot coals in his fireplace. Wai and his wife Koina then unwrapped the *mumu*, pork, bananas, sweet potatoes and *kumu* (green leaves), they had cooked in the ground earlier that day. We shared this feast among us, Wai, his wife Koina, his three daughters and me. I ate blissfully, savoring the pork fat. I must have fallen asleep by the fire. I don't remember how I got home that night.

All our children's games consisted mostly of adult activities like hunting, working gardens, building houses, cooking in earth-ovens. The normal activities of a little girl are to follow her mother to the garden to learn about different types of crops. So I learned to wash sweet potatoes, to sort out what should be given to the pigs to eat and what needed to be kept for us. I also learned to get fibers and dyes from the bush to make my first string bag. However, one of my favorite pastimes in this period was hunting. We knew the habitat of our target and the children would divide into several groups to form a triangle and chase the target into the point of the triangle, where two of the oldest and strongest children were ready to catch the animal and kill it. Our catch would be our treat at the end of the day.

We would usually divide into two teams for hunting. I always wanted to be on Noah's team because he was the tallest among all of us and the eldest of the boys. Several girls were older than him, but they would let him boss them around. I always insisted on carrying the catch. If Noah did not let me, I would threaten to leave his team. Sometimes Noah would say, "Yes, you can carry it, but only for some of the way." If he allowed any of the other children to carry the catch I would go berserk and try to bite them. Noah would always give in to me and say, "*Kanda* (okay). Everybody, today we will let Wia Tilgil carry the catch all the way." I would then poke my tongue out and wiggle my body with pleasure.

One day Nikints snuck up from behind and pinched me really hard to make me drop the rats we had caught. He pushed me around a bit and said to Noah, "Look, it's like I said, Tilgil is too young to carry the catch. She has let the rats go. Let me carry the catch!"

As I write this, forty years later, Noah and Nikints are still living in our village; our houses are very close to each other. I have created Haus Poroman Lodge ("House of Friends"), which encompasses ten huts built on my tribe's land. Nikints is working for me as a general maintenance man and Noah comes around often for a chat with me or the tourists.

Although I was an average child, there was something about me that was quite strange. Why did I have a different type of hair, of a color unlike that of any other child in the village? Why did my family make such a big fuss about my hair? Whenever we were going to the Catholic mission or any white settlement, *ma* and her co-wife Grimel, would shave my hair off the night before with a bamboo knife and rub charcoal on my head. At the time, I never understood what was happening, but later I realized that they were trying to disguise me from the white people. I always longed to go to the places where the white people were stationed, to see where the wondrous things came from that other children showed me and talked about when we played. However, whenever I asked *wutta*, *ma* or Grimel to take me to these places, they would always offer other attractive options. They would suggest, for example, that we go and visit our cousins in the Nebilyer Valley to get some *marita* pandanus fruits. It was always a special moment in the year when our neighbors harvested and cooked these greasy, blood-red fruits.

I was six at the funeral. Suddenly our home and the surrounding area was crowded with people from all over the valley. Large groups of people carried live pigs, large bunches of bananas, *bilums* full of sweet potato, tapioca, taro, long bundles of sugar cane and firewood. Some people were covered in red clay and others in white ashes. Everybody was crying and pulling their hair out. I was fascinated by the way people were wailing and chanting my *wutta*'s name over and over again. Every now and then, someone grabbed me and cried out loud. I pulled away.

This sort of thing repeated itself for several days and when new groups of people arrived and the others got up to meet them, someone would throw him or herself on the ground and roll around in the dirt. It seemed like a big party to me. All my favorite relatives were in one place and I feasted on all my favorite foods. Again and again, people pulled me close to them and patted me under the chin. One of my aunties, Melka Amp Tumul, dragged me under one arm, jumping up and down, wailing, "Kuan, why did you leave Tilgil, who will Tilgil turn to?" I felt important then. I ran off to the river where the other children were playing and bragged about Aunty Tumul composing about me and not them.

After the death of my father, I became less spoiled. It was a traditional practice at the time, that *ma* and Kuan's second wife Grimel would remarry Kuan's younger brothers. My two mothers both refused to remarry such a short time after my father's death, but the men of my tribe threatened them. If they didn't remarry immediately they would have to go back to their maiden tribes without me and without all their personal belongings. The only way for the two women to stay and have time to grieve properly for Kuan without remarrying was if Kut, his youngest brother, agreed to take them under his wing, at least for a while. But he refused to do that, even though both Jara and Grimel had been like mothers to him. Kut was newly married and did not want the responsibility, so my mother had to marry Tugl and Grimel had to marry Penapil. The main reason Jara and Grimel married Kuan's brothers, who already had wives and their own children, was to stay with me.

Ma would sit staring at the cemetery for hours and her tears would fall like rain. This made me very sad so I would cry, too. My grandmother and Grimel cried, crooning poignant songs in memory of Kuan.

I am very privileged to have been the only girl in the village to wear the *omak* sticks. Traditionally only sons wear these sticks.[3] My *wutta* put each stick together with extra love and care, ensuring all the sticks had the same coloring, size and length; he told me that they looked really pretty on me. The length of the *omak* at this time was just below my breast line. For each stick *wutta* added to my *omak*, he had a story to go with it. For instance, one stick would represent eight *kina* shells he had given to a girl cousin who in turn gave him a very big pig for a feast. It seemed like ages before he could add just one more to the list.

I did not want to dig sweet potatoes or look after the pigs any more. I got very tired of fetching water for Tugl. Before, when Kuan was still living, these things were not work. His praises and encouragement made everything enjoyable. I used to take pride in making things so that I could show them to him at the end of the day and he was always so proud of me. I missed him terribly. I fully realized what it meant to lose him several months after the funeral, when it dawned on me that his *omak* would not grow any longer.

"Your father, your father.... Don't you know the colour of your hair? Your father is white!"

"No, you giaman, liar, my father is Tugl."

This afternoon, as I was about to write this book, Tugl came to see me. He sat quietly for some time, watching me writing while enjoying a candy and smiling contently. He was a good father to me. The only problem with him was that when he married my mother he was already the father of seven other children. He tried to give me the kind of love and attention that his older brother Kuan gave me, but it was impossible. If I got special attention, his children missed out, and if they got the attention, I missed out. Tugl demanded that I behave myself like his other children did and do as I was told. He would continuously remind me that I was not a boy and that I should carry out girls' chores. I couldn't stand his bossy ways and would sometimes run away to my Grandpa Kentmel's village. I resented Tugl for ordering me around. At the same time, I hated the days when he did not have his evening meal of sweet potatoes and *kumu* in our house with my *ma*, grandma and me. I thought that perhaps he cared more for his other wife and children.

Tugl had a men's house. Sometimes he invited some of us children to sleep there. He built a long women's house divided into three sections. Each wife lived in the two extremities of the house with her children. The largest part of the house, the center, was occupied by the pigs of both wives. One evening when we were playing marbles, Tugl called out to his daughter Lauie and me to come quickly and fetch some fresh water for him to drink. We did not want to interrupt our play so we snuck out to hide in the *pitpit* grass, but Tugl kept calling out, "If you don't come, I'll belt the shit out of you!" He was an impatient man and everybody was a bit scared of him. Finally, my mother and our sister Tali went to fetch his water, and then he went to sleep in his men's house. Later, Lauie and I snuck back home to eat our sweet potatoes, but I could not keep quiet. I started to mimic Tugl's impatience. Lauie started giggling, and my grandmother could not restrain herself and joined in, burst-

5. My Village Childhood

Maggie as a child, c. 1958. Maggie's kin are not able to identify the woman on the left (Wilson family collection).

ing out with laughter. Of course Tugl woke up and, jumping over the fence, kicked down our door and burst into the room. We were huddling in one corner, shielding ourselves with a *pandanus* mat. It did not take him long to find us. Tearing the mat away, he belted the two of us furiously with a bundle of sticks.

"Tugl, you tried to be a good father to me. But from whom did I get the colour of my hair?"

REFLECTIONS
Rosita Henry

After her marriage to Tugl, Maggie's mother Jara had two children with him—Rita and Thomas. Tugl had seven children with his other wife, Aip—four daughters (Prul, Poning, Tali and Laui) followed by three sons (Kuipa, Kawa and Pora).

Maggie developed a special bond with her sister Tali as they were about the same age. As they got older they started to go to *tanim hets* together and it was Maggie who eventually accompanied Tali to the village of Tali's husband-to-be during the transactions for her marriage. It was customary for a young girl to be accompanied by one or two other young girls during the period when her father and other clan members were negotiating her brideprice. If her father was happy with the brideprice the girl would remain at the groom's village and her companions would stay with her to help allay any fears and provide comfort and companionship while she came to know her husband and his family.

In the course of my research, I met with Tali to ask her about her childhood days with Maggie. Bernadine and I called on her in Palimbri Village, close to Hagen town. Tali was at home caring for her baby granddaughter, while her daughter-in-law worked. Tali was no longer able to work in the garden because she had lost the use of her legs due to an illness. She sat on a mattress on the floor while her granddaughter contentedly crawled around her. She was thrilled with our visit and happy to recall her childhood days with Maggie.

> I was about the same age as Maggie. We were [the] best of friends. We shared everything and slept under the same blanket. When possums and birds and all that got cooked by the boys in the village, they would give Maggie her share and she would take it and then give it to me. I was happy to have double meat. One day Nikints got suspicious and told us to eat while he watched but Maggie said, "Oh, I've got a tummy ache and can't eat my meat." The only meat she liked was chicken and she would also eat pig meat, mostly young piglets that Kuan would kill for her.
>
> One day, Maggie and I walked from the village to the Leahy place at Kuta and saw Danny Leahy. He said that it was good that we came [and] told us to go and hang around with his wives, Mancy and Biam. Sometimes Dan killed pigs and cows for his labourers and he told us, "They will put your name on the list to get a share of the meat." Mancy and Biam made us tea and coffee and gave us biscuits. They gave us soap and towels and said that we could come back any time we wanted.
>
> When we brought the soap and towels home, Tugl asked us, "Where did

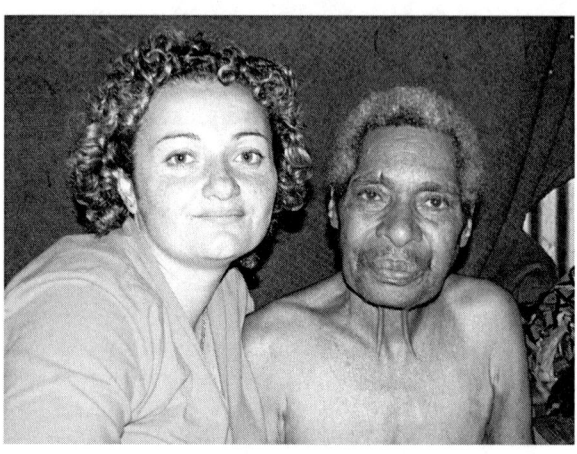

Maggie's sister Tali (right) with Bernadine (left), Palimbri, 17 September 2009 (photograph by Rosita Henry).

5. My Village Childhood

you get the soap?" Tugl got angry with me and said, "Tali why did you take Maggie to Kuta? Old Dan will see that Maggie is mixed. He will see her white skin and take her away from us for good." We explained that that he was not going to take her but only wanted to give us a share of the meat.

Maggie knew that she had a white father but never spoke out. She always kept her hair tightly covered with a piece of cloth and would ask me to make sure no hair was sticking out before we visited Danny Leahy. We did not know who Maggie's father was. Even Maggie didn't know, but his brother Danny Leahy must have known and began slowly to establish relations with her.

There was also a Sepik couple in Hagen who invited Maggie to stay with them. She went to visit them but Tugl got worried that she might get lost or killed or something so he brought her home. But Maggie was clever and found ways to keep in touch with her Sepik friends.

When Maggie was young, the Catholic missionaries and Danny Leahy wanted Maggie to go to school but Tugl didn't want her to go to school. He wanted her to get married so he could get the brideprice.

At the time when I was to get married to Mogei Pangamp Pius, Maggie went along with me to the Mogei Pangamp village at Palimbri. We were there for a day and the next day there was another girl from the Mogei Akelika tribe who was also there to marry.

Maggie was a little bit rough at that time and called out to Pius'[s] father, Temba, "You told us to come, we are here, and now you have told somebody else to come too, why?" Maggie threatened to leave straight away because there was this other girl there, even though all the Mogei Pangamp men were already gathering pigs and shells and putting them in a line. After Maggie said this, I was prepared to go home with her but Temba got up and said to Maggie, "No, no, no, *amp kundul*,[4] I did not tell this other girl to come. Others asked her to come. You were the first girls here and we are just getting ready to pay you now. We will send the other girl away, so don't worry."

I did not know my husband Pius beforehand, but I recognised him when we came to Palimbri for my brideprice. He was one of the guys that came up to Kuta for a *tanim het*. I agreed to get married to Pius because I was scared that Tugl would belt me up if I did not stay with him. If a girl's father and his clansmen are happy with the brideprice, they let the girl stay in the man's village; if not, they take their daughter back home with them. Tugl was happy with the brideprice so I stayed at Palimbri and Maggie stayed with me to keep me company.

Maggie was already going to *tanim hets* at this time and the guys usually called her *kundul*, which means white or light skinned. They called her *kundul* Tilgil. One time Maggie told a guy with one eye that she didn't want to *tanim het* with him. Tugl got up and told Maggie that she had bad manners and that what she had said was shameful, that it had embarrassed the visiting group. "You are young. Who told you to go and *tanim het*? You should stay on the side and look. Just because you *tanim het* with a guy does not mean that you have to marry him. All these guys here have come along to support just one guy to get a girl." One of the guys that came along as support then got up and said, "We see that you are light skinned, you have a long nose and you are pretty but when you say things like that it's really embarrassing for us. You're a tough girl."

When Maggie accompanied me to Palimbri, all the guys wanted to *tanim het* with her and they made up a special song for her at the *tanim het*. They sang about the river that flows through their village at Palimbri and they called Maggie's name and sang that where Maggie is, there is light. It is a love song.

The pigs that Tugl and his brothers received from my brideprice payment were slaughtered up on our mountain at Kuta and some of the cooked meat was brought down for Maggie and me at Palimbri. We had not yet finished eating the meat when the Bishop sent word for us to come to the mission at Rebiamul. When we went to see the Bishop, he told Maggie that he wanted to send her away to school and he told us to go back up to Kuta and tell Tugl and his brothers.

The next morning we went to Rebiamul to see the bishop and the nuns told me to go back home and kept Maggie there with them at Rebiamul. I was so sad to leave Maggie, I cried. I went back in the afternoon but the nuns told me to return home and come back the next day. The next day, Tugl and Jara and all the people from Kuta came down to Rebiamul. When we gathered at the Bishop's house, Father William Ross said, "I told you people to come because Maggie is going to go away to school." We saw that Maggie had already been changed into a modern girl. All her hair was cut and they had dressed her up in clothes with shoes and all that. When we saw she was dressed like a white girl and that she was more like one of the nuns, we were shocked.

Father Ross said, "Tomorrow she is going to school but now is the last time you will see her." It was very quick. The next day she got onto the plane and went away to school. Tugl really cried, but Father Ross said, "Don't worry, I am here. Whatever information I receive from her I will always let you know, so don't worry," and he tried to calm down Tugl and Jara.

They drove her along the road to the airport and we all ran after her, taking the shortcut to keep up. We all cried and cried and cried and Maggie too cried and then got on the plane and went away. We didn't see her for two or three years then. But one time she sent me a radio from Rabaul. Father Ross had the radio and sent word for me to come and get it.[5]

Tali's story left me with much food for thought. Perhaps Tali's marriage had precipitated Maggie being sent away to school. Hearing about the brideprice and that Maggie was at Palimbri already attending courtship ceremonies may have led Danny Leahy and the Catholic missionaries to realize that time was of the essence if they wanted to prevent her from being married, like Tali, at a tender age. Until then, Danny Leahy had been content to allow his niece to remain in the care of her Penambi kin, discreetly keeping an eye out for her welfare from afar.

6
Off to School

I did not know at the time, but Danny Leahy knew that I was his niece. When I was about nine or ten and looking for adventure, I used to sneak off to the plantation and my uncle would give me work. He was going blind and needed a guide and we used to walk him back to the house from his factory. On payday, he gave me more money than he gave the other women. I did not tell anyone as my father Tugl did not want me to go to the Leahys. He was worried about brideprice. Girls were raised to get married for brideprice as a way of entering into a relationship with another tribe or making a new connection. It was also a way of raising status in the community.

I was with my sister Tali at Newtown, a suburb of Mount Hagen, at the time of her brideprice, when Father Ross sent for me. The catechist Mogei Uk went with me to my village to tell my family that the bishop was going to send me to school. When Catechist Uk told Tugl the news, Tugl started screaming, "I don't want her to go!" I stood at a distance and said, "But, I want to go." Shouting, "No!," Tugl jumped over the fence and tried to hit me. Everyone came out of the house and my grandmother began to wail. Uk argued with Tugl. I stubbornly said, "I am going," and started walking. At that time, I didn't have many things. My mother ran after me and said, "Don't go, you eat first and go." Tugl saw me leaving and ran after me, crying, "Don't go now! We'll have a meal together and we'll take you tomorrow."

The next morning the whole village accompanied me to Rebiamul. In those days, my people did not have a lot of money, but they all contributed some coins, about ten kina in all. They put the money in a tobacco tin and gave it to me. They did not know where I was going but they advised me not to accept food from strangers. When we got to Rebiamul the bishop and some priests came out to meet us. Tugl said he was planning to get brideprice for me and asked the bishop, "Why are you taking her away from us?" A missionary woman brought me a little red suitcase and some dresses from the mission shop. I had a wash at the priest's house and put on my new clothes.

I didn't have any underclothes so I wore the priest's underpants. They were too big for me and I had to get a safety pin to pin them up.

Those of us going to the airport squeezed into a Land Rover while my sisters and other villagers ran after us. It was very emotional. My people were crying but some of the Mogei tribe said, "This is a good thing, let her go." My people smeared mud on their faces in mourning and *ma* kept hitting her hand on the ground and crying. The only person that I did not want to leave was my grandmother. I remember thinking everything was perfect but that she should come with me.

At the airport, which was near present-day Chinatown, we waited for the plane—a DC3. A loud, heart-rending funeral cry erupted as I boarded. All my cousins and the girls from my village were weeping and wailing, but I did not shed a tear; I was too excited.

As Tugl tells the story:

> The Priest sent word through Mogei Uk for us to bring her down to them. I started to scream at her mother and grandmother. I did not want her to leave because several men already wanted to marry her and one had offered me money. Nowadays people go and come, but those days I thought they would take her away forever. Later, I thought, "The priests have sent for her many times and she wanted to go," so after seeking advice from her mother's parents, I gave in and agreed to let her go.
>
> We all went down to Father Ross's house and waited while she had a shower. We were all in one room waiting for her. When she came out she looked very different. She was without her *purpur* [grass skirt] and all dressed up with a nice necklace on her neck. Father said, "I will take her away," and we were all shocked. I didn't know what to do and started jumping up and down and crying.
>
> On the plane, she had a flower in her hand and looked different. She got in the plane and as we watched the plane disappear, we thought she had died and gone in the sky and we all cried. We came back to the village and put mud on our faces and mourned for her. Then we killed a big pig for a funeral feast.
>
> I couldn't believe the way the Bishop dealt with her. He did not give us anything for taking her away. I was expecting compensation from them for taking her away. Mogei Yaga, a village leader asked me, "What's going on with your daughter?" I told him and he said it was a good thing. I couldn't believe it! "What's good about her being taken away?"

We stopped over at Alexishafen in Madang. Once there, I thought of Hagen. "I've had my plane ride; now I want to go back," I thought. I stayed in Alexishafen for one week and the teachers there were worried by the fact that I was already a grown girl and did not know English, so they got some of the other girls to teach me the alphabet. I used to help in the kitchen in my plain blue dress with a white collar. It was my favorite dress and I wore it all the time. I had my first taste of salt water there. I didn't realize people used the toilet in that part of the sea. The other girls came and told me not to drink there.

After a week, I boarded the plane again to go to Rabaul. On the way, we stopped at Wewak, Kavieng and Manus. In Rabaul, I was taken to a dormitory at the back of a church. It wasn't a boarding school but all the girls lived there while we waited to go to Vunapope, near Kokopo.[1] I stayed there for three days and then finally the car came to take us.

When I got to Vunapope, the nuns looked for clothes for me. There were mixed-race kids running around everywhere; some were older than me and some were only about five or six years old. I was excited to be there since there were other kids that looked like me. There were some mixed-race highland girls there, one from Chimbu and two from Enga. They had started a couple of years earlier and had been civilized so they were a bit embarrassed to see me. I think I must have reminded them about themselves when they first got there. Three older Leahys had gone to school in Vunapope before me. The nuns asked me if they were my brothers and I told them they were not because I was not aware that I was a Leahy at the time.

There was another mixed-race coastal girl there, Roslyn Morris. She had finished grade six but didn't leave to further her education. As she had no family and nowhere else to go, Vunapope was home to her. She was given the tasks of teaching me the alphabet and how to read. She was good and tried her best. I picked up reading and knew the alphabet within three weeks, but confused meanings of the words that sounded the same, like cotton and cousin.

Some months later, I joined an official class—grade three. I could not speak English properly and the other kids used to pick on me. I became very good at handicraft work, probably because of my experience at home making *bilums*. I also did well in my religion classes, which impressed the nuns.

In those days, Vunapope was a town full of religious institutions. There was Palaram High School, which was Our Lady of Mercy High School, the Nursing School, the Vunagunan Boys' High School and the Technical College for mixed-race boys. We used to have movie nights together with the students from the other institutions. I was impressed at everybody getting dressed up and going to church.

Every Sunday the nuns would take us swimming at the wharf. Someone pushed me into the water once and I nearly drowned but a girl saved me. On Sundays, we sometimes would go on long walks with the nuns to the cocoa and copra plantations to pick guavas and other fruits. I enjoyed those walks because I had two uncles working on one of the plantations and there was a chance that I might see them. I used to walk way ahead or well behind the others so I could have a quick talk with my uncles when nobody was looking, as we were forbidden to talk to men, especially highlanders. In those days, people on the coast used to refer to all highlanders as Chimbus. Highland men had a bad image and people used to run from them. One day, one of the other girls caught me talking to my uncles and reported me to Mother Deofilia. She scolded me and gave me two hits on the leg with a ruler, cautioning me never to do it again. Mother did not give me the opportunity to explain who they were. I felt that I should be allowed to talk to my uncles because I was missing home. I really needed them to comfort me in my homesickness.

The hitting did not stop me. My uncles somehow knew that I was forbidden to talk to them so we used to have our own secret signals. For example, sometimes in the shops in a crowd they would come and stand close to me and bump me. I would put my hand out without looking at them and they would put money in my hands. Sometimes they would whistle or make signs to catch my attention and we would look for hidden places to talk. Although we were only ever able to talk for a short while, it was still comforting and I looked forward to it.

A girl at school had a thing against highlanders. She said we were grass cutters, dirty and primitive. She used to provoke me by calling me Chimbu. In those days, the color red was associated with highlanders and my little red suitcase added to that. I got fed up one time so I attacked her in the shower block. I held her down and told her that her mouth was dirtier than us Chimbus. Then I scrubbed soap into her mouth with a clothes brush and bashed her around until some other girls came and broke us apart. She never dared torment me again. I also gained the respect of the other girls. I lived up to the Chimbu name and no one ever pushed me around again.

The toilets at the school were outdoors. Once, there was a huge earthquake, with tremors that continued for three weeks. I was sitting on the toilet when the earthquake happened. I ran out with my underpants down thinking, "This is the end, I won't be able to see my family ever again."

I was not allowed to return home during the holidays like the other girls. The bishop and my uncle thought that I would go back to the village and never return to school. However, Raphael Got, a Mogei tribesman, went home for the Christmas holidays and my Penambi people asked him to visit me upon his return to Vunapope. They had collected money for him to give to me. Raphael held the money and waited for the opportunity to meet me and pass it on to me. He came across me at the Kokopo show. I was with a group of girls, one of whom was the one that reported me to Mother Deofilia all the time, so when Raphael approached me, I walked away and ignored him. That really hurt his feelings. I was hurt too but I could not explain that I had to walk away because the other girl was there. Raphael took it personally and thought that I did not want to know him as I was attending an "A" school.[2] He later sent me the money with a very bitter letter reminding me that I came from the same grass hut background as him. Even then, his letter caused me trouble. The nuns thought I had encouraged him to write the letter. I was called and questioned about it and they took the money and kept it for me. Today Raphael knows the reason why I ignored him and we have a good laugh about it. He understands why I acted as I did. He knows the right approach would have been to write to the nuns first.

By year five, I had become an average student in reading and English and other subjects. Finally, at year six I did the IQ test that determined whether I got to go to Australia and passed. However, much to my disappointment, only students who were twelve years and under were accepted for school in Australia and I was already over age. It was decided that I should be sent to Marianville College in Bomana, Port Moresby. I spent 1968 and 1969 at Marianville, after which my Uncle Danny Leahy decided to send me to boarding school in Australia. But first, let me tell you about the time I returned home after two years of school in Vunapope.

REFLECTIONS
Rosita Henry

Maggie was full of stories about her early school days, many of which were shared with me during our time together at boarding school in Australia. In turn, I told her of the eight different primary schools I had been to, three in Australia (in Cairns and Mareeba), then two in Germany, and finally three in Papua New Guinea (two in Port Moresby and one in Kerema). The school I attended in Kerema, in the Gulf District, in 1966 was a one-room building with a single teacher who taught all the primary grades, from one to six. There were only two of us in grade six, the other being the District Commissioner's daughter, Dale Murphy. Four of my younger siblings were in the lower grades. Among the other children in the school were the police officer's children, Paul and Gillian Fyfe. The A (Australian Curriculum) school would have had to close that year for lack of students, except for the arrival of our family in town. My father had a job in the Public Works Department (PWD), which came with the promise of a residence large enough to house his wife and children. There was no building in town with enough bedrooms, so the department converted a four-bedroom building that had been single men's quarters for our use.

While there were only about 12 children in the A school, there were many more in the T School (Territory Curriculum) next door. We were discouraged from mixing during school hours, but on the way home we would meet at the creek to joyfully take turns swinging and jumping off a rope into a waterhole. Over the holidays we roamed freely, playing together in the village and on the nearby beach fringed with red Poinciana trees. We would run as fast as possible across the black sea sand, risking burnt feet, to wade to a cave on the other side of the cove before the tide rose.

Maggie and I had much in common, in that we had both faced many rapid changes during our early school days, and had to adjust continuously to making new friends across cultural divides. Maggie enjoyed my stories as much as I did hers and we fell in love with each other's families. While I was a rather serious teenager, with a tendency towards compliancy born of a need to please others, Maggie had a feisty resistance against subjugation and a *joie de vivre* that excited me.

In 1974, after we finished school and I started my first year at University, Maggie invited me to visit her in the highlands. She insisted on meeting me in Port Moresby before the flight to Mount Hagen so she could take me to see her old school, Marianville College. The Catholic high school was established in 1966, so when Maggie attended in 1968–69, it was still in its infancy. Maggie had great respect for the nuns who taught her and was keen to introduce me to them. I remember walking around the grounds as she proudly pointed out the dormitory and the refectory, savoring the tales she told of her adventures there.

Maggie's story that her family had thought she died when she was first sent away left me teary eyed, but she did not express any sadness herself. She told the tale in a matter-of-fact way, flavored with wry humor. I wondered what her family felt, so I asked her sister, Rita.

> I was just a little girl. My grandmother and I were in the house when my grandmother heard that she was going. My grandmother cried. She got mud and put it on her face and wiped it on her body and cried and cried. I was there when she was doing that. I did not know what was happening.
>
> My grandmother cried and sang songs with Tali and the other women. They composed songs about Maggie and would sing them and cry. Now we know that children go for school and come back, but [at] that time we thought she had gone for good and mourning songs were sung at night time around the fire. One of the songs I remember went like this:

6. Off to School

> Here at Kunguma Village,
> Our hearts are sending light signals
> From the top and the bottom
> I send the lights over the hills and far away.
> Who is there to see it?
> My sister must have seen it
> My sister who listens to me
> My sister who shares with me
> The clouds and the mountains are in the way
> She has already turned her back to us
> But the memories of her are in our hearts
> Because of this I cry under my pillow.

Every time we used to hear aeroplanes, we used to think of her and another song was composed about this:

> The plane in the sky is noisily flying over
> The wireless on the ground is sending messages
> The clouds moving above bring messages back from her.³

Maggie's sister Rita Tul (right) with her brother Councilor John Kawa (left), 12 September 2009 (photograph by Kanawi Danomira).

7
My First Return

At the end of my second year at Vunapope, I was finally allowed home for the Christmas holidays, this time on a TAA (Trans Australian Airline) flight. It was 1967 and a lot had changed within the two years I was away. The Mount Hagen airport had been moved to Kagamuga. I remember getting off the plane at the airport and thinking that the plane had taken me somewhere else. At the time nearly all the workers at the airport were white people. I said, "This is not Hagen," but the airline staff assured me it was.

I was taken in a car to the Highlander Hotel, which was at that time a little *kunai* house. As my luggage had grown from the little red suitcase I had left Hagen with two years before, I left it there and walked all the way to Rebiamul. I met Bishop Bernading there. He and I had grown quite close as I used to correspond with him from school. He was at his typewriter and did not recognize me for a while. I stood at the door and waited, starting to feel disappointed. He looked up and asked, "Who might you be?," and I replied, "I am Magdalene." "Oh Magdalene you have grown and look at the color of your hair!" he exclaimed and came around the desk to hug me. He took me to collect my luggage and then to meet Father Ross and have lunch with him in the dining room before driving me to my Uncle Danny Leahy's place at Korgua. The bishop had planned with my uncle that I would stay there over the school holidays rather than return to live in the village.

Before we left for Korgua, I walked into town to see my friends from the Sepik. I met my father Tugl and my brother Kuipa there. We walked together to Wilya, but then I quickly went back to the mission, as I had wandered off without informing the bishop where I was going.

Here is Tugl's account of my homecoming:

> After she left we kept her friendship with her Sepik family alive. I went with Kuipa to visit her Sepik family. They used to call her Maria. The Sepik family

cooked a meal and we ate with them and were sitting down when the children started calling, "Maria, Maria!" I couldn't believe it! I thought she would be gone for years.

Kuipa ran out to see who it was. She came in and we hugged and cried. It was as if she had come back from the dead. We spent the whole afternoon together and then Kuipa and I left to go back to the village to tell all our people. The next day we all went to see her; she was in Church then.

I was in Church when they all came in. My mother was carrying my brother Las. I didn't know of his existence until that moment. *Ma* came into the Church crying. I went back to the village with them. They killed chickens and pigs and we had a big feast. I took Gerry, the young son of Clem and Agnes Leahy, up to the village with me. Like me, Clem is a mixed-race offspring of one of the Leahy brothers. His father was Michael Leahy, who led the first expedition to the highlands in search of gold. Like his brothers, Joe and John, Clem was never acknowledged by Mick Leahy, but Danny Leahy knew he was his older brother's son and gave him a job on his plantation. Clem's mother's name was Yamka Amp Wenta. Wenta's husband was from the Kopi clan, whose land neighbors my Penambi Wia clan's land, close to the Leahy brothers' settlement at Kuta.

This is my sister Rita's story of my return:

After a long time she came back. The village people said that Tilgil had come back so I ran to the *singsing* ground to see her. She was walking towards us and when I saw her she looked like a *missus* and I got frightened. She looked different without her *purpur*.

All the village people were holding her and crying but I was still scared and kept away. That night she stayed with us in the house and we slept together. After that, I wasn't scared of her any more.

The next time she came back she brought me a little radio with a long rope for a handle. I used to put the radio around my neck and carry it around with me everywhere I went.

When she was staying at Korgua I used to trick *ma* and carry my brother Las to go see her. *Ma* got cross with me for doing that and hit me. One Christmas the Leahys killed a cow and pigs and made a feast at Korgua. We went and feasted with them and came back.

As Tugl was not happy with the Leahys, he did not come to Korgua to see me. He sent my mother and Las. They brought a pig and killed it and we had another feast. They went back and told Tugl that I was in good health and that the Leahys were treating me well. The next holiday Tugl came to Korgua himself with a pig. He killed it and we had another feast.

REFLECTIONS
Rosita Henry

During my many research visits to Maggie's home in Kunguma Village after her death, I spent much time with her brother Thomas Las, seeking his reflections on his sister. Thomas was born after Maggie left for school in Vunapope. Here is what he remembered:

> By the time I was born, Maggie had already gone. From what I heard, she came back one holiday when I was a baby and my mum had a little *bilum* on her back and Maggie asked, "What's that in your *bilum*?" She said, "Oh I've got a baby boy," and Maggie was so delighted that she had a brother.
>
> When I was about five or six years old, my mother said, "We are going to go a see this white woman." We went down to Korgua, where Dan Leahy was staying, and I saw this woman with really big hair and I was scared of her. It was Maggie. She would try to hold me and I would really struggle. After some two or three days I got used to her. We would live there for as long as Maggie was there. We would live with one of Dan Leahy's wives and we would wait until Maggie went back to school and then we would come home to the village.
>
> While we were visiting Maggie, old Dan's family did good things for us. We would sleep in the house and there was plenty of food. Old Dan would wait for all his kids to come home from school and he would always kill a cow and make a big *mumu* for the kids and we would have a lot of meat. We would bring a lot of meat home too.
>
> So I knew I had a sister and every holiday we would go and visit her. Rita would come too, but sometimes my father did not let Rita come with us because she was a young girl and he wanted her to stay home, so it would be just me and my mum. Maggie would bring me toys. She

Maggie's brother Thomas Las (right) with their sister Lauie (left), 17 April 2010 (photograph by Rosita Henry).

would come home with a little round ball or something for me to play with and I would have these toys that no other kid in the village had.[1]

Thomas spent his childhood in Kunguma Village with his other siblings, mothered by his father Tugl's two wives, Jara and Aip. Maggie was away at school during most of his childhood, and was already a young adult before he really came to know her.

After Maggie finished school herself, she decided to give Thomas a similar opportunity. She paid his school fees in Hagen and sent him to school in Australia during his final years of high school. Being fluent in Temboka, Tok Pisin and English, Thomas proved to be very helpful in assisting me as I went about the village meeting Maggie's kin and conducting research on her life.

Maggie's brother Kuipa had taken her death very hard and lines of grief were etched deeply onto his face as we greeted. He was also still grieving the death of his wife Tress, who had passed away not long before Maggie. Tress had been digging for gold at the old Leahy mine site at Kuta, as many of the villagers do to earn cash, when the mud tunnel collapsed and she was buried

Maggie's brother Kuipa weaving a blind for the walls of a men's house, Kunguma Village, September 2016 (photograph by Rosita Henry).

alive. Maggie and Tress had been very close, so close that Tress and Kuipa had given one of their children to Maggie to grow up as her own. I, too, was heartbroken to hear of her death. Tress, Maggie and I had spent much time together during my visit in 2001. She had spent hours dressing me in *bilas* (traditional finery) for a dance at the Hagen Club. I was mesmerized by Tress's attention to detail as she dressed me. She lovingly placed layer upon layer of shell necklaces around my neck, and carefully arranged a possum skin so that it hung down my chest. "How wonderfully restorative to be dressed this way," I thought, and I felt a special connection to Tress for this gift of care.

Kuipa, who is renowned among his clanspeople for his expertise in weaving blinds from *pitpit* grass, reminisced about his childhood in *tok ples*. Thomas waited until he had finished before translating for me.

> Maggie would take me by the hand and lead me around the tracks and give me food. I remember she got mushrooms from the rainforest and gave them to me. Then she grew up and started to *tanim het* with other tribesmen who came to court our girls in the village. She teamed up with other young girls who were actually older than Maggie.
>
> I remember one time they were having a *tanim het* up where Noah lives. There was a big long house. All the women in the village got together and Maggie was there. Normally the girls in the village at a *tanim het* would fold their legs and sit upright. Maggie folded her legs and sat upright for a while, but then she straightened her legs and sat with them out straight and an old woman got up and said, "Hey young woman. Young women never put their legs straight, fold your legs back!" Maggie said, "Well I folded my legs for a long time and my legs are aching so that's why I put my legs straight but if you want to come and *tanim het* with this guy, you come and do it!" Yeah, so everybody burst out laughing at Maggie's response.
>
> The day Maggie went away to school, she had this bundle of flowers tied up with string in her hand. She went into the plane and took a seat on the window side. She had these flowers and she waved them at the window. We could not see Maggie but we could see the flowers waving. We came home very sorrowful that day.
>
> One time the old man, Tugl, said we should go to town to visit these people from the Sepik that were friends with Maggie. The family welcomed us and cooked us some rice and fried dough and as we were about to eat the food the family's kids got up and said, "Magdalene, Magdalene!" and we thought they were talking about someone else and then suddenly right in front of the door stood Maggie. I threw the food down and hugged her. We were so happy to see her.
>
> Then Maggie said that she was leaving to go back to Rebiamul and said goodbye to the Sepik family. As we walked out of the gate all our sisters were

7. My First Return

there. They all hugged her. There were tears of joy and then we all walked back to Rebiamul with her.

During that time, I was still in traditional clothes but when Maggie came, she brought me two little shorts and T-shirts and she brought a box full of toys. I was so rich in toys. We lived in Knep Village at the time and I would make these little roads for the toy cars. I was so happy. After that, she went back to school but we were not as worried as we were the first time, because we knew she would come back.

Those days, there was only one guy in the village Konga (married to Wai and Koina's daughter, Lut) who had a radio. Konga wouldn't let us listen to the radio unless we worked for him. I got sick of cutting firewood for Konga and used to dream of having my own radio. One day as I was walking towards our house I heard a lot of noise that sounded just like the radio at Konga's house. I thought, "Who would bring that radio into our house?" When I entered the house everyone said, "Hey Kuipa, Maggie has come to Korgua and she has sent a radio for you." I was shocked. I grabbed the radio and went all the way to Kunguma to show the boys in the village. I was really joyous inside because before that only Konga had had a radio and we had to work hard for him to listen to it. I was overjoyed that I had my own radio.

Maggie would live down at Korgua when she came back from school and at times, the old man and I would visit. One time we brought two pigs down and we had a big *mumu* down there.[2]

8
Life with the Leahys

I knew I was half white before I was about eight years old. I am not sure how I knew. Maybe some kids told me in a nasty way, but somehow knew. Once I went with my sister Tali to Kuta and we encountered my father, Patrick Leahy. We returned with all these gifts—soaps and towels—and my family wanted to throw them in the fire. They said they were smelly and we shouldn't touch them. My village family used to cover me up whenever we walked past Kuta. To disguise me, they used to cut my hair at night with a bamboo knife when I was asleep.

Grimel told me that once when I was a baby and had problems going to the toilet Patrick Leahy bought medicine to pump me out. They put me in the hospital and he used to visit me. The Leahys had made attempts to send me to school when I was younger but my village family refused to part with me. Uncle Dan even offered to buy me with pigs.

Although my family did not like me mixing with the Leahys, they trusted the bishop and allowed him to send me away to school. The Leahys used the bishop as a go-between. They gave money to the bishop and he would give it to me. When I returned from school for the Christmas holidays in 1967, instead of going back to my village home, I was taken to live with my Uncle Danny Leahy at his coffee plantation at Korgua. I don't know why this happened. My uncle allowed my parents to visit me but he would not let me visit the village. Perhaps he wanted to reduce the village influences and increase my Australian influences, but when my uncle went to town for the day, I would sneak up to my village.

To give him his due, Uncle Dan was not totally against my contact with my traditions. He encouraged me to keep speaking *tok ples* and when he had important village visitors he would call on me to interpret.

On the border of Korgua lived some of my clan members. Living there brought me into closer contact with these people. I found that all the boys and girls from my village who were the same age as me had become laborers on the plantation. Some had quite prestigious jobs like shop keeping, working as kitchen hands or supervising the coffee pickers. On their payday, they never failed to hand me a few kina. I would have been in serious trouble with my uncle if he knew I was taking money from these people but if I had not accepted their friendly offer of money, it would have been like rejecting their friendship. I wouldn't dream of doing such a thing. One thing I knew for sure was that I valued my relationship with all the tribal people related to me. They were always warm and loving towards me. Their love was unconditional.

Uncle Dan was a bit rough on me. He used to say to me, "You're a no hoper like your father." His sister told me that my father, Patrick, was my grandmother's favorite. My father and Uncle Dan used to live together in Australia and when Uncle Dan said the place was getting crowded and that someone should move out, my grandmother told Uncle Dan to move out while my father was permitted to remain with her.

According to the family history, Patrick was the black sheep of the family, but he was his mother's pet and she spoiled him. He became a heavy drinker later in life and died around 1963, unmarried, with no other known children.

While staying with Uncle Dan at Korgua during school holidays, I also got to know other members of the Leahy family. Clem and Agnes Leahy had a young son named Gerry who took a liking to me and I would play with him when I visited their house. One day I went to visit the Catholic Mission at Rebiamul and took Gerry with me. We had fun raiding the nuns' gardens.

Agnes was a kind and motherly woman from the Papuan coast. She recognized the special bond her son and I were establishing and encouraged it by building her own relationship with me. Clem was very caring and referred to the three of us as "his whole." We became very close. When Agnes died, I wrote this poem in tribute to her.

Mudmong (Sweet Heart)

In life's mystic journey
I was a little afraid
And a little lost.
A lovely lady reached out
Her arms to me
And took me under her wings.
Her warm sweet smile said it all.
There's room in her heart for me.
Knowing that she cared
Gave me the confidence
To build my life's nest

Inspired by her.
It's a fact of life
Life is given and taken.
And I shall not ask
Why her?
But no one will take from me
Her warm, loving and caring ways.
She planted in my mind
The treasures of many people.
The memories of her are
Lingering
High in the mountains
The home of her youth and beauty
And down by the deep blue seas
Her childhood playground.
Her smile will abide
Until life's journey
Comes to its crossing.

REFLECTIONS
Rosita Henry

Maggie was proud to be a member of the Leahy family and deeply respected her Uncle Dan. During our schooldays, she would fondly tell me stories about each of her Leahy cousins. One year, when I was about sixteen, Joe and George Leahy came to visit her at Mount St. Bernard College. Maggie was keen to show them off to me and I was excited to meet them, as I had already heard so much about them. Moreover, it was a rare thing for us to see anyone of the opposite sex at this girls-only boarding school!

I recall shyly shaking Joe Leahy's hand and being somewhat entranced by his winning smile. Thirty-five years later, I find myself sitting with Joe Leahy at the Hotel Poroman in Hagen town, sharing memories of Maggie. I had fortuitously met Joe in the main street of Hagen town as he was passing through in his 4WD and arranged to meet him at the Hotel. Joe recalled,

> It was only after Maggie went away to school and came back and stayed with us at Korgua that I got to know her better. Old Dan told me that she was Paddy Leahy's daughter and then we started to grow closer.
>
> I was closer to Maggie than to Danny's kids because she came through the same way as I came, through the village. She was a big girl already but she had a bit of schooling at Vunapope and they could see the potential there so they continued.

> At that time, Paddy Leahy died and he left his property to his brothers. They sold Paddy's plantation and the brothers shared the money but Danny said, "I will use my share to educate Maggie." He was a hard bloke, but a good bloke too.
>
> Danny told Bishop Bernarding,[1] "Paddy left some money to me so I'll use that money to pay for Maggie's education in Australia." But his wives, Biam and Mancy, they got it all wrong. They thought, "Why is Danny sending her to school?" They were jealous you see.[2]

Joe Leahy had his memories and interpretation of events and his brother Clem Leahy had others. Clem offered to guide me on a walk from Kunguma up to Kuta and down the mountain to the Korgua plantation in the Nebilyer. I gladly accepted the opportunity to ask him about his life and times along the way. Clem proved an excellent guide and wonderful raconteur. In spite of having suffered a heart attack that led to bypass surgery, he walked strongly and surely, pointing out the sights and chatting all the way without any loss of breath although I struggled to keep up.

> Joe and John were born up at the station at Kuta, but me and Maggie were born in the village. All Dan's kids were born after us. After his children were

Clem Leahy at Maggie's house, April 2010 (photograph by Kanawi Danomira).

born that must have been when he decided to also look after his brother's kids. That must have been what he had in his head.

He took care of all of us. He was the best, old Dan. My father, Mick Leahy, was useless, a bloody womanizer. He was useless; he wouldn't even look at us. But old Dan, he had time for us. He told the bishop to send us to School and all of that. He did the right thing because he knew we were his brother's children. And then he had his own. He had nine of them. George is from his first wife, Koka's son. Then he married Biam and Mancy. Mancy got four, Biam got five; that's all his kids.

I used to be with all the Chimbus in Goroka; in the school up to 1954. That's where I went up to grade six and then in 1955 I went to Vunapope and repeated grade six. I did the scholarship test to go to Australia and passed. I was very, very happy. Next minute the head nun, Sister Deofilia, came, patted me on the shoulder and told me, "Clem you can't go to Australia. You're too old." I had tears in my eyes. I could have been the same as Julius Chan.[3] He went to Australia. He was in the same class as me, he passed, I passed, but he was younger than me. The Leahys are very smart people. Very smart.

Old Dan never liked me very much because Joe ran away from Vunapope and he thought I ran away from school too, but they closed school and sent me home. He didn't know that and he thought that I ran away just like my brother did. He brought me to Tom Ellis's office (Tom Ellis was the District Commissioner) and he said, "Put this bastard in jail. I sent him to Vunapope to learn something and to become something but he ran away and his brother ran away too." I was very young. That was in 1961. Tom Ellis looked me up and down; he looked at Dan and looked at me; but that Tom Ellis guy was very smart. He told Dan, "Ok Dan, I'll fix him up. I'll tell the policemen to come and take him down to Baisu," and Dan really thought I was being sent away to jail in Baisu and drove away. Then Tom Ellis said, "Ok son, you tell me what happened; why you left the school." I said, "Mr. Ellis, they closed the school. Joe, yes; he ran away. He had trouble with girls and they kicked him out, but me, I was there until the last day." Then Mr. Ellis phoned Rabaul and found out it was true, that they had closed the school. He said, "Son, I think your uncle is out of his mind." Then I felt better.

He said, "You know how to do anything?" I told him, "Oh yeah I know how to drive the biggest truck." I used to drive all the big trucks in Vunapope, go and collect all the coconuts, copra, and bring it to the factory. I would fix the trucks, grease them up and all that. For two years I did that. So when I told Tom Ellis that, he said, "That's good. You can be my mechanic," so he put me into the transport department to do an apprenticeship.

We learned the hard way. Uncle Dan really taught us. I am not sure what Joe and Maggie thought, but me, afterwards, I realized that Uncle Dan was right. He was teaching us, but in a very mean way. I worked for him as a plantation manager and I went and asked him for a car just to drive to town and he said, "Go and buy your own, ya bastard. I pay you for what you are

8. Life with the Leahys

Leahys at Korgua Plantation, c. 1966. Left to right: (back row) Kathleen, Rhona (married to Joe Leahy), Maggie, Agnes (married to Clem Leahy); (middle row) Terry, Gerry Chrissy; (front row) Margaret, Bryan, Nancy (Leahy family collection).

doing for me. I am not going to give you everything. Who are you?" And then I said, "Jesus, what is this?" and then afterwards, I realized, "He was right; he was paying me, feeding me and then I go and ask for a car! If he gave us everything we wanted, then we'd be spoilt." We worked for everything we wanted. When he told me that, first I bought a motorbike to go up and down to town to have a beer and then I got a Volkswagen. Then I realized, "Dan is not wrong. I can buy my own bloody car!"[4]

I wondered what Maggie's younger Leahy cousins remembered of their early days with Maggie on Korgua Plantation.

At school, Maggie would especially tell me stories about Clem's son, Gerry Leahy, and his mother Agnes. Gerry and his wife Sally invited me to dinner at their home in Hagen town. We talked in the living room of the high-set house while Sally prepared us a tasty meal. Like Maggie and Gerry, she is also "mixed race," the daughter of a Chimbu woman and a white Australian who happened to be the schoolteacher in her mother's village. Her father, just like so many other genitors of mixed-race Papua New Guineans, left the country. Gerry relaxed in his armchair and quietly began to reminisce.

> I was an only child; then all of a sudden there was this lovely girl. I was probably four and she was thirteen. I particularly remember her taking me up to Kunguma Village. It was such a long walk and she carried me up there. We went up there because there was something happening, a feast, a *mumu*. When we got there they did for us what we do for kids now, looked after us and spoiled us.
>
> My dad, Clem Leahy, was working for Uncle Dan and my mum had a working role on the plantation as well. It would have been around 1968, so from age four to eight, that's the next set of memories I have of Maggie. We were living at Korgua and she was going to school at Vunapope and had come back for holidays. I remember she was a really good cook. She'd make pastries and cakes and, of course, because I was her pet I'd get the best when she shared it out. I remember her making sure that we'd pray every night. We'd go into the room and I'd kneel on the floor and she would too and she'd say the prayers.
>
> My childhood memories are just wonderful. It's probably what has made me very conscious of giving children an environment that's happy, full of love. That's what it was like out at Korgua. It was a wonderful place to grow up and I can recall Maggie being a part of that. I think probably, rather than being an aunty, Maggie was more like a sister to me and to her I was like a brother and that connection was because of mum as well. I think it was because of dad and mum that our relationship grew. Dad was endearing and charming and very nice and I guess all throughout their lives he and Maggie related not only as brother and sister but also as friends.
>
> Then as I became a teenager, Maggie was always there and when she was at boarding school we'd write to each other. I think Hagen was a wonderful place at that time. There were a lot of young people who'd been to school in Australia and had come back, and there was so much to do. We younger ones would always be tagging along. If there was a picnic or a BBQ or a party we'd be on the fringes, or I'd always be. Everywhere Maggie went she'd take me.[5]

After a pleasant evening with Gerry and Sally, I was eager meet with Maggie's other cousins, children of Danny Leahy, who might be willing to relate their childhood memories of the days they had spent together with Maggie at Korgua Plantation. Of all Danny Leahy's children, I knew his two youngest daughters, Margaret and Nancy, best as they used to spend holidays with my family in Cairns, while they were at school in Australia. Through her friendship with me, Maggie had arranged that they had somewhere to stay when it was impossible for them to get back to PNG for the term breaks. Maggie knew that my parents would make them welcome and that they would happily fit into our big family life. Being around my eight younger siblings would make it almost like being back at home for them!

8. Life with the Leahys

Since then both Margaret and Nancy have married and have had families of their own. Unlike their sisters, who have settled in Australia, they chose to stay and make lives for themselves in PNG.

Nancy drove up with her son and his baby daughter to meet me at Maggie's house. We sat on the front veranda drinking coffee and admiring her grandchild while she filled me in on her life since she had returned to PNG after school in Australia. I remembered Nancy as a very cute little girl, plump and healthy with a shock of blond fuzzy hair. She had grown into a big mama, with a generous spirit and a warm heart in keeping with her ample bosom. Nancy had married a man from Manus Island and had four children with him. She had lived for some years in Manus but her marriage was not a happy one and she had returned to Hagen with her children to live among her own kin.

Nancy had clearly been through hard times. In response to my request to relate some of her childhood recollections of Maggie, she began by picking up the threads of her own life story, weaving them into a pattern with her memories of Maggie.

> I had my first joint with her. I remember one night we went to Banz. That's where all her friends were and the Banz club was the in spot. Actually dad was away at this time and my brother Bernie was looking after us at Korgua. I was frightened because it was my first time out to a club at night. After a few joints at Banz, Maggie drove us back and as we were coming towards a single lane bridge, I said, "Maggie, you're going off the bridge!" but Maggie replied, "No, no." Anyway she had to stop the car because I was ready to hit her. I said, "We are going to die Maggie!" When we got out we saw that the car was almost half way off. We could have gone over the side completely.
>
> Maggie was just like my sister. She and my sister Kathleen were the two eldest girls. She was more relaxed than Kathleen. Maggie was the hippy, she was a hippy all her life, and Kathleen was more *missus*. Maggie would do the wild and adventurous things, and she'd talk about boys and we'd all be listening to her and Kathleen. Maggie was outrageous. Oh, we all know that!
>
> When Maggie lived with us at Korgua she was treated equally. Maggie and Kathleen had the same of everything. My brothers George and John are older than Kathleen and Maggie. John used to give Kathleen and Maggie hell. Oh he used to really boss them around; but he was the same with all of us.
>
> Dad really loved Maggie, because Maggie used to sit and listen to him. She was always interested. I don't know any of Dad's stories. I only know the stories Maggie passed on to me.
>
> She had a lot of dad in her, Maggie. She was strong headed, very strong headed. Dad treated her well, but she was stubborn. Maggie always voiced her own opinions, whereas the rest of us were too frightened. If you didn't do what dad wanted, he would say, "Well, I am not talking to you!"
>
> Dad was very strict with us all. Even when we were young adults, we were

still treated like young kids. There was that side to dad. He could be a mean man, but he was a good man. All of us used to do sneaky things, because that's the only way we could get away with it, by waiting for him to go to sleep or go off somewhere.

We had to make our own entertainment at Korgua. We played Chinese checkers or cards. Maggie's all-time favorite was Chinese checkers. We'd have concerts, sing and do performances for dad. We'd go bush walking and swimming. Dad would always make sure we did things as a family.[6]

I met with Nancy's older sister, Margaret, and her husband Pat Duckworth at their comfortable high-set house in Hagen town. Margaret reflected:

> For me Maggie was just always there. She was just part of our family, like a sister. I saw her as a sister. As we got older we became closer. Rather than calling her Maggie, I called her *ana* Maggie, which in Hagen means sister.
>
> My fondest memories of her are as an adult, as a mother myself and her being a mother. It was great for us living here in Hagen. I would ring Maggie and say, "Oh the kids and I are coming up." We'd take off to her place up on the mountain. Rather than us just being in town, we'd stay up there. The kids would swim; that sort of thing.
>
> Even after the kids went away to school I would ring Maggie and I would say, "*Ana*, get the BBQ fired up and I'll bring some lamb flaps." Get some corn and some ginger. We'd both be wanting to eat lamb flaps or something like that. We'd sit there and make pigs of ourselves; eat to our hearts content.
>
> She was very good. Whenever she went to a pig kill or anything, she'd always remember, always. You'd hear the car come in at night, didn't matter what time. The pig meat would have been given to her, but on her way through she'd call in and say, "*Ana, i no bikpela* but I've cut some and carried it straight to you." She'd do that.[7]

The eldest of Danny Leahy's children, George Leahy, invited me to his spacious house in Mount Hagen, located on a huge compound surrounded by high walls. He had agreed to meet me in spite of the heavy weight of business responsibilities that he bore. That day, he was particularly worried because a woman who ran across the airstrip at Porgera had been hit by one of his fleet of aircraft while it was taxiing for takeoff. We sat outside by the pool while he reminisced about his childhood, his life on the plantation, and about being "mixed race."

> The first time I became aware of Maggie was when we moved down to live on the plantation at Korgua. I was already at boarding school in Australia, at Charters Towers, probably about 1961–62. She would have been about twelve or thirteen. It was Bishop Bernarding that organized with dad to have her move in with us. She was just a village girl.
>
> Maggie was part of the family, you know. From what I can recall, she was a

young woman when she moved in with us. So she had reached puberty I guess. And usually in the village they start looking for a husband for them so that was the next stage of her life if she had not moved in with us.

We were probably roughly about the same age. I was baptized in February 1950 and I was a two- or three-month-old baby so I must have been born in November 1949. My mother is Koka. She is a Jiga. I was born in the village too. Some Lutheran missionaries took me in and I must have been seven or eight years of age when dad eventually got me. The Lutheran missionaries were going to go back to America for their long leave and they contacted dad and dad was quite happy to take me in. He was already married to Biam and Mancy. I got the benefit of learning English with the missionaries, so I could speak well with dad. It wasn't a natural thing being his son. It took a bit of time. Because I could speak English, very quickly he started leaning on me a bit. I became his right-hand man, not his favorite at all, just his worker really.

I guess it was not easy for Maggie because she'd been brought up in a village all her life, but she learned how to integrate with us. She was just part of the family. Maggie was like a big sister to the others. She did her best to fit in and it would have been very difficult to do that because she was a village girl. That's what she was. And it's amazing to see her achievements, considering. She definitely had that Leahy go in her. She was born of the right blood I guess. She was full of go. No one was going to hold her back, once she got a chance, you know, and I guess my father gave her that chance and she never looked back.

And Uncle Jim from Goroka helped out too. He helped out in a big way, because dad was pretty stretched back in those days. He had all of us, ten children, and sending us all to boarding school. He was a moderately successful farmer. The plantation was a small plantation really. He had a bit of a struggle there and I do remember Uncle Jim helping out quite a bit.

Paddy Leahy left 500 pounds to each of his brothers. Yeah he left a bit of money in his will, not much. And dad used that money to help educate Maggie. He was a wild man, Paddy. That is another book in itself, Paddy Leahy. I don't think he knew he was Maggie's father. He may not have known. He was up there at Kuta building the house but they could not get on and in the end dad kicked Paddy out. In his younger days he was a boxer, used to cut cane in North Queensland. He was a drunkard and just a really wild person. Dad said Uncle Paddy was the worst person on earth, but their mother used to dote on Paddy. She was the strength. She was a Stone. That's where the strength came from, not the Leahys. She totally dominated; she was a strong woman.

Dad really instilled so many of his values in us. He was a strong character. We didn't seem to be that much affected by being mixed race. We seemed to fit in wherever we went, at boarding school, up here. I think it was the way dad brought us up. Dad was tough on us. We never had any problems. But you do get mixed race people who have chips on their shoulders, a lot of them do.[8]

9
Australia in the 1970s

At first, I couldn't believe my luck when I was told that I was to go to school in Australia. It was a dream come true to be able to attend Mount St. Bernard College in Herberton, North Queensland. I could barely contain my happiness.

I started in grade nine and continued until I graduated high school at the end of grade twelve. Uncle Dan also paid for extra-curricular classes for me. I was taught how to play the piano and the guitar and had speech training sessions.

While at boarding school, I was lucky to meet and make friends with three nice Australian girls from different backgrounds and cultures. Rosita Rusch was a brilliant student whose parents were residents of Papua New Guinea at the time. She was the eldest of nine children in the family. Her father was German and her mother a mixed Sri Lankan woman. Her mother was very artistic. Their home was loving and warm. Usually, conversations were based on intellectual topics and there were often quite heated debates around the dining table. They struggled to give their children the best education. When Rosita was in grade eleven her parents moved to Cairns. Often I would spend time at their house in Cairns on weekends. They made me feel part of the family.

Marie Collins was an average student of mixed Aboriginal, White and Thursday Islander background. Her parents lived in Kuranda. Her father was a truck driver. She had four brothers and one sister. Hers was a happy-go-lucky type of a family. Meeting Marie's family and being invited to stay with them over the holiday weekends was a blessing in disguise for me. It was almost like life back in Kunguma Village.

Marie Martin was from an upper middle class Australian family. They owned a sugar cane farm in South Johnstone, near Innisfail. They lived in a beautiful old house built by Marie's mother's father, who had migrated to Australia from Spain. Marie's mother had also attended Mount St. Bernard

College in her school days. They were very strong Catholics who attended Church every Sunday. She had an older brother and two sisters. All the children were very smart at school and had dreams of becoming professional people. Both Marie and her older sister Carmel became medical doctors.

These girls took me under their wings and introduced me to the very diversified far north Queensland. I couldn't have asked for more. They were caring people like those I left back home in Kunguma Village. I fell in love with North Queensland and the people I came to know at a personal level. Their love for me gave me the strength and courage to enjoy life to the fullest, in both good and bad ways.

Though I liked most subjects at school, I hated accounting. I couldn't understand what they were teaching us. I went to the principal and told her that I wanted to drop that subject but she got in touch with Uncle Dan and he told her to force me to do it. As I had no choice but to continue attending the class, I spent my time there ruling pages for the teacher.

In grade eleven, I had no sense of direction; I was just floating around. Once I was sitting for exams at a desk that had a flip up lid. The nun came by and I put the desk up and accidentally hit her on her face. I was sent to Sister Mary Jude, the principal. She was very understanding. She just said, "What, change of weather or?" The nuns were generally very good to me, but they always called me a "nitwit."

We used to play sports at an oval about eight kilometers away from the school. We would walk there and back. I used to really enjoy the walk. Once, Rosita and I were offered a lift by an Italian guy, who was the father of one of the girls in our class. We refused but he practically forced us into the car and took us to school. I was so annoyed that when we got there, I walked back to the place he had picked us up and then walked back to school again.

I used to come home once a year, for the Christmas holidays. For other holidays, I used to stay with Rosita, Marie Martin or Marie Collins. Sometimes my uncle would pay my fare for me to visit my Leahy cousins and family on the Gold Coast and elsewhere in Australia. As I did not know my Australian cousins well, I felt like a stranger. I felt comfortable with my younger cousins but not with the older Leahys as they made me self-conscious about whether I was doing the right thing. I preferred to spend time with Uncle Dan's children (Nancy, Margaret, Bryan and Christine) as they had grown up in PNG like me. Uncle Dan used to give us all pocket money and we used to go shopping for clothes, flares or bell-bottom trousers, and shoes, such as clogs, that were then the latest thing in fashion. I loved the shops, social life, dance and music in Australia.

We used to have fun traveling back and forth between Cairns and Port

Moresby. The flight always left at midnight and would get into Port Moresby at about 3:00 a.m. A Papuan family of friends used to put me on the plane to Hagen and look after me while I was in Port Moresby.

A careers guidance counselor visited the college when we were in grade eleven. I liked the idea of sociology because I liked to talk to people. I decided that I wanted to study sociology and come back to PNG to do that, but Uncle Dan said I had to go into nursing and stay in Australia. Uncle Dan was trying to turn me into an Australian. He was influenced by other members of the Leahy family. They did not give me a choice. It was the eve of Papua New Guinea Independence and they thought it wasn't safe for girls in PNG. My uncle probably meant well for me. All the Australians were leaving PNG, as they were panicking that the country would go back to tribalism and could not survive without Australian administration.

I got my Australian citizenship when I was in grade eleven. Although becoming Australian was not really my idea, at the time it seemed quite convenient and I did not resist. I was at a stage of my life in which I was waiting for whatever was going to happen to happen. I just went with the flow. My friend Rosita had tears in her eyes because she thought that becoming an Australian citizen might not be the right thing to do. I had not felt one way or another about the event, until I received a letter from some friends at the University of Papua New Guinea. They said that I would be deserting our country in its hour of need if I became an Australian citizen.

Racial prejudice did not really worry me when I was in Australia. However, there was a time when I went to buy fish and chips and there was a girl serving who went to my school whose parents also lived in PNG. When it was my turn, she refused to serve me and put up the closing sign. I called her names so she called the police and gave them the number plate of the car I was in. There was a police car coming down the range from Kuranda and another one was heading the other way, so we were caught in the middle. The police officer asked who was swearing and as I did not want my friends to get into trouble, I owned up. He asked why I swore and I explained that the girl did not want to serve me although she had served the other nine people in the shop. I noticed that Australians in Australia were much more down to earth than those who lived in Papua New Guinea.

After I completed grade twelve at the end of 1973, I began as a trainee nurse at the Calvary hospital in Cairns. I made friends with a nurse from Thursday Island. We used to stick together as we were the only dark nurses. I was living in the nurses' quarters where you had to sign in and out. I got into a lot of mischief. I liked to go to the "House on the Hill" nightclub with Rosita and her sisters and our group of boyfriends and I was getting into the social life, going out to dinner and dancing the night away. I used to jump over the fence of the nurses' quarters. One night I got in late and the nurse I had gone out with had decided to stay overnight with some friends. I got the blame and was told that I was a bad influence.

That wet season there were bad floods in North Queensland and about seven people drowned. Many nurses couldn't come to work and there were only a handful of us working. I was terrified during night shift as at the time my mind was full of ghosts and that kind of thing. Under all that pressure, I realized nursing wasn't for me.

Reflections
Rosita Henry

During the late 1960s and early 1970s, when Maggie and I attended Mount St. Bernard College, it was a Catholic convent school for girls only. All the teachers were nuns from the order of the Sisters of Mercy. They wore veils and full habits, black in winter and white in summer. We too wore uniforms: grey box pleated skirts, white blouses and blue berets for daily wear and for special occasions we added ties, gloves and white panama hats. After school hours, we changed into blue and white checked dresses for sports activities.

The majority of the girls who attended the school were the daughters of Italian farmers who had migrated to North Queensland and established cane farms around the small coastal sugar towns such as Innisfail, Silkwood and Ingham, or tobacco farms near the inland towns of Mareeba and Dimbulah. There were also some girls from dairy farms near Malanda in the Atherton tablelands and from beef cattle stations in Cape York.

A handful of girls at the school were from the Torres Strait Islands and, in addition to Marie Collins from Kuranda, there were a few Aboriginal girls from Palm Island. Maggie and I were among only about five girls from Papua New Guinea. Most Australians living and working in Papua New Guinea during the 1960s and '70s sent their children to private boarding schools in Australia to complete their high school education. The Australian government at the time provided a subsidy to help pay the boarding school fees, but most of the schools charged much more than the subsidy. There was competition about the status and reputation of the schools that parents could afford to send their children to "down south" (generally schools in, or near, the cities of Brisbane, Sydney or Melbourne). During the school holidays when we returned to Papua New Guinea, I often heard teenagers boast about their different schools. At teenage parties, there was a clear hierarchy based on where one went to school. Fortunately, I did not have to compete as few had even heard of Mount St. Bernard College, which was located in a remote old tin mining town west of Cairns.

The Sisters of Mercy ran the school with temporal efficiency. Bells regimented our daily lives and the occasional use of the cane for punishment ensured obedience to school rules. The day began with one of the sisters ringing a little bell at the dormitory door. Each girl had a bed and a chair with a white cotton curtain to pull across for privacy when we dressed. At the sound of the bell, the nuns expected us to jump up, dress, strip our bed sheets, place our chair upside down on the bed and drape the sheets over the chair to air while we went to morning mass or to the classroom to study before breakfast.

Mealtimes were highly regulated, with everyone sitting in unison only after saying grace and leaving the room in unison only after saying thanks to God for His bounty. At each table was a head girl whose role was to oversee table manners and serve the food. After breakfast, we went back to our dormitories to make our beds before a bell call sent us to our various classrooms.

The school day was punctuated by further bell calls to morning tea, lunch, afternoon tea, sports time, dinnertime and study time. After dinner, one of the sisters would distribute our mail. The nuns reserved the right to open and censor our mail, particularly if they suspected that the letter was from a boyfriend! On Saturdays, time was set aside to respond to our mail, only one letter each week, which had to be to a parent or a guardian, and a second letter every three weeks to another family member, such as a grandparent.

It was against rules to leave the school grounds except on official excursions and on sports day, when we walked to the sports ground on the other side of the town. This was not really a hardship as the town had only one main street with a couple of shops. There was nothing much to tempt us, apart from perhaps catching a glimpse of the boys who boarded at Woodley College across the road. We were forbidden to associate with Woodley students, as they were not Catholics. Instead, once a year a school dance was organized for the older girls with the boys from St. Augustine's College, over 100 km away in Cairns. The boys would travel up by bus to Herberton.

The event was strictly supervised. During the dance that Maggie and I attended in grade twelve, one of the nuns walked around the hall with a ruler inserting it between each couple to ensure we were dancing at least 12 inches apart!

I had already been attending Mount St. Bernard for two years before

9. Australia in the 1970s

Maggie arrived in 1969. We immediately became the best of friends, spending much time together during the next four years until graduation in 1973. I had great admiration for Maggie's strength of character. Although she had started school late, she caught up quickly and was better at her work than many of the other girls in our class. I thought she was brilliant. She sometimes asked for my help in checking her spelling and grammar, but she was a keen thinker, sharp-witted, intelligent and quick to learn.

While some of the other girls were miserable about being imprisoned in a boarding school, Maggie and I treasured our days there. We felt that the school offered us the luxury to dream and prepare for the future. Boarding school presented Maggie with opportunities that she could not have imagined if she had stayed in her village in Mount Hagen and it gave me the chance to bury my head in books, which was impossible at home with a bunch of noisy younger siblings to care for while my parents struggled to make ends meet. Although the nuns were strict, they were kind enough and most of the other girls were friendly. We enjoyed a caring circle of friends. It was a time to share our girlish hopes and wonder where our lives might lead. Our heads were filled with romance and we read whatever love stories we could lay our hands on. Georgette Heyer's regency novels were all the rage. Maggie too was enamored with them. I had forgotten all about this until I rediscovered *Devils Cub* and *Frederika* on her bookshelf in her house at Kunguma Village after her death.

The nuns turned a blind eye to us reading these romances but on Sunday mornings we were expected to read only biographies of the saints. There was a large library in the college devoted to saints, such as Saint Thomas Aquinas, Saint Katherine and Saint Francis of Assisi. I cannot remember reading too many because Maggie and I soon discovered Father Brown hidden among the books—a collection of short detective stories by G. K. Chesterton. Perhaps it mistakenly found its way into the library, or some other student before us hid it there, but each week Maggie and I would take turns secretly reading these mysteries while virtuously pretending we were pouring over a very different kind of mystery, the miracles of the saints.

On Sunday afternoons, parents who lived close enough would visit their daughters at the school. They would bring picnic lunches and treats for their daughters and the families would sit companionably together around the school grounds. This is when Maggie and I felt most homesick. We would console ourselves with sweets from the tuck-shop, while listening to pop music on Maggie's transistor radio and talking about home. Because our families lived in Papua New Guinea, they were not able visit us. On long weekends and mid-term holidays when the other girls went home, we had to stay behind

Mount St. Bernard College School photograph, Grade 12, 1973. Left to right: (back row) Josie Tiepo, Maggie Leahy, Rosita Rusch, Louise Cable, Frances McNeil, Faye Pini; (front row) Joy Marino, Rosa Lanzo, Marie Martin, Margaret De Campo, Angelina Murano.

unless one of the Australian students took pity on us. Over the years, Maggie and I spent many school breaks with friends, becoming very familiar with small town life in North Queensland. We learned about cane and tobacco farming and the social hierarchies that characterized the cattle stations in Cape York. We also had the privilege of experiencing Aboriginal family life in Kuranda during the early seventies, at a time when a wave of hippies seeking an alternative lifestyle inundated this "village in the rainforest," about which I was later destined to do doctoral research (Henry 2012).

In 1972, my parents left Papua New Guinea to return to Australia and live in Cairns. Thus, during the last two years of high school, I was able to invite Maggie home for the holidays and she came to love my mother as her own. They were kindred spirits in that both were a bit of a rebel. Maggie admired my mother's creativity and mum loved Maggie's feistiness, her joyful spirit and her sense of humor.

9. Australia in the 1970s

Maggie and I spent the Christmas holidays of 1973 in Cairns, after we completed our final year of school. Maggie began her training as a nurse and I was headed for Canberra to study at the Australian National University. It was a heavy wet season that year but in spite of all the rain, we had a wonderful time together going out on the town, meeting boys, dancing, partying and enjoying our freedom after all the years we had spent spirited away at school.

10
Picking Up Threads: Back to PNG

Upon my return to Hagen in 1974, the first thing my village family tried to do was to sell me off for a Land Cruiser. My father, Tugl, came to see me and said, "All your age group has been married off. You'll end up a spinster!" "Get to the point," I said, suspicious of his intentions. He confessed that one of the lineages of the Mogei tribe had decided to put all their coffee money together to buy a Land Cruiser to pay for my brideprice. "The Mogei man is a good match for you," he urged. Tugl was used to people giving pigs, kina, steel axes and knives, oil and cassowaries as part of brideprice, but not a Land Cruiser!

"I'll choose my own husband," I insisted, refusing point blank to be married off. Instead, I got a job at the pharmacy in Hagen and remained a single woman, developing platonic relationships with a number of men in Hagen. I partied and went out to hotels as I had done in Australia. In Papua New Guinea women were not supposed to act this way but more and more women had begun to do so.

In late 1974, I went to Port Moresby and worked as a trainee public relations officer in the Office of Information. During my employment, I was involved in radio talk shows and was responsible for answering inquiries from tourists and doing tourism promotions. During that year, I also worked for the Highlander Hotel as an accounts clerk.

REFLECTIONS
Rosita Henry

I left home in Cairns for university in Canberra in February 1974, expecting to see Maggie again in Cairns during the term holidays. Instead, Maggie decided to return to PNG and suggested I join her there. I excitedly took up her invitation not only to spend time with her but also because I was keen to

10. Picking Up Threads

meet the people she had told me so much about and whose lives, as I discovered during my studies, happened to be of great fascination to anthropologists.

Maggie met me in Port Moresby and we spent a couple of days there before traveling together to the highlands to stay with her Uncle Dan on his coffee plantation at Korgua in the Nebilyer Valley. Dan Leahy was kind and hospitable but very strict with us. He was hard of hearing and barely able to see, but he was still fit and strong enough to run the plantation. He took us on a long and arduous walk from Korgua up the mountain range to Kuta Ridge and down into Mount Hagen. Although I was only 18, I was not particularly fit and, unaccustomed to the thin mountain air, I struggled behind, puffing and panting. If Maggie was also short of breath, she did not let on. It was a relief each time we came across people walking in the other direction, because they would stop and shake hands, giving me time to recover.

I noted that the men carried only axes or bush knives, while the women lugged huge loads of firewood and sweet potatoes in *bilums* on their backs. The woven handles of the bags were slung over their foreheads, while I carried the finely made red, white and blue *bilum* that Maggie had given me, over one shoulder. I tried carrying it the Highland way and immediately felt more balanced as I walked.

The framework of the original house that Maggie's father, Patrick Leahy, had built at Kuta, where Dan had his old gold mine, was still standing. We were able to make our way around the shell of the house and peer through the window openings to glean what it must have been like living on the mountain ridge before the gold mine became unprofitable and Dan moved down to the Nebilyer Valley to grow coffee. The view was spectacular—an intricate patchwork of village gardens and larger fields of plantation coffee, in several shades of green and brown. Thin spirals of smoke rose from the hearths of houses clustered across the valley.

While staying at Korgua plantation I met Dan Leahy's two wives, Biam and Mancy. The women were friendly and fun loving. They appeared to be companionable with each another. I noticed that they shared the household tasks and would take turns brewing us steaming cups of freshly ground, home-grown coffee. It was unfiltered, so I had to wait for the coffee to settle in order to avoid a mouthful of coffee grains.

Maggie was eager to take me to meet her Penambi kin but Dan Leahy refused to let us leave the plantation. Frustrated, Maggie waited until he went into town one day and then took me for a walk to a hamlet close to the plantation. We scrambled uphill along a well worn, muddy pathway until we reached a cleared area with a cluster of small houses. The roofs were thatched with grass and the walls were neatly woven. There were hearths inside but no chimneys. Through the smoke in one of the houses I could barely make out an old man lying on a small platform. He was thrilled to see Maggie. He appeared to be suffering from a chest infection. He showed us a stinging leaf that he had been rubbing on his chest to relieve the pain. Maggie wanted to give him a gift before we departed and asked me if I had a few coins, but I had none with me to give.

One night, Maggie and I waited until Uncle Dan was asleep before tiptoeing out of the house. Maggie had heard that a special event was being held in a village nearby. We walked with our kerosene lantern to attend the traditional courtship ceremony, a *tanim het*. By the time Maggie and I arrived, the event was in full swing. We were eagerly ushered inside. There were several pairs of young men and women sitting in the center of the room with a crowd of men and women around them. Each pair knelt with their foreheads pressed together, swaying from side to side in rhythm to songs sung by members of the audience.

Sensing my fascination with the performance, Maggie asked one of the young men to *tanim het* with me in order to show me how it was done. I sat down beside him and awkwardly gave it a go, to the amused appreciation of the audience. Maggie told me later that the young man went around Hagen town for years boasting to everyone that he had turned heads with a *kundul amp* (white woman). The story seems to have become part of local folklore, as one of my students, while doing research among a neighboring tribe over 40 years later, was told that his teacher had participated in *tanim het*!

All too soon, my holiday drew to an end and I had to return to my studies in Canberra. Because my flight departed from the coastal town of Lae, Maggie arranged for Joe Leahy to give me a lift from Mount Hagen down the highlands highway in his coffee truck. Maggie saw me off at Joe's house, where I also met his wife Rhona, who was pregnant. The highway took us on a fascinating tour through the highlands and across the flat Markham Valley. Joe was excellent company and a wonderful raconteur. He stopped the truck frequently to allow me to take in the scenery and photograph village houses and people along the way. Regrettably, I did not keep a diary of that trip.

I was not to see Joe Leahy again until more than ten years later on television in Australia. During the late 1980s, the film *Joe Leahy's Neighbors* was screened and as I sat watching the film in my living room surrounded by my own three children, I was surprised and touched to hear Joe calling his eldest daughter Rosita. His wife Rhona had given birth to their second child, a baby girl, and they had named her after me! Somehow, in the many letters and cards we had exchanged since then, Maggie had forgotten to tell me this.

I returned to Australia after my all too brief holiday, but Maggie stayed in Papua New Guinea, against the wishes of her Uncle Dan. She stayed not only because she had realized that a nursing career was not for her, but also because it was the eve of Papua New Guinea's Independence and she felt a strong calling to contribute to the growth of the new nation.

In 1975, during the semester at my residential college in Canberra, I received a long and distressing letter from Maggie explaining that she was pregnant. She did not mention the name of the father, but wrote that Uncle Dan was furious with her and that the Leahys had ostracized her. She said that some of her male cousins had threatened her and had called her a *pamuk* (prostitute) because they thought she had shamed the family. As Nancy Leahy remembered,

> Dad and Maggie went through a period where they never spoke. Dad wasn't happy when Maggie quit nursing in Australia and after she became pregnant with Bernadine he refused to associate with her. He didn't talk to Maggie for about eight years, something like that, but when they got back together they really bonded again and became very friendly.
>
> We are a stubborn family; we are all very stubborn. I know Maggie went through a hard time with my brothers. Oh, they all gave her heaps, even Joe and Clem. They all said real mean things, but at the end of the day, Maggie was the one that kept this family together. She'd bring us all together at Christmas time. She'd have *mumus* and invite everyone. To me, she was like life itself.[1]

And Joe Leahy revealed, with his usual candor,

> Old Dan became really nasty with Maggie after she got pregnant. That's when she came out to Waipip, where I had a house. My wife Rhona took her down there and she stayed with us until she gave birth. I am her brother so my wife took her in.[2]

Without question, Joe and Rhona invited Maggie to stay with them during her pregnancy. A couple of weeks after my meeting with Joe, I visited Rhona in Brisbane to hear her side of the story.

> I married Joe in 1968 and I used to see Maggie when she came home from boarding school. We lived out where the factory is at Waipip. When I gave birth to Paddy she was one of the young girls, my sisters, who came to babysit Patrick. I was pregnant with Tots (Rosita) when you came over in 1974. Then when I was pregnant with Jim, she was pregnant with Bernadine. So I took her in. We were both pregnant. She looked after the kids too and helped me. Then she gave birth and, of course, I wanted Bernadine. I wanted to adopt Bernadine, but Maggie wanted her baby.[3]

It seems there was no shortage of people willing to adopt Maggie's baby. Clem Leahy and his wife Agnes also offered to adopt Bernadine.

According to Bernadine, her mother told her that Kerry Foley, whose father used to be the District Commissioner in Mount Hagen, was very supportive during her pregnancy. If Maggie had shared her intimate feelings and experiences with anyone then it would have been with Kerry, but Kerry had died tragically in an accident in 1980, so I decided to arrange a meeting with one of their mutual friends, Lois Logan, who was the wife of a *kiap* (patrol officer) stationed in the Western Highlands, to see if she could help shed light on some of the mysteries of Maggie's life at this time.

> I first saw Bernadine as a young child sitting in the middle of the nature strip with these village people. You know, people who were dressed in traditional attire, not Western clothes and stuff. So I started asking around. It was unusual to see a little white girl with village people. It was usual to see them maybe with a house boy or house Mary but not with real villagers. Then I heard that she could speak and understand the language and I thought, "Where does this little girl come from?"
>
> I asked Kerry Foley and she said, "Oh that will be Maggie Leahy's little daughter." I was curious because I hadn't heard about a female Leahy. I had heard about Joe and Clem and John but I hadn't heard about Maggie."
>
> I was curious about her because of the cultural things, what it meant to be a mixed-race person living in Papua New Guinea at that time. I was interested also because I thought she might make a good friend. My husband was a patrol officer and it was really hard making friends with expatriates working in New Guinea; you would make friends with someone and then they would leave.
>
> Kerry Foley was a key link in my relationship with Maggie. After Kerry died, Maggie and I became much closer. Kerry's death was very traumatic. She was decapitated by the rotor of an airplane.
>
> The day before the accident, a plane carrying the premier of the Southern Highlands had gone down and people were out looking for it. Kerry was at our house the night before and she said, "I just want to go and help; anything I can do." That morning when they all got on the plane the pilot jokingly said, "Oh there's oil on the windscreen can someone get out and wipe it off?" Kerry said, "I'll help," and got out and was decapitated. It was terrible.
>
> I had a dream before Kerry died. I dreamt about a metal frame being taken up to the sky, like on a crane. It wasn't moving. There was a person in it wearing a pink dress. Suddenly, the person in the pink dress fell out and was killed. I didn't know who it was.
>
> The day that Kerry died was very traumatic for everyone. I put my daughter Opal in the pusher and I wandered around the streets with her. I met Maggie. She just walked up to me in the pink dress that I had seen in my dream. I remember saying, "So you know?" and she said, "Yeah I know." I told her my dream and she said, "I'm wearing Kerry's dress." It was a pink chenille dress, really unusual.[4]

11
Motherhood: Bernadine

My daughter Bernadine was born in 1975. My relationship with her father was short term. When I discovered I was pregnant, I was nervous and scared but at four months, I accepted the situation I was in and prepared for the birth. At that time, I had a good group of male friends. One night we were drinking and I told them not to give me anything to drink as I was carrying a baby. They were shocked and each one felt my tummy to feel the baby kick. After that, they took on a responsible role and started looking after me and helping me get the things I needed.

When the Leahys heard, they were not happy. They advised me to adopt out the baby. Joe Leahy said, "Why are you having the baby? Where's the father?" but his wife Rhona was very kind. They invited me to live with them and they would take me to the hospital for my visits, but Uncle Dan refused to talk to me for many years.

Bishop Bernarding was very nice to me during my pregnancy so I told him that if it was a boy I'd name the baby after him. The bishop helped me pay rent for my flat in town after I had the baby and on the first day we moved in I radioed him to come and help me light the gas stove.

When she was born, I had two choices, Bernadine or Anita. I asked Rhona which name she liked best and she said Bernadine because it's unusual, so I chose Bernadine, after the bishop. I also named her after my mother Jara and me. She was christened Bernadine Jaralyn. Her village name is Lauie.

I took Bernadine to work when she was only three weeks old. I was working as a ledger clerk with South Pacific Bank. Because I needed money to feed the baby, I also took jobs with the ANZ Bank[1] and with a coffee buying company. The boss of this company was a really awful, colonial type and used to bash the boys.

If my village family was embarrassed about me being a single mother, they did not show it. They were supportive. One time my father Tugl went around asking my cousins and aunties for money. He collected about $80 and brought it to my flat to give to me. At that time, my breasts were running out of milk and I needed a fridge to store Bernadine's milk.

Although I had adopted church values from Bishop Bernarding, because I had a baby out of wedlock, I began to revert to my childhood beliefs, such as appealing to spirits for the strength to continue and for the courage not to be a pushover. However, Bishop Bernarding continued to be like my "father" in life until we broke apart after a big argument.

The argument was over me reporting a priest, who had molested some village boys, to the police. The bishop said I should have gone to him instead of the police and that now the Catholic Church's good name was ruined. I said he should give the boys 400 kina to go to the hospital for counseling. He told me that I had "bitten the hand that fed" me and refused to talk to me after that. I replied that he was a hypocrite as he preached one thing and did another when he was trying to protect the Catholic institution.

On another occasion, a Catholic priest asked Bishop Bernarding to give him dispensation to marry a Canadian girl he had met. Bishop Bernarding was very ashamed of this and wouldn't give me a lift to the airport to say goodbye to the priest and his girlfriend. I was learning that people I'd idolized all my life were only human.

Nevertheless, I am pleased to say we made up before he died. At his funeral, I was busy filming and did not shed any tears. It was only later when I was editing and looking at all the footage that I cried my heart out. I realized that he had truly been a father to me.

REFLECTIONS
Rosita Henry

Bernadine and I sat on the verandah of the house that she and her husband Kanawi had built on the mountain beside Maggie's place, talking about her early childhood memories. I remembered Maggie sending me a photograph of her daughter in a Christmas card and wondered whether Maggie had ever told Bernadine who her biological father was.

"What if in the course of my research for this book I find out who he is?" I asked Berni. "Would you want to know?" Bernadine recalled:

> I went through stages as a young person wondering who my biological father was and when I was in high school I thought that I would go and find out who I am. Mum gave me a name. She said his name was Wayne Wright. Now I think that she made it up. I don't know why. There could possibly be a Wayne Wright, I don't know.

11. Motherhood

Maggie (left) and Bernadine, Kunguma Village, c. 1982 (Wilson family collection).

Mum told me that it was really hard for her and that the Leahys were disappointed in her for getting pregnant. She had a difficult time during the pregnancy and afterwards but her friend Kerry was supportive and Uncle Clem said, "If you don't want to have the baby, then I'll have the baby and I'll look after her," but mum decided that she was going to keep me.

I guess one of my earliest childhood memories is of going to visit Bishop Bernarding. Mum would be really happy. You could tell that she was excited. It was a cozy little home right next to the church at Rebiamul. Now it's bare but when he was alive there were flowers growing. He had this coffee table in the middle of the lounge and under the table were all these stuffed toys. I was fascinated and always wanted to go so I could play with them and he would say things like, "Dance for me and I'll give you a lollie." I was maybe three years old. Mum told me that she had named me after him.

He died in America and then they brought his body back and they buried him at Rebiamul. It was a big deal. I remember going to his funeral. It was packed. Everybody went, I guess, because he was the Bishop for the Western Highlands. I remember mum making a big fuss, making sure she had flowers and really wanting to be there. She was really sad.

> I remember that wherever mum went, I was there. When she went out partying she'd take me and I'd end up falling asleep somewhere. Mum always had people around, especially her sister Rita and her mother Jara. She was never on her own, never parenting on her own. That's probably why I grew up knowing the language.[2]

The smell of wood smoke from the cooking fires in the village drifted our way. It was an agreeable smell, homely and comforting. Old Elizabeth Ump (Api Ump) sat nearby weaving a *bilum*. She had been working in the garden all morning and had come to rest and enjoy a cup of coffee with us, as was her custom. She was one of a few remaining women of the village who were of Maggie's mother's generation. No one could tell me exactly how old she was but she looked ancient. Her face was deeply lined and her body thin and stooped with age. As she sat and listened to us talking in English, I wondered how much she understood. Sometimes she tried to join in the conversation but I found it hard to understand her. I assumed it was because of my poor grasp of the language, until Berni told me she had a very bad stutter and that even those who had known her all their lives found it difficult! Yet, while she struggled to weave sounds into comprehensible utterances, Elizabeth was an expert weaver of *bilums*. Her hands were never idle. Whenever and wherever she sat down to rest, she would start to work on her latest creation. She had developed a distinctive style, combining a rainbow of colored threads into a complex pattern that was recognizably her own.

As I pondered over Berni's account of her early childhood, I pictured her being carried around in just such a *bilum*, woven with loving care by Maggie's mother Jara, or her other mother Grimel, Jara's co-wife. While Elizabeth Ump sat with us companionably weaving, Berni continued with her story:

> I was six when we moved from Hagen town up to Kunguma Village and I could already talk *tok ples*. In the village house, we had to go to the toilet outside. Mum was scared of the dark so when we wanted to go to the toilet, she'd open the door and just make us squat just outside the door. She did not want to walk us down to the toilet because she was scared of ghosts.
>
> When we went to sleep at night, I remember being thirsty and wanting a drink and she couldn't get me a glass of water. I don't know why; maybe it was dry season and the tank was empty and we'd have to get the water from the river. She said to me, "Just go to sleep with your mouth open and the angels will come in the night and in the morning when you wake up you won't be thirsty because you'll know that the angels gave you a drink." I felt frustrated because I really wanted a drink but in the morning when I woke up and wasn't thirsty I thought, "Wow, the angels really did come!"
>
> When I ran to her crying and scared at night after a nightmare, mum said,

11. Motherhood

"You know, when you get scared do you feel your heart jump? Well that's your heart growing bigger and bigger, so you need to have nightmares so that your heart can get bigger and bigger as you get bigger." After I had my daughter Jaradeenah, who was born deaf, I really wished that I could share that with her, because it was comforting for me.

I have other vague memories of when I was a child. They are not really memories, but based on feeling. For example, I feel that Nancy Leahy's mum, Biam, was full of love. When she got sick and died, it was really sad. That was the first time I saw Nancy. I guess she had been at boarding school in Australia. She was crying and crying and crying and I had no idea who this person was who was just sob-

Elizabeth Ump weaving one of her fine *bilums*, Kunguma village, 2011 (photograph by Rosita Henry).

bing her heart out. After Nancy came back from Australia, she came here and lived with us and that's when we got to know her and became really close.

We also spent a lot of time with other Leahys, like Uncle Joe and Auntie Rhona and Auntie Agnes and Uncle Clem. I have many memories of being with them, but then they were suddenly not around and I didn't know why. Maybe that was when they had a falling out with mum and were not talking.

After we came up here, Api, mum's mother Jara, lived not far from us. I remember running in and out of her house, getting *kaukau*. Api was always around taking care of us. We would come home from school and run off to the river and have a swim and she would be there at our house to take care of us, have a fire lit, and give us *kaukau* and Milo. She actually lived with us for a while. Grimel, her co-wife, didn't live with us, but she was close and she would come over a lot. She was a lovely woman.

I don't think Grimel and Api really liked each other; they tolerated each other. I didn't see them being best of friends. I don't remember my grandmother being close to any particular woman in the village. When I think about the women in the village, I'm sure that they have certain preferences, but I don't see the alliances. Maybe I'm not around enough to notice.

Tota, my grandfather Tugl, used to scare me. He would walk around with his big stick and just whack us with it every now and then when he felt like it, just to put the fear in us. He was a tough guy but he was also really caring. His other wife, Aip, was nice to us too.

I was really close to mum's sister, Rita. I would go and stay with her and her first husband who was from the Jiga tribe. I loved that man; he used to spoil me rotten and Rita did the same, so much so that I am really close to Rita now. I know I am going to take care of her; whatever she needs. You know how you have that extended family and your mother's sister is your mother as well? I really feel that with her. She would go to sleep with me at night like a child goes to sleep with her mum. Another of mum's sisters who was around a lot was Tali and I was close to her as well. I did not see much of mum's three older sisters because they had married and left the village.

I don't have a lot of memories of mum's brother's wives, except for Agnes, Pora's wife. When I was younger, I was really close to them as well. I would go to Knep Village and stay with them. Agnes made me *bilums* and gave me gifts and took care of me. And Pora, I just loved him. I thought he was the nicest uncle that I had and I looked up to him. I still have a soft spot for him.

We felt free to go anywhere in the village. Mum had strawberries, broccoli, cucumbers, and sweet potatoes in her garden and we could just go and pick

Bernadine carrying Pora and Agnes's daughter, Anita, Kunguma Village, c. 1983 (Wilson family collection).

11. Motherhood

whatever we wanted. You were never hungry; you never needed anything; you never wanted for anything.

Our relations always fussed over us. I hated being fussed over; I just wanted to be the same as everybody else, but mum would say, "You are different so just accept it and get on with it." For example, because my relations in the village didn't want me to sit on the floor, they would go out of their way to find me something to sit on. I just wanted to be treated the same as everybody else; I didn't want to be treated special.

But being fussed over has its perks as well, like when we had a pig kill. Apa Noah and others had a big *moka*. They got dressed up and they did a *singsing* and killed their pigs and *scaled* it (shared the meat) and everything. We were running up and down, jumping into the *mumu* holes and asking for the pigs' bladders and blowing them up; they were our balloons. We had so much fun. I was maybe ten or eleven. The whole *singsing* ground was full of pigs.

At that time we owned a shop in town called Jara Clothing. My grandmother would come to town sometimes and then would sit outside the shop to wait for us in the afternoon until it was time to go home. One day I stopped outside the shop and complained to Api, "Oh I'm hungry"; because your grandmother is your grandmother and you can ask for anything you want. She said, "All I've got is a cucumber," and I said, "Ok, I'll have that." By this time, people in the street had gathered around. I think this was the first time I realized that I could speak the language and it was strange to them because I was white. I realized then that I was a little bit different. Not in a bad way, but as a conscious thing.

My main friends in the village were Kai, Noah's daughter, and Glant, Epetua's daughter. I went to school in town but they went to the village school and I would play with them on the weekends and holidays. I'd get them to come over and we'd have tea parties. We'd go swimming and catch frogs and birds and then go into the village and decide who was going to eat what part of the frog after we'd cooked it on the fire.

Once they convinced me to steal some cucumbers from down the road. This old woman had laid them out to sell but she wasn't around. They lied and told me the cucumbers belonged to a witch. The woman told mum some time later and then I realized that the kids had tricked me.

On another occasion we decided to get tattoos. Kai got me to steal some tobacco leaves. She said she needed the sap from the tobacco leaves to mix with the ash to make the tattoo, but she just wanted to smoke the tobacco leaves. I was naïve because I was a couple of years younger.

Sometimes mum would take us to the Nebilyer Valley; we'd walk from Kunguma down to the Nebilyer because there was a *singsing* on. We'd get there and everybody would be fascinated by us and our long hair. We'd be excited to be in the *singsing* atmosphere with everybody dressed up and happy and dancing.

Once, mum took me with Gerry Leahy and Joe Mek Tiene[3] for a walk down to Korgua in the Nebilyer. On the way, when we got to Kugulwe, mum just skipped off. When we finally caught up with her, she was picking cucumbers from a garden. She handed them to us and we ate them. Then she skipped around saying, "I was born here." Finally we got to Korgua and swam in the river, and had a great day. That night, after we got home and went to bed, I woke up to mum screaming. Dad said mum was bumping into the walls in the bathroom. Then in the morning when she woke up, the side of her cheek right down to her neck was swollen. She went to the doctor but he did not know what was wrong with her.

You know, when you get sick in the village there is a reason. People are worried that you are feeling badly towards someone, or you have a grudge, or you are unhappy about something. Everyone was concerned and worried about mum, so they all came, all the older people as well, Tugl and all her old uncles (Kuan's brothers).

At that time mum's brother Kuipa was the security guard and he told everyone that he had seen a light travelling and going to the bathroom. He said that he had been so scared that he took off and went home. Mum said that she felt that someone had picked her up in the bathroom and thrown her against the wall. I told her that she had skipped off at Kugulwe to pick cucumbers during our walk but she had no memory of that at all.

Mum's uncles put everything together and said that mum's father Kuan must be cross with her. When you die, people make a feast for you and although many years had passed, she had not held a feast, so he was cross. They said that she should kill a pig in honor of Kuan and the other people from Kugulwe who had gone. So then, mum killed a pig and did the right thing and the next thing her face was back to normal.

I hate the thought of that though. It is just scary that they can be cross with you from the outside. You wouldn't want anyone cross with you from that side because you wouldn't even know. Traditionally they say that you are stronger when you are outside; the *tok ples* word means "outside." They say "*pena*." You can see everything and know everything and your force is stronger when you are out there.

When I was younger growing up and right until just before mum died, I always felt like I didn't achieve what she wanted me to achieve. I just felt that I was never good enough. I remember her telling me, "You have to be a lawyer. Otherwise you're just a mixed-race bum like the rest of them." I only just understand that now. At the time growing up I was really sensitive and thought, "Why is she so mean?" I'd bring home my report and she'd look at it and I'd be really proud of what I had done but she would say, "You can do better than that."

I think it comes from the fact that she was one of the first mixed-race people in this country. She didn't fit in with the Europeans or the Western people and she didn't fit in with the national people and she had to prove herself in both cultures. She had to work extra hard in both worlds to prove herself so

11. Motherhood

that's why she didn't want us kids to be lost. I can understand that now but at the time, I didn't understand it. I thought she was harsh.

Thankfully, she believed in me. When I was in year ten, I had an English literature teacher who told me I was never going to be a lawyer. I wanted to do work experience in a law firm and she told me to be realistic and just do work experience at the Highlander Hotel, because maybe I'd be good in the hospitality industry. This was a white Zimbabwean woman. When mum heard that, she was ropable. She wanted to go to the school and tell that teacher a thing or two. I was in tears and said, "No mum!" and dad was kind of siding with the teacher and said, "If the teacher said that, then the teacher knows," but mum just said, "No way! No daughter of mine is going to finish school at Year 10. She is going on to Year 11 and 12 and then she's on to University and the world is at her feet."

So mum really pushed and pushed for me to make it to Mount St. Bernard College. They had to get a bank loan. Because mum and dad made sacrifices to send me to college in Australia, I worked hard. I studied all the time and then got accepted into James Cook University (JCU) to do law. Mum and dad couldn't pay for it so I went to the University of Papua New Guinea (UPNG). Mum really fought for me to get in. They denied me because they give preference to the kids that go to school in PNG. We flew down to Moresby and mum went and saw the Dean and the Chancellor of the University and made a really big hu ha and said, "I'll sue you for denying my child her right to an education." They put me into an arts foundation, bridging course. While I was doing that, I applied for an AusAid[4] scholarship and won it. I went to JCU to study law and mum was really proud.

By this time I had already met Kanawi, partying away at UPNG and having a really good first year, enjoying my life. When I went down to JCU, I felt really awkward and out of place. I was homesick and unhappy. I didn't feel like I fitted in. When I say that it was cultural, that I was not

Bernadine (right) and Kanawi (left) Danomira, Kunguma Village, 17 September 2009 (photograph by Jaradeenah Danomira).

fitting in because I was from here, people laugh and say, "How can that be because you're white?" But I feel at home in PNG and my identity is with the people here. I struggled being in a group of Australian people that know what they want and are direct. I had a hard time making friends, so I didn't try. I didn't apply myself. I just went through the motions of being there. I went home for the semester break and came back pregnant.

I couldn't tell mum so I rang dad from the payphone near the JCU bookshop. Dad said, "Ok, you better tell your mother." I said, "Can you?" So he told her and then she rang me up and said, "Have you got anything to tell me?" and I said, "No," and then she got really angry. She said, "You know what you are? You are a baby having a baby, so you'd better grow up, look after your baby yourself, and don't bother coming home because if you come home we will argue and it's not good for your baby. You go and live with him and his family in Port Moresby." So I did.

I had met Kanawi's mother only once before. Kanawi told his uncle and his uncle told his mum and dad and they were really quite good about it. I flew back from Townsville and they picked me up from the airport. They moved out of their bedroom and gave it to Kanawi and me.

I was lucky because the overseas student advisor guy at JCU was really good and said, "You can go and take a year off and then come back," and worked it out with the AusAid scholarship people.

I think mum was disappointed because she didn't want history to repeat itself. She wanted me to be successful and in her mind that meant getting a degree. But when I did finally have Jaradeenah mum came down to Moresby and she was beaming; she was absolutely happy.

Then I went back to JCU and Kanawi came with me. We got married. I finished the law degree. It wasn't easy being married, being told your daughter is deaf, going through all of that, but we managed and we got through it.

Then, just before mum died she told me that she was proud of me. She told me I was a good daughter. I think that the way that she pushed me was just her trying to motivate me because she didn't want me to be lost or not know who I was.

12
Working Woman

I had to support Bernadine and myself so in 1976 I decided to start my own business. I began with "scratch and smile" T-shirts and denim jeans. I had $800 to spend so I telephoned one of my friends in Cairns and asked her to find me some T-shirts and colonial jeans. I sold these to expatriate wives for a big profit.

Eventually I had enough funds to rent a space to set up a retail clothes shop. Instead of painting the shop, I decided to line the walls with woven blinds. I asked the village blokes to make them for me. Mike Bromley gave me a gramophone for the shop. He also gave me some big plastic jewelry to sell. The village women saw what I was wearing and came to buy.

Later, I placed an order in Singapore for batiks. I was learning about business and moving on. Keith taught me bookkeeping. He was a better teacher than the nuns at Mount St. Bernard College! We were not yet married then. I had a ball running this business. My friends used to come and story with me. They used to dress up in scarves at that time and looked very nice.

Bernadine was upstairs so she used to come into the shop and I was always with her. She became my possession, my companion, and I used to love having her around me. My sister Rita, my mother and my best friend Kerry Foley were the only ones that I'd trust with Bernadine.

Once there was pig kill at Newtown at Tali and Pius's place. *Ma* went there with my cousin Metang. I came back from work to find Rita at the house with Bernadine but *ma* hadn't yet returned from the pig kill. I sent Rita to quickly go and get her, as I was hungry and craving to eat pig.

There was a heavy rain shower that afternoon. Rita put a towel on her head, walked to Tali's house and called out for *ma*. *Ma* came out with a plastic sheet over her head and said, "Let's wait for the rain to stop and then we can go." But Rita insisted that she come quickly because I wanted to eat before going out that night, so *ma* and Rita hurried home, bringing Metang with them. When she got home, *ma* complained angrily, "Why are people moving around in this big rain?"

It was my cousin Metang's first time in a modern house. She saw the telephone on the table and she said, "Ai yeh! This thing when you are cold you put it on your ear." Rita told her it was a telephone but she kept insisting in was an ear warmer.

Metang then followed Rita into the bathroom. Rita took off her wet clothes and got under the shower. She ordered Metang to put their clothes into a bucket before joining her under the shower. After their shower, Rita asked Metang where she had put the wet clothes. She replied, "In the bucket in the bathroom." Rita saw that Metang had bundled the clothes into the toilet and closed the lid. She told me about this later and we had a good laugh.

REFLECTIONS
Rosita Henry

Maggie knew that my grandfather had an import-export business in Cairns who might be able to help her source clothes for her shop. I remember her contacting me to ask if I could assist by putting her in touch with my grandfather. I am afraid that my studies kept me too busy at that time to pay attention to whether or not he ever did help Maggie, and I did not follow the growth of her business interests. However, many of Maggie's other friends and family members witnessed her blossoming business acumen firsthand.

Lois Logan was particularly forthcoming, as this was also a significant time in her own life. She was happy to share with me her memories of life in the Western Highlands as the wife of a patrol officer.

> When I went to Hagen in 1970, nobody sold jeans. The Chinese stores had clothes but most of the expatriates would not set foot in the Chinese stores. I found I could get jeans there but the tops were not appropriate because they were Mary-blouse kind of tops and I wanted fashionable clothing.
>
> Maggie first had a shop with clothes out the back in Hagen Chinatown called *Jara Clothing*. She was on to a good thing because she'd buy a couple of bales full of Indian clothing and there were enough of us younger people in town who wanted to buy them. Then Maggie moved to the front of the town so her shop had a better profile and a window display. There were still glass windows in Hagen in those days, not the metal security screens you find today.
>
> Later Maggie started getting bales of used clothing from Australia. That was a separate shop. She still kept *Jara Clothing* and then moved it into a building that was like a little mini shopping complex. She employed a

Chimbu woman, Anna Dinbi, to work it. Anna was someone you could trust. If you employed a *wantok* they would steal from you. It wasn't really stealing it was just taking because it was your *wantok*.

Maggie's businesses were developing well so she started a little coffee shop, which didn't really make a lot of money, so it wasn't the ideal thing to go into. There was probably more money in secondhand clothes. Maggie had to compete with the big guns like Mike Bromley. It was always a struggle for Maggie because hers was a comparatively small business. Mike Bromley had lots of trade stores and became very, very wealthy. He's sold out now. His father was a teacher down in Morobe Province, so Mike grew up in New Guinea.

Lois reflected on Maggie's generosity in helping others. She provided work not only for her own kin and other Papua New Guineans, but also for Lois.

> Sometimes, because I needed a bit of extra money, Maggie used to let me work in the store. Then I could get my clothes free or get them at a discounted rate or something. We were struggling financially a bit. After I had my third child, I quit full-time work and started working for a little newspaper called *Hailans Nuis*. My work time wasn't nine to five. It was somewhat relaxed, which meant I could go and have chats to Maggie at different times. We'd hunt each other out. Or I'd hunt her out. If there was something going on in the villages that I needed extra information about I'd go and ask her and if she knew about it she would tell me. I suppose we developed a kind of trust in each other. I was often very unsatisfied with my husband in those days. When I was distressed, I used to go down and dump on Maggie.
>
> My husband wasn't such a good friend of Maggie's. He thought that because he was a patrol officer he needed to keep this independence from anyone who had village affiliations, whereas I thought, "That's your deal but I want a friend."

To get a different perspective on Maggie's early working days, I sought out one of Maggie's brothers, Pora, who now owns his own small trade store in Hagen. He recalled the employment that Maggie created for her kin from Kunguma Village:

> I can't remember much, but I remember that she started her own business in town getting snooker tables. She put Noah and Kuipa on the job to look after them. Later on, she had secondhand clothes. I remember she was employing Nikints and Tep and all the guys in the village.
>
> So Maggie was a woman leader. She started small doing little things from the village, running backpackers, tourists and then in town her own hard work paid off when she worked to buy Hotel Poroman. She also represented the women of the province, of the country, of the village. She was president of the Western Highlands women's association and she was also invited to Moresby as a women's representative. She did things that other women couldn't do.

She had plenty of employees working for her, in town and at the lodge up here—laborers were cleaning around the place and planting flowers and they were getting paid and we were working with her too so we could build up new our own houses.

Maggie employed me as a security guard at Haus Poroman Lodge and I worked night shifts for about four or five years. I got tired of working night shifts so I asked Keith and Maggie to get me a proper job. They offered me a job in town at the secondhand store.

When I was working in town, I had a good relationship with Keith and Maggie. I was honest in what I did. I trusted them and they trusted me and so we built up a good relationship.

After some years working at the secondhand, I was promoted to be overall supervisor. I looked after about three secondhand shops in town and whatever Maggie needed, I helped her. For example, when she built her new house up there I gave her K3000 and I helped her with pigs too; so we helped each other in many ways.

I learned a lot from Keith. Whatever Keith did I watched and followed, so when Keith saw that I did everything well, he gave me a little room at the shop and said, "You should sell what you want to sell." So I decided to sell Coca Cola and oil. The shop has a small kitchen and I've done that business for about nine or ten years now and the business has grown. I also bought a PMV[1] bus to take passengers and built my own house. I too am a leader in the village now.[2]

13
Tying the Knot

I met Keith at a party in Hagen. It was a fancy dress party and I felt super wearing my new red stockings. Kerry Foley had a friend visiting from Australia and we all got dressed up together. There were only white people at the party. Keith was with his "bank Johnny" friends. My girlfriend asked me why I wanted to talk to Keith. I replied that I liked him. I had just broken up with my Canadian boyfriend who was a CUSO volunteer.[1] He was "going finish," leaving PNG, and wanted me to go to Canada with him but I refused.

After the party, the others all went to a private party and I was left behind with Keith. When my friends realized I was missing they sent the car back for me. They advised me not to get involved with a bank Johnny but I did just the opposite.

Bernadine was only nine months old and Keith was very good with her. We were together for eight months before we got married. Keith said we might as well tie the knot and I replied, "Why not?" When I told my father Tugl, he exclaimed, "At last!"

I told Tugl that instead of the groom paying brideprice, according to Western tradition my family must give Keith a present. They gathered money together and bought a stereo worth about 200 kina and killed six pigs.

The wedding took place at Rebiamul Catholic Church. Tugl gave me away. My bridesmaids were Kathleen Leahy and Meg Taylor.[2] Annette Leahy was the flower girl. The page boys were my two nephews from my village family, Tom Konga and Petrus Pius. Bernie Leahy and Jeff Hausler were the groomsmen.

I wore a pink wedding dress. Bishop Bernarding conducted the ceremony and gave a lovely speech. His speech went something like, "I first met Magdalene at Kuta Catholic Church. Today I stand here in front of this congregation and I see before me a beautiful bride. I can say I know Magdalene well as she is like a daughter to me. Today I feel proud. Her story is like *My Fair Lady*. The Leahys would join me in wishing her happiness in her marriage."

Maggie and Keith Wilson on their wedding day, Holy Trinity Church, Rebiamul, Mt. Hagen, 28 May 1977 (Wilson family collection).

After the church wedding, most of my village family went back to Kunguma. Only a few selected members of my village family came to the reception, which was held at the Hagen Park Motel. It was paid for by Joe, Clem and John Leahy.

We had a live band, *The Waghi Hellcats*, and danced and drank. Clem's two wives, Agnes and Josephine, fought a fight that continued into the next day.

Another unexpected event from my wedding night included rescuing Tali's husband Pius at the Police Station in my wedding dress with my husband of less than one day in tow.

Reflections
Rosita Henry

"What do you remember of your wedding day, Keith?" I asked, as we savored our freshly brewed mugs of coffee. Keith had lit a fire to warm the room against the damp, cold afternoon outside. He began with telling me how he came to be in PNG in the first place.

13. Tying the Knot

I got an interview with the Commonwealth Bank in London and then they sent me out from England to Australia, straight to Melbourne. I had the travel bug. They were still sending guys up to Papua New Guinea so I put my name in for that. They were winding down because Papua New Guineans were taking over. I was one of the last ones to come up who wasn't an accountant or a manager.

The Bank here had already been handed over to the Papua New Guinea government. It was called the Papua New Guinea Banking Corporation. I came straight up to Mt. Hagen. I came up here for what I thought was only one or two years but before long I met Maggie.

We met at a party in town. I went with some other bank Johnnies. We weren't invited but we turned up. I had seen her before at the bank, at the other end of the counter, but not to talk to. I told her I had seen her at the bank but that she hadn't seen me and she said, "I saw you!"

When he saw I was admiring her in the bank, another expat guy said, "You don't want to mess with her." The funny thing is, I went back to Maggie's flat after the party and when we came out in the morning, he was coming out of the flat next door!

It seems like Maggie and I were living together virtually straight away. We'd go out to dances. The Hagen Park was the place to go in those days. We lived in Maggie's flat. She had a little clothes shop downstairs, *Jara Clothing*. It must have been towards the end of '76. I know it was after the Goroka show and that's in September.

My family back in England were a bit concerned because we were different culturally. They did not meet Maggie until about a year after we were married. It was too expensive and a bit short notice for them to come to the wedding.

Maggie did most of the planning. Her cousin Kathleen Leahy helped with the dress. Maggie arranged for her father, Tugl, to come and give her away. He was all dressed up in his traditional dress and there were two page boys all dressed up in traditional dress as well.

On the night of the

Maggie and Keith Wilson at their wedding reception. Mt. Hagen, 28 May 1977 (Wilson family collection).

wedding the husband of Maggie's sister Tali got drunk and we were told to go down to the police station to identify him. We looked at him in the cell but Maggie just said, "Yeah, that's him; leave him there." Maybe the next day somebody else bailed him out!

We had another reception up here in the village the next day and they gave us gifts. Normally brideprice has to be paid by the groom but Maggie explained that I was English and that it was the other way around.

After we got married, we rented a duplex in town that was owned by Joe Leahy. Maggie's sister Rita was there with us all the time with another girl and Maggie's mother was there a lot of the time.[3]

"What did you think about that? Did you ever feel invaded by Maggie's extended family?" I asked, intrigued by the way this rather quiet and gentle Englishman had managed to adjust to a household very different to the one in which he had been brought up.

They did all the housework so I thought it was great. If we wanted to go out, Rita was a permanent babysitter and there were no worries about who Bernadine was with.

After we married, I continued to work at the bank and then I worked for Joe Leahy for less than a year. After that Maggie and I worked together in her clothes shop. It didn't take us too long to work out that we couldn't work together as well as live together!

When the shop had to support us all, it became hard financially so we decided to move up to the village to save rent. Maggie knew that the village courthouse was not being used so she asked if we could live there and they agreed. They told us we had to pay for all the materials they had bought to build the house. We agreed and then moved in.

We'd drive down to Hagen each day, so maybe what we had to spend on fuel and stuff for the vehicle was not saving any us money on the rent! But I was happy to move to the village because it was like another adventure.

Keith clearly had taken in his stride the fact that Maggie already had a daughter when he met her. I wondered how Bernadine had responded to Keith. How had she felt about him becoming her father? Like her mother before her, Berni enthralled me with her talent for storytelling. As we sat munching on freshly boiled peanuts and fat little cucumbers from the garden, I asked Berni to share with me some of her memories.

On the occasions that I would get teary for whatever reason, mum would emphasize the fact that I was loved and that dad was my dad because he took care of me and that my biological father was just that, he was just the biological father and dad did everything that he did for me so therefore he was my dad.

My relationship with dad was like any father and daughter, I imagine. Once or twice or whatever, I'd cry about not knowing who my father was, but I never felt that dad treated me any differently to Olivia. When Maki came and Nadia came along, it wasn't any different. He didn't favor one child over the other. It really takes a special person to father somebody else's kids and not be a little bit biased.

During my early high school years, I thought, "I'll go to boarding school and when I finish boarding school, I'll take a year and go look for my biological father, whoever he is." But when I got to year 12, I decided that there was no way I was going to look for someone who was never there for me. I realized that dad was more than any father I could have hoped for and I didn't want to hurt him. I felt that if I did go looking for someone else, it would mean that I thought he was not good to me or he wasn't my father. So I wrote him a letter saying that I had thought about it but was not going to do it.

He didn't reply but mum told me that he wouldn't share the letter with her. He told her that it was a private letter between a father and his daughter.

One time I was hurt because my grandmother, dad's mum, gave Olivia a really nice old English ring that had been in their family. Dad and I were in the car driving somewhere together, just the two of us and I said, "If I was your biological child, then she would have given it to me," and he just said, "Yes."

He never said anything after that. We didn't talk about it. I wanted to talk about it but I guess dad didn't want to talk about it because what can you say? There's nothing you can say.[4]

14
A Village Baby: Olivia

Olivia was born on 24 June 1979, two years after Keith and I got married. When I was pregnant I wanted to have an unusual name for Olivia. I thought most names begin with letters like A and E but O was an unusual letter so I said I would name her Olive. Keith and his friends disagreed and suggested that if her name had to start with O then it should be Olivia.

She was a cute looking baby and I breast fed her for about six months and then she went on the bottle as I did not have enough milk. I weaned her off the bottle at age two. We had gone to George Leahy's place and I had forgotten Olivia's bottle. She started to cry for the bottle and I didn't know what to do so we took her for a drive in the car until she fell asleep. The next day, she didn't ask for the bottle.

Olivia was a village baby. She was a tough child. She was eighteen months old when we moved to Kunguma, so she was always in the village playing with the other children.

She did everything that all the other children in the village did. When she was hungry she would go to my mother's house for a sweet potato.

When I got home from work she would be naked, covered in mud, with her hair flying everywhere. We used to have bucket showers in those days and Olivia and Bernadine used to bath in the kitchen near the wooden stove in their red bath.

Reflections
Rosita Henry

Although over the years Maggie had sent me photos of her beautiful fair-haired daughter, it was not until my field trip to Hagen in 2000 that I met Olivia in person. By then she was already a self-confident young woman, two years out of high school, working for her parents at Haus Poroman Lodge. Olivia's boyfriend Denis was also working for Maggie and Keith at the

14. A Village Baby

Olivia Wilson, c. 1983 (Wilson family collection).

lodge. Denis was a tall handsome young man with a gentle smile whose mother was a Papua New Guinean woman from the coast. Denis had come up to the highlands after finishing high school to join his British father, who was at that time working in Hagen. I could see that Maggie had developed a soft spot for the young man and had taken him under her motherly wing.

When I went back to Hagen in April 2001, Maggie and Olivia were in the midst of raising funds for Olivia's Miss PNG campaign. Much has happened in her young life since then. At the time Maggie passed away Olivia was pregnant with her third child. Just a few months after Maggie died, she gave birth to another baby boy, Aidan, who would sadly only ever know his grandmother through the memories of others.

During a quiet moment in her busy day, Olivia sat with me on the veranda of Maggie's house to flesh out some of the missing details in this chapter that her mother had specifically dedicated to her.

> I was never at home. I was an outside girl. I spent most of my time in the village or with animals, or just time by myself. We were never restricted to being at home at a certain time or indoors for lunch or anything like that.
>
> We moved to the village when I was a baby. My mother's brother's daughters, Ai (Arolyn) and Mai, were my two closest friends. We're all the same

age. We did everything together. I would often stay overnight at Mai's house. Mai is Kuipa's daughter and Ai is Kawa's daughter.

I remember that we'd sneak into my house and take some meat or something and we'd make a small *mumu*. Ai and Mai were always keen on doing that. Having noodles was a special treat for us all. If we could get our hands on a packet of noodles it was the best thing. It was the day's mission. We would cook the noodles ourselves over a fire.

I spent a lot of time by myself and I really liked that. I wandered freely everywhere. I would walk up to the church or to Knep. I had a secret little hiding place, a tree that had a sitting place within its branches. I would sit there by myself forever, just day dreaming, just me and the world, me and nature.

I knew that we were different but it wasn't an issue for me. I felt that we were very special. Up here in the village, you just fit in with everyone else. But in town I'd know, because people would want to touch my skin when I walked past, or they would call out. It was never anything negative. Everywhere I went they'd say, "Oh that's Maggie Wilson's daughter, that's Maggie Wilson's daughter."

When I was younger I could talk the local language. Ai couldn't speak any pidgin at that time but Mai could, so we'd talk in a mixture of both. I've forgotten the language now. I can speak a little bit but I'm quite embarrassed because I'm not able to speak much of it. That holds me back. However, when I am on my own with the old women, I'll give it a go and we'll laugh and it feels comfortable.

As I got older my relationship with Ai and Mai started to change. When I was about ten or eleven, I became more interested in what I was doing at school and with my friends at school. I was still close friends with Ai and Mai, but it was different. I guess I was just doing different things. They started school a lot later than I did. I was in grade six when they were in grade two.

I remember the day my mum brought my brother Maki home. I've just got an image of us driving up the road together in the back of a white ute and me looking at him feeling quite proud that this boy was coming [home] and that I was going to show him where I lived. I didn't know he was going to be my brother. I just thought he was somebody coming to stay with us. It was not unusual to have somebody come and stay with us.

Maki is a year older than me. That's just the way mum guessed it. Maki and I celebrate our birthdays on exactly the same day. I think he's found a record of it now, but he still celebrates his birthday on the day that we have together. It was mum who gave him his birthday on the same day as mine. Isn't that strange? But it was nice. We were in the same year at school, so we had the same friends. We were good friends because he was an outdoors person like me. We did everything together.

Then mum decided Nadia would live with us. I remember her as a baby in

14. A Village Baby

nappies. She was really adorable and we all liked her. We had a family meeting about it. I don't know if mum got us kids on [her] side first and then we had a family meeting with dad or if we all had it at the same time. But we knew Nadia was coming before she came. We had a meeting and we all got to say what we felt about it. I think dad was a bit worried but all of us kids said, "Yes, we want her, we want her!" For family meetings we all had to sit together at the round table after dark.

We still call such meetings. When we were younger it would be one of our parents that would call it, but now any of us can call a meeting. That's how we've always done it; whether there is problem or whether it is good news, or both. I really like the round table; it's close and comfortable.

For example, if mum and dad were having financial problems or something like that, we would have a meeting and they would say, "This is what's happening now, so go and get a part time job." We'd say, "What do you mean get a part time job? Okay."

I think they lived from wage to wage. It didn't affect us. A lot of people were worse off. We were not down and out. If we had financial problems, dad and mum just took up more work. It was never detrimental to our happiness or anything like that.

We also had a meeting about the last two children mum took in, Malt and Magdalena. We said, "What if you go? What happens to them? You're a bit old to take in these ones. We're not going to grow up together. We're not going to live in the same house. It will be a different relationship." Mum had Magdalena and Malt for about two and a bit years before she passed away.

However, even though we weren't into the idea, when she did take them in, it was easy for me to get to know them and like them. I think dad purposely kept his distance because he didn't want to get close to them, but it could have worked. Any situation can work if you are open to it.

Not long before she died, Mum also took in Jaralyn. Jaralyn's father is mum's youngest brother, Thomas Las. When her mum and dad went down to Moresby to work, Jaralyn was left up here on her own so mum brought her to live with Malt and Magdalena and sent her to school. With Jaralyn, it was only temporary, but she meant to keep Malt and Magdalena forever. I think she cared for them to help the village people. She wanted them to get properly educated so that they could come back one day and contribute to their families.

I think she also thought it would foster our relationship with the community, so that we would always have something in common. This also may have been partly her rationale for making Nadia her daughter. She had a special relationship with Nadia's mother, Tress, and she wanted us to be close with our cousins in the village.

I went to high school in Hagen first and then I left for England when I was fourteen. I overheard my mum and dad talking about it at the table one night. My dad said that he had spoken to my grandparents and that they'd be willing to have me. The next night mum and dad asked me to sit at the table with them. I said, "I know, yes; I'm going, I'm going!" Dad said, "You can think about it and tell us tomorrow what you really think," but I said, "I know now! I want to go!" However, when the time came, I didn't want to go. I cried and told mum but dad said, "No we've made all the plans now and you can't change your mind at the last minute."

It was really hard to be in England for the first eight months or a year. The way my grandparents ran their house was stricter than I was used to. I lived two years with them and then I spent two years at boarding school where I did my A levels. I was away for five years altogether. I would come home once a year for the summer holidays. The first time I came home it felt really strange. All year long I had wanted to come home and then when I did it felt so awkward.

I felt a tie with England, the same as I do here. I didn't feel that I was a foreigner in England. I felt like I was from there but also from here. When I finished school and came back to live here in 1998 I felt that I belonged here but that there was something missing that was on the other side of the world that I missed as well.

Mum wanted me to go to University in England but I wanted to come home. After I got back, I worked with a real estate company in Hagen for a few months. During this time, I met Denis at a party. He had also just finished grade 12 and was here on holiday for three weeks to visit his father. I met him during the first week he was here so he decided to stay and get a job. I guess we both didn't have a plan for what we were going to do after grade 12. We went out a lot, to parties and that kind of thing. Life was exciting. Eventually, mum offered us the chance to run the lodge together.

Mum would always ask for help, ask us kids to work with her and to be part of her projects, including those in the village, such as the women's group and the birthing house project. She would say, "If you want to live in a community you have to be part of it."

If we had to be disciplined it would be dad that did it. Mum was very forgiving. She was open; she'd want us to go and tell her anything. I felt more reserved, but Bernadine and Maki, I don't know about Nadia, had a really open relationship with her. She used to say to us, "Do unto others as you would like them to do unto you," if we had done something out of line. That's what made her special, actually being able to feel what the other person was feeling. I think that's why she was so successful and why so many people liked her and wanted to know her. She was genuinely empathetic.

The main difference between mum and dad was that Dad was content with the way things were. He didn't need this big house or anything. As long as he had his radio, a roof over his head, running water, he was happy, whereas mum wanted to do more because she felt life had so much more to offer. She kept having more ideas and wanting to do more. I think maybe it's because of being mixed-race. Maybe she thought, "I have got an advantage and I should be doing something with it. I've been educated properly and I can run a business and I can contribute to the community so I've got to do it. There is no point having skills and having knowledge and not doing anything with it."

Also, mum was naturally creative. She always had a million things going on in her head and a million ideas about what to do. She was a keen gardener and she designed and produced her own furniture fabric and her own clothes and lots of different things. When we were younger she used to bake bread, make soap or make candles. She was always making something or trying something new.

Just after I started working at the lodge, I was asked to run for Miss PNG. None of us, Bernadine or myself or Nadia, ever thought that we wanted to be Miss PNG. It was never a childhood dream or anything like that. Two of my school friends, Sarah Timbi and Rose Kay, who were working at Courts furniture store in Hagen, suggested it. They rang me up and said, "Our Manager at Courts is looking for a person for this year's entrant." I was thrilled and excited but wasn't sure I had the confidence. I was a bit of a tomboy, still am.

I sat down and talked it over with mum and she encouraged me to do it. I was actually quite thrilled that I had been asked. I think there were nineteen of us who got interviewed and they selected me. So I joined the Miss PNG quest as Miss Courts.

We were judged mostly on fundraising ability. We were also graded on our public speaking, traditional dress and traditional dance performance.

I did a Hagen dance, with the *kundu* drum. Mum wrote the song. Then she organized for the village women here to sing it and put in on a tape. We had practice sessions and full dress rehearsals with the women here in the village. It was really exciting. It's weird, even though I grew up in the village, I'd never done a *singsing* and it was a big thing for me, whereas Ai and Mai would have known exactly what to do. It wouldn't have been hard for them to learn something like that, but for me it was. It was new and I felt shy about it at first, but afterwards, I was quite proud of myself.

Mai's mother, Tress, and mum's sister, Rita, danced with me, so the three of us went on stage in Port Moresby. I

Olivia Wilson in Hagen body decoration for her Miss PNG performance, 2001 (Wilson family collection).

wore the traditional dress, with the *purpur* and all the beads and the *kapul* skin and the big, big headdress. Mum came down from Hagen for the performance.

Mum also designed the dress for the final [event], the evening wear. No one else had ever worn anything like that. They had always picked a Western-style dress, never anything that was in any way traditional. My dress took about six months to make. It was made out of traditional materials. My mum designed it and then made it with about six other women.

They would sit here working late into the night, telling stories and making *bilum*. They used traditional dyes from the plants around here. They sewed strings of beads (Job's Tears)[1] to the bottom of the dress. It was supposed to resemble a *purpur*. There was also an *omak* on the bodice. The hat was a kind of beret, a variation of the traditional hat that everyone wears around here with a *guria* pigeon[2] feather on the front. The whole outfit was really amazing. People were astounded when they saw it.

Each entrant was also expected to pick a song. Everyone picked a Western song, whereas I picked a song by Nadya Golski sung in our local language. It's a campaign song, actually, so it was appropriate. We used it as our theme tune wherever we traveled for fundraising. Courts wanted me to go where their branches were so we went to Madang, Goroka, Lae, and Rabaul. We raised 55,000 kina in six months. Wherever I went people would say, "That's Maggie Wilson's daughter." It made it easier for me. People knew who I was and were really quite proud to have me in their town, because they knew mum. They'd ask, "How's mum?" I was given a lot of attention and therefore I was able to speak more than the other entrants, get to know people better. Because of this, I had an advantage over the other entrants.

Dad was the treasurer on my fundraising committee and we made him DJ switch. Bernadine was in Moresby but she was quite involved as well, writing speeches and so on. I really didn't have to do too much myself!

I won Miss PNG 2001 and I was charity runner-up by 200 kina. I also won Miss Friendship. The contestants chose the winner of that title themselves. After I won I was expected to work for the Red Cross. However, the office was in Moresby and I lived in Hagen so they didn't want to give me that position. Instead, I was asked to travel for them, go to the other provinces, to the schools or the hospitals and talk about the work of the Red Cross. But it was not organized very well. I said, "I'm at work so you've got to tell me when you want me to go." They'd say I was going and then I would get ready to go and then they'd cancel; that kind of thing. All the prizes that I was supposed to get didn't arrive either. It was disappointing. I did some of what was expected of me and then it fizzled out. I said, "Oh well, I don't want to do it any more." Mum was quite disappointed. She understood, but she said, "If you take on something, you do it to the end."

I continued to work with Denis at the lodge but eventually we broke up, so I decided to leave. It was a really hard thing to do because I thought that

14. A Village Baby

mum and dad needed me. I felt guilty that I needed to leave because Denis and I weren't working out.

Denis and I had been living in each other's pockets. We lived together, we worked together; we went out together and did everything together. I confided in mum that I was unhappy and that I wanted to go. I was really nervous to tell her as I didn't want to disappoint her, but she said, "That's okay, if you don't like it you can go. We can find somebody else." She said, "Whatever you want, you do it." I thought it was a big deal that I was leaving the family company that kept us all going and to which I owed something back, but she understood. She was always like that with me. She would never tell me what I should do and what I should not do.

Olivia Wilson and Denis Doyle with their children, Cohen, Patrick and Aidan, Kunguma, 1 January 2013 (photograph by Rosita Henry).

Bernadine I think feels quite differently. Mum made her feel that she had to go and do Law. Sometimes I think Mum didn't push me as hard as she pushed Bernadine and that's not fair. At the end of the day, I think it's just our personalities. I need my space and I need to make my own decisions. I need to feel that I've got space. I can't have anybody too close.

After leaving the lodge, I ran a shop in Hagen and then I decided to return to England. I stayed there for nearly a year and when I got back Denis was still here. After I had left he ran the lodge for a while and then he worked for a coffee plantation. I think mum liked him not just because he is a nice guy, but because his mum died and he was so young and he was here with his step dad. She always felt for people. When mum started Hotel Poroman in Hagen, she offered him a job there.

At first my dad was running the place with mum and then he left so my mum and Denis were running it when I got back. Denis and I began seeing a lot of each other again and got on really well, even though I never thought I would get back with him. In the beginning I thought, "No it's not going to work. We've already tried." But then, the more time we spent with each other, the more it worked out.

My working relationship with mum was really strained. I used to think, "Hang on, I want to do what I want to do, and you are making me do what you want to do and how do you know if it's want I want to do?" Especially towards the end, I was thinking, "I can't do all of the things you want me to do. I've got my kids and I want to do what I want to do as well." She was always giving everybody jobs.

I resigned from my job at the hotel just before she passed away. We weren't getting on. It was hard I think because there were three of us: Denis, me and mum. I said, "I am taking six months off work full stop, because I am pregnant and I don't want to work." Every other pregnancy I was working up until the day or two days before I had the baby and I felt that I was always rushed back into it and I felt they both, Denis and mum, did not give me enough time to be at home.

After mum died, Denis wanted me to go back to work at the hotel. He really needed the support, without mum there. It is working all right. I think he's doing a really good job. The only problem is that we are short staffed at a management level. We are spread thin, in terms of our maintenance, kitchen, and human resource and housekeeping staff. It's just ridiculous. You can't do a good job with anything, because you are doing everything.

Denis has got to oversee everything. He feels a lot of stress from work. However, we want to keep on going because the hotel has got potential and it's going to do really well. At the end of the day we both really want it to work.

We love living up here in the village. We wouldn't move into town. We definitely do really like being able to come home. Sometimes we think we would be much more productive if we were down at the hotel in Hagen full-time but we would be stressed all the time, if we lived down there full-time like mum did.

There is a kind of buzz about this place. When I am walking in the evenings from my house to Berni's house or something, there is a buzz in the air. It feels like I am going to walk around the corner and that place, the lodge, is going to be there. Even if there is nobody there, it still feels the way it used to. It feels like somebody is there and something really exciting is going on. It's nice.

It would be nice to still have the lodge for our kids so they can experience what we did growing up. The hotel is a totally different experience for the kids. It's not the same thing. The lodge was very family oriented and had a different atmosphere altogether. It would have been nice to keep it going for them. We met so many people. We had so many people coming through our lives.

15

Here Comes Maki

In 1983 I went on a campaign trail with Clem Leahy deep into the Nebilyer Valley towards the furthest hill slopes. I had never been there before. I was doing my part helping Clem in his election campaign, talking to people, when after one gathering I noticed a woman and a child with blond hair walking towards the crowd. The child was about two or three years old. As soon as the little boy saw me, he hid behind the woman. I was determined to see his face as his unusual blond hair attracted me.

I shook hands with the woman and asked if they were on their way to the campaign rally. She said yes so I told her that it was already over and we were returning. I then touched the boy, trying to get him to face me. I asked him in his language what his name was. He was very shy but whispered "Maki." I was fascinated seeing a mixed-race boy in such an isolated area and it brought back memories of my own childhood.

I asked the mother how many sons she had and she replied that Maki was the youngest of three boys. I became curious about his destiny. What would become of him growing up in an isolated place like this, as a mixed-raced boy? Would he get a chance to go to school? I felt a sense of affiliation with this child.

Without thinking, I advised the mother that the boy should be with other mixed-race children. I told her that I had two children who were his color and that if she'd like it, I would look after him and send him to school where all the other mixed-race children go. While we were talking, Maki kept smiling and biting his fingers. I think he lost his shyness and kept smiling because I made him feel at ease by speaking his language.

I found out that the woman's name was Noma and I asked her to think seriously about what I was saying. She agreed with me that it was a good thing and she said she would talk to her husband. We then arranged to meet in Hagen town at my work place.

Sometime later, Noma came in to Hagen with Maki to tell me that she

15. Here Comes Maki

and her husband had agreed that Maki could come and live with me and that they would be happy if I adopted him. I was not in the shop at the time, but Keith was there. He said to Maki that he could come and visit us and stay for a few days. I had not told Keith yet that I wanted to adopt the boy.

The next time Maki came with his parents, I was there and I asked him if he would spend some time with us. I think he was excited about getting in the car and so he agreed to come with me.

Olivia and Bernadine were playing outside when I brought Maki home. They had friends staying with them at the time. As soon as she saw Maki, Bernadine came and held his hand and took him around.

Maki was excited and speaking in the language and Olivia and Bernadine were speaking a mixture of Tok Pisin and Temboka and confusing him. The children ran around for a while and then Maki came in and I coached him how to take a shower. He called me *Punt*, an affectionate term of reference to loved ones who share with you. The shower water was warm. Maki had always had cold baths in the river and this was his first shower. He was really impressed and said to me, "Punt oh! This rain is really warm." It reminded me of my reactions to Western things when I was young and I burst out laughing.

I asked Maki if he wanted to stay. Some days he would say he wanted to stay and other days he would say he wanted to go. Before long he got used to the girls and was having fun and fit in and wanted to stay for good.

We made the adoption arrangements based on the traditional way and agreed that he could go and see his parents from time to time and that they should feel free to come and see him. I said I'd pay for the school fees and they promised to contribute with money they earned during the coffee season.

I initially enrolled Maki in the Kuta Community School near the village and later I sent him to school in Mount Hagen and then Port Moresby. At first, he did not know any Tok Pisin but soon spoke like the girls—broken English, Tok Pisin and Temboka all mixed together. These were the languages of our household.

Now that Maki is an adult, when he comes home we sit around the dining table at night and story about our first meeting. Maki says he thought I was Superwoman. He thinks that I have a wonderful aura about me and admires the easy manner in which I relate to people from all walks of life. He has seen me give speeches to large crowds of highlanders and has observed me relating to both old and young people. He has seen how I am able to share jokes with women of my age group as well as comfortably communicate with our Highland big-men.

Maki (left) and Maggie (right), 1983 (Wilson family collection).

Reflections
Rosita Henry

Although Maggie had told me much about her son Maki over the years, by the time I actually met him in person, he was already in his early twenties. A handsome, well built young man, he had not yet decided what career path he wanted to pursue. Maggie thought it would be a good idea to keep him busy working for me as a translator during my fieldwork with the Ganiga in the Nebilyer Valley in January 2000.

Maggie came across Maki in 1983 at Kailge, the remote village in the Nebilyer Valley where anthropologists Alan Rumsey and Francesca Merlan did the fieldwork that resulted in their book *Ku Waru* (1991) and numerous other publications. Maki spoke the language that Merlan and Rumsey call "Ku Waru" (meaning "steep stone" or "cliff") but Maggie and he could understand one another easily because Penambi people speak a dialect of the same language, or *mbo ung* (literally "seedling human talk"), as the people who live at Kailge.

The metaphor of planting, growth and fertility is cosmologically important for peoples of the Western Highlands and people refer to themselves as *mbo*—

planted beings (seedlings, cuttings or offshoots). This is also reflected in naming practices. From the time Maki first came to live with Maggie they called each other "Punt," after the edible root of the wing bean (*Psophocarpus tetragonolobus*). Such reciprocal naming after favorite foods is a common cultural practice among people of the Western Highlands. Two people will share a piece of food and vow from then on to call each other by the name of that food. In a sense the two people enter into a contract with one another. The quality of the relationship that is signified by the use of these reciprocal names I think justifies calling them "terms of endearment." For example, *kennga*—a type of banana—also means "sweetheart." No longer do the two people address one another by their proper names, or autonyms. They reciprocally address one another by the name of the food that they have shared. Through the relinquishment of their personal names in favor of the name of a shared food the parties mark a close social bond.[1]

Maki proved to be a great translator for me during my fieldwork in 2000 and his youthful enthusiasm and confidence made the journey all the more enjoyable as we traveled back and forth to the Nebilyer from Maggie's lodge in Kunguma Village. But when I tried to pay him for his help, Maggie refused to let me do so, saying that he was working for her and that she had directed him to help us in order to give him work experience. It seemed to me that Maki and Maggie had a fairly typical mother-son relationship, the mother trying to guide her son and the son trying to please his mother but at the same time seeking a means to independently spread his wings.

I was fascinated by Maggie's story about how she came to make Maki her son, but it was not until after she died and I began to work on this book that I had the opportunity to sit down with Maki and find out how he felt about having been given by his birth mother to Maggie to grow up.

Maki and I met to reminisce about Maggie at his rented apartment in Cairns in August 2009. It was also where I had last spent time with Maggie, four months earlier, planning our research together on women and politics in PNG.

Maki had left PNG some years earlier to train and work as an aircraft engineer. By now he was the father of a very bright, beautiful and engaging daughter, Jada, whom he was committed to bringing up on his own.

Jada was at school the day I visited Maki so he had time to sit with me in the garden and talk without interruption:

> I had heard of Clem Leahy's rally and people said he was coming and that along with him there would be some *kewa*[2] people. My understanding of *kewa* people was that they eat human beings. I didn't want to go and see them but my mother did and she tricked me, saying we will just go and visit [my] grandfather.

A True Child of Papua New Guinea

Maki Wilson (left) watching his daughter Jada (right) dancing at Maggie's house in Kunguma, 31 January 2012 (photograph by Rosita Henry).

At first we took the back track but before I knew it we were going alongside the main road so mum would catch a glimpse of Clem Leahy's party. Finally Clem Leahy arrived and at the back I saw that red hair. I was very scared and had nowhere to go except behind my mother's hip.

The party went to the school where a large crowd was gathered. They gave speeches there and then moved down to where the *singsing* ground is where more speeches were given. I didn't want to go near the scene. Again my mother tricked me, saying all the people had already gone.

I wasn't too fond of white people, sort of scared, you know. My world back then was the village and probably Chinatown in Hagen. I don't remember anything else. All I could see was mum's (Maggie's) red hair and I was really scared.

My birth mother, Noma, is from the Kopi Kumbuga tribe. The place is Kailge, which is where Drs. Alan Rumsey and Francesca Merlan did their research. Noma's got photos of them and me when I was probably about four or something. That's funny, because I wasn't scared of them.

I think Noma said my biological father was an Italian man who was working down on the roads back in those days, but I am not one bit interested in who he was. My mother's husband Mek accepted me as his son. If I had a choice I would have preferred to have just known Mek as being my biological

15. Here Comes Maki

Maki and Noma at Kailge, 1981 (photograph by Alan Rumsey).

father. But obviously he can't be my biological father. He was really good. He is an amazing man when I think about it, because my older brothers Paul and Lucas are his sons as well but from a different man. From Mek's other two wives I've got another two brothers.

It was probably a few days after the campaign visit that Noma and Mek took me up to see mum. Mek was very happy that mum had offered to take me and send me to school. Mum and dad (Keith) had a little secondhand shop and we went there. I just liked the bus rides to Hagen. We tried that for about three times, back and forth, back and forth so that I would get to know mum and dad and agree to stay. The first time I cried and I just wouldn't let go of Noma. I knew something was happening so I just clung to her. So they agreed to just take me back home and bring me back again later. And I thought it was great because I was getting bus rides back and forth! Mek used to make the long trip each time. From the bus stop it was another 30–40 minutes into Hagen and he would carry me the whole way.

Then I saw a little toy car in mum's shop. That was, I think, on the third day. I really liked it and started to play and then mum said to come into the office and play. I got carried away and when I looked up Noma and Mek were gone. They couldn't say goodbye because I would have got up and said "bugger this" and insisted on going with them.

I can't remember being upset. I had my little car and it was like a whole new experience. And mum was really good, you know. She was speaking language to me and reassuring me and I thought she was okay. Mum and dad had this white Ute and we jumped in with Olly [Olivia] and Bernie [Bernadine]. We went to mum's house at Kunguma. I remember having a shower and I was just amazed. I think I got up and said in my language, "Wow this rain is warm," and mum had a good laugh. That was my start.

I stayed for about a year or so before I went back to the village. I can't really remember exactly how long I was up at Kuta, or Kunguma, before I went back for holidays. Mum first sent me to the community school at Kuta. When I was there I started to learn pidgin. I had no clue what school was. Everything was over my head. Growing up in Kuta and going to the community school was good because now those boys I grew up with still know me. They are boys from the Kopi tribe. It cemented my relationship with them. They'll see me on the road and they'll stop the car and say, "How are you?" So I'm glad mum sent me there. I don't know if she was aware when she did it or if she just sent me there because I didn't know pidgin. It fell into place I suppose.

I can't remember being scared about anything really. It was a whole new experience. A whole new life, you know. Yeah, I was just really fascinated that the whole thing was happening. Some memories are really clear. I remember mum's hair. I used to just look at her and stare at her because of her hair; I used to be really fascinated. And I remember the smell of bread too. That always hits me, even today, just the smell of bread, ordinary sliced bread. It was new to me. I had never had bread in the village, so when they gave me this thing called bread I was just like, "Wow!" It felt funny but it tasted nice. So I remember the smell and the texture of bread. It really amazed me and fascinated me that people ate this. When I smell it now I remember mum's long table and think of her.

Our nickname for each other is "Punt." Punt is *as bin*. It's a root; people *mumu* it and then peel the skin off. It comes in a big bundle. It's a kind of bean. We eat everything off that plant, the bean, the flowers, the leaves and the root. It's probably one of the best plants. It was comfortable calling her Punt because then I didn't have to call her mum, you know what I mean? It was my way of calling her mum, I suppose. I always called my birth mother Noma; as far as I can remember, it was always Noma and Mek. None of my brothers called them mum and dad. We always addressed them by their name, which is really funny. I don't know why we did that.

It took me a long time to call Maggie and Keith mum and dad. It took me a long time, well past my teens, until I was comfortable enough. Dad was really good. I can't fault him for anything really. He was probably one of the best father figures, both of them were. Mek in his younger days was your typical highlander and Keith was awesome, come to think of it. Mum wasn't a typical mum, you know, a get up in the morning and make you breakfast mum. In that way we were lucky. It was easygoing living with mum. The food was there and she was there.

15. Here Comes Maki

Once she was using soy sauce to cook. I was in the kitchen and I was watching her cook on the stove and thinking, "Geez, what is that? What did she put in the stir fry?" It's the same story, as when that man in *First Contact* was taken by the white man and they said, "Don't eat the food because it might be poison." I felt like that too. I thought, "Man, what if I was poisoned?" Mum just turned around and smiled at me; and then I thought it was beer or wine. I remember the bottles of wine that mum had and the soy sauce bottle looked exactly like wine.

I think I was your typical kid growing up. I didn't feel like I didn't belong. No one in Kunguma Village was ever cruel to you and said, "What are you doing here?" Everyone was really accepting. I remember Thomas Las, mum's younger brother. He was very good. I used to really admire him because he was young and tall and really solid. I remember that I sat on his lap the very first day I was taken in mum's car to Kuta.

I think the good thing with mum and dad was that I still knew where I belonged, as in I was still allowed to see Noma and Mek. It was their responsibility to come and pick me up for the holidays and feed me while I was in the village and they'd come and do that. Mum and dad didn't complicate things for me. I didn't have to try to be their son. You know what I mean? So it was smooth sailing. As far as I was concerned, I was there and I didn't have to try to be mum and dad's son.

People who know my past have asked whether I felt I was caught between two worlds, but I didn't feel I was trapped. I think mum was very smart the way she handled that one. There wasn't a title to me. I wasn't made aware that I was being either accepted or rejected. I didn't look for that.

Mum also adopted my sister Nadia. All of us kids wanted Nadia because she had this cute little face. We all agreed that she was going to be our sister. Mum's brother Kuipa is her father. I've never asked Nadia about how she feels. Same thing, we just accept her as our sister and that's it.

The special thing about my mum was the number of friends she had, the way people were drawn to mum and she made them feel easy, I suppose. We met so many different people both foreign and Papua New Guinean through mum. Some had just come to stay for a little bit but then ended up staying, living with us for like half the year.

Mum had this friend called Don, a Canadian traveler, who lived with us a long time and helped mum build the lodge. He was a carpenter by trade, or joiner. Then there was this young Singaporean man. His name was Richard. I used to think he was cool because back in the eighties he had that big hairstyle. It would be really funny to see photos, you know, the tight sort of jeans with the pump-up shoes. He lived with us for ages.

And then mum had her favorite cousins. Gerry Leahy was very close to us when he was a young man before he got married. Nancy Leahy came and lived with us for a long time as well; and Annette Leahy was up there and she'd come to visit every night. That's one thing I remember about mum, just the incredible number of people that came through our lives.

After mum got into filmmaking we also met some amazing people through her being a filmmaker. I don't know if it was just a kid's perspective but I thought they were the nicest people. Mum made our lives more interesting. She pursued all her ideas, whether they were successful or not. She always pursued what she wanted in life. She was happy about that during the weeks before she died, when she was down here visiting me. She wanted to buy a house in Australia. Not just any house; if she wanted to buy a house it had to be one with a huge acreage around it. Mum wanted to buy a place like that so her kids wouldn't disturb the neighborhood, not as a status symbol or as an investment. That's the difference with mum and a lot of other people I know. I said, "Oh mum, you should buy a unit and start getting into real estate," and she said, "Why would I want to do that? I want a place where I can live and then we can do something." In those last days I think finally she felt like everything was going well and she was very happy.

Mum was really good at speaking. I remember mum standing up and talking at a lot of places and the men in Hagen were very respectful of her. Again, she'd do things and it wasn't that she wanted to enhance her own status or reputation, but it was because she felt duty-bound to say something. It was not because, "I'm Maggie Wilson and I have to stand up." She did things because she had to do something and because it had to be said, and with that came her status.

Prominent highland men would come and see mum and have coffee with her. She'd do things like show them a flower or show them her garden and say, "I'm planting this." You don't see that normally and when you see it it's really sort of funny and cute at the same time. They would take the time to listen to mum, her ideas and her opinions. I think she had the respect of most of them. They recognized that she understood the language and knew her people and other people really well. I think because she was interested in them they were interested in her and showed her respect. She actually showed interest. There was never a hidden agenda with mum. Hagen back in those days was a small place; everyone knew everyone. She knew where a person was from, his village or her village. She took an interest.

There was one time when mum took us to stay at our grandmother's place, mum's mum's mum's place. We went and stayed there for a whole weekend. It is quite a far drive there and we had to walk in. It was good because mum still had her connections there.

Mum had a special relationship with her mother. She was always mean to her mother, I thought, really short with her. I asked her about it when she was down here. I said, "All I remember is you being short with Api." And she said, "Because my mother wouldn't let me do anything." It all started with her wanting to dig her own *kaukau* and plant her own garden. "Api would say no and she was always trying to boss me around." It was really cute hearing her say that, at her age. I thought, "Well your mother was just trying to be a mother." But in the end mum was really good to her mother. Mum brought her to live with us and she passed away while in mum's care.

I think I was shown heaps of love by both mum and dad and Noma and Mek. I can't remember anyone being mean to me in both places. I think as kids it's a pretty straight road. Life's either good or bad. It's only when you get older that you start analyzing.[3]

16
The Gift of Nadia

Nadia was offered to me as a special gift and I was so thrilled I said yes on the spot. She was a cute addition to the family and the older children loved her and spoiled her. Bernadine was like her mother. They would all do anything for her.

Nadia's father Kuipa is my brother and he is about ten years younger than I am. Kuipa and his wife Tress already had four children, born very close together. They thought that it was about time I had another child so they offered Nadia to me.

Keith saw it as a big responsibility. Initially we had decided to have only two, Bernadine and Olivia, but I had gone ahead and adopted Maki. Keith had his reservations because we were not financially stable then, but we managed and, in the end, Keith became the adoring father of four children. I guess he doesn't regret that at all now. He is very good with all the children and treats them all the same.

REFLECTIONS
Rosita Henry

Keith, Nadia and I sat around the dining table. Nadia was home in Kunguma for the holidays and was trying to finish an assignment that was due for a subject she was studying as part of her tourism course at the Divine Word University in Madang. I could see that Keith was indeed a caring father as he patiently helped Nadia complete her assignment and save the file on the computer so that she could email it to her lecturer. Although Maggie's death the year before had hit her hard, Nadia had gone back to university and was working even more diligently to complete her degree.

I had returned to Kunguma for the one-year anniversary memorial of Maggie's death, as well as to continue the research on her life. It was a time

16. The Gift of Nadia

On her way back to Divine Word University, Nadia (middle) flanked by her father Keith Wilson and Maggie's sister Rita, September 2009 (photograph by Rosita Henry).

for remembering Maggie and therefore an opportunity to sit down with Nadia to talk about her relationship with her mother. I began by asking Nadia to reflect upon the title that Maggie had given this chapter.

> I'm not sure why mum called me a gift; maybe because I was given to her. I think for Maki she went out and asked for him, but I was given to her, offered to her. Mum must have told me when I was very young, because I grew up knowing who my real parents were. To me Maggie and Keith were my parents. I never really thought of Kuipa and Tress as my parents. I knew it but I did not really act or express myself as their child. I knew that Maki was adopted, because his parents lived far away and if they wanted to see him they'd come and spend time with us. So I knew that Maki was adopted and I knew I was adopted, but we never ever felt out of place. Our parents were our parents and my brother and sisters were Maki, Olly and Berni. I never felt out of place or had any questions about it; I never went through that. Some of my friends who were adopted do feel out of place, but I can't remember a time when I have felt out of place. I've always just felt that this is my home and this

is my family. I don't think I feel more connected to the village and the Wia Ulgamps because of my birth parents. I think I belong here because I'm Maggie's daughter. If she had trouble or was going to move away then I wouldn't find it difficult to go with her.

I relate to Kuipa and Tress more like an aunty and uncle. Kuipa has always been more distant. He has never made it very obvious that he is my father. Tress would sometimes make it obvious. I noticed that it was when mum wasn't there. She would make comments if I was with her alone or we were with other people from the village. I think I was pretty stubborn. I guess I didn't really have a good enough relationship with her because I didn't appreciate her making comments like that. I got embarrassed. It kind of pushed me away. I avoided contact because I didn't like thinking about it. But Tress was good overall; she was always there. I knew if I went to the village and wanted to buy something I could just ask and she would give me what I wanted.

I think some people give up their children for adoption because they have financial difficulties. For others, it's in order to build a strong relationship between two tribes. Or maybe it's about giving a child to a more well-off family, thinking that the child will get educated and then help them in the future. I think sometimes Tress expected that, which pissed me off sometimes. But I don't think Kuipa expects anything. Kuipa and Tress have seven children, eight counting me. The last one was adopted out too. I see them all as cousins. We just act as cousins.

I looked up to mum. I always thought that I wanted to be like her one day, because I love the way people respected her. When we went to places, she'd talk and everyone would listen. It just really shook me that they're respecting my mum; these are people that we don't even know and they know her. And I think people respect me because I'm her daughter. That's something great that she gave to all of us.

Dad is very humble. He's such a great person. I think he was just so supportive. I don't remember any arguments or anything. Whatever mum said went. If he thought differently, I don't think he said it. He probably told her but he wouldn't carry on. He'd just express what he thought and leave it at that. He was a very cool dad; you could tell him anything. He knew where he stood. He is a very calm person. I don't think he was strict with us. We knew what the rules were and that's it. If you did something wrong then you knew that you'd have a sit down. He'd be reasonable; there'd be a discussion about it.

I got on great with Maki and Olly and Berni. They all spoiled me rotten. I remember being small and they'd always be happy and trying to hold me. I can say I'm closer to Berni. I used to share a room with her. She was more like a mum and I looked up to her. Olly and Maki were the same age and would pretty much do their own thing, so I'd just hang around with Berni. I still look up to her now, especially with mum gone. If I had something to discuss I'd talk to Berni about it first. Maki and Olly were very similar kind of people when they were growing up. I saw them as the same; if one did some-

16. The Gift of Nadia

thing, the other one would do the same. They'd always be a team. If one got into trouble then so would the other and they could always support each other.

Because he was the only brother, Maki was caring and protective, but not overprotective. Mum always emphasized, "Do something and get out of here. If you have the opportunity, go and work and see the world," and for me, Maki was the first person who actually did that. I think she'd be proud of him for going and doing something for himself. But when mum had trouble and was getting upset with different issues, I'd always wish that he'd be here to support her; with the land and things like that. I'd think, "If Maki was here, people won't say that kind of thing or act like that."

My childhood was awesome, growing up here in the village. My first language was English and then I learnt pidgin afterwards. I can understand *tok ples* but I'm not very fluent in it. Just seeing both sides, having a life in the village and being able to associate with the European life as well is great. The lodge was always full with tourists, so as kids we'd go down and socialize with them and ask questions. We were pretty open with everybody. It was very exciting meeting people from different places and they'd tell us about their places. I remember tourists always being impressed with our English. When we went down to school in Mt. Hagen and back there were always tourists in the car, so we were used to them. We'd say things like, "That's a coffee tree." We were already tour guides.

The JICAs would come to do their Tok Pisin course at the Lodge. They're very interesting people, the Japanese. I've always been fascinated by the Japanese, because I went to Japan when I was about ten years old with Annette Leahy and a group from our village. We were displaying traditional dance costumes. Although mum organized it, she didn't come. One of the bosses of the JICAs that came here was there and took us around and was really happy. My impression of Japan was that it was so fast, the bullet trains, and everyone was so busy. When the JICAs came here, I was always keen on telling them that I'd been to Japan and showing them that I could count to ten.

There were other people we met over the years because of the Lodge. I remember Tara[1] who lived in the house on the hill. I was scared of her. Bernadine always hung around her and was fascinated by her. Her house had really old, kind of creepy stuff in it. She had a

Nadia Wilson dressed for a traditional dance performance, c. 1990 (Wilson family collection).

little bottle with a child's hand in the house and Berni used to go look at it. She must have given that bottle to Berni and she used to put it in the room. I was so scared. I didn't like it. Because she had things like that, I didn't really like to go to her house much. And she had lots of dogs.

There were lots of people who came through. There was a guy called Grant who was one of mum's friends. He used to come to the house. I think he lived with us for a while. There were always people that she'd find somewhere and bring home. There was Raz, who is a tour guide. He's an Israeli, and he always came and went with the tourists. He'd stay with us at the house and he pretty much watched all of us grow up.

Mum and Dad sent me from preschool to grade six to Mount Hagen International and then I went to Highlands Lutheran International School which is in Enga country. I went there for three years. It was a really good school, American-run, and the curriculum was very high, higher than the PNG standard. But there were tribal fights when we were in year nine and it wasn't very safe so I came back to the International school here in Mount Hagen for grade ten and then did grade 11 and grade 12 at Coronation International in Lae. Then I spent a year working at the hotel before going to Divine Word University in Madang.

Mum wanted me to be a pilot, because I always wanted to be a pilot and I was trying to get into a course here the year that I was working. But there were so many of us and they only short listed eight people, who already had degrees in physics and stuff. So then I applied to Divine Word University. My first choice was IT, which I didn't get because you needed straight As for that. So I applied again for tourism and got in. I am glad now because tourism is an enormous industry and there is so much to learn. Mum was happy when I got into tourism. I guess she was thinking I would come back and help out here, but she never said anything.

I appreciate everything that mum did for me. She was a strong person, but also very tough with us; you work for your money and nothing's for free. Hard work, she taught us all that. My friends' parents just give them money.

It got into a routine so that when I came home for holidays, I'd just come and see what I had to do to help out. I'd know that mum would have something for me to do. I was not allowed to just do nothing. She'd know I was coming and she'd say, "Nadia's going to be here for this long so she can do this." For example, when I was in second year, I used to buy stuff for one of my class friends because he was not very well off as his father had died and his mum was single. Mum must have found out and she asked me about it and I said, "Oh he's my friend." So she said, "Ok, you guys come for the holidays." The very next day after we got here, mum said, "All right guys, you know the block of land I bought at the airport? You guys are here for two weeks. Make the fence." She didn't sit down and make a design or tell us exactly what she wanted. All she said was, "I want it two meters in from the road," not what kind of fence, nothing. Because she was always busy, she didn't have time to

16. The Gift of Nadia

explain. So we said, "Yeah, yeah, ok, ok." Mum said, "Here's a car, here's a check. Get some guys to help you guys out. Two weeks. Do it." I asked my friend, "Woody, do you know how to make a fence?" He's like, "No, I thought you knew." I said, "You were nodding your head and saying yes! I don't know how to make a fence." So we asked one of my uncles to help and then we had to find guys to help us. She gave us money and the car and we had to budget and pay for all this stuff and she just expected the fence to be done in two weeks. And it was. The same year that my mum died, my friend, who did the fence with me, passed away of an overdose. So now that fence is really important.

After mum died and I was back for holidays I thought, "If mum was here she would have something for me to do and I'm guessing no one is really going to give me anything to do, so this is the time to start something and see how it goes." I thought I would try to do something small, so I started growing and selling chickens. But then there was a bit of confusion in the village about me doing chickens, because they had their own story about why I shouldn't do chickens. It had to do with the land that I was going to do it on. My cousin already had chickens there and her chicken house was really old, so I suggested to her, "I will make a new house and then I will put my chickens in with yours and in exchange you can look after them while I am away at school." And she said, "Oh that's a great deal, no problem," because you need the house to be warm all the time and it's really cold up here. But her father, Noah, had passed away a week after mum and some people have stories about why that happened. They say that he passed away because mum wasn't happy with him. People said that if I do chickens on his land, mum is going to curse me. I didn't know that people were thinking this way about Noah. So then I told Berni and she talked to Apa Kawa, and he said, "It's fine, just do it," and Berni said, "As if mum's going to curse you! She's probably going to be happy you're doing something with yourself!" Then when I went to the village and they were saying something bad will happen, I said, "Oh bugger you all. It's not a million-dollar company. It's just a chicken house!" I just went ahead and did it. I bought the chickens in the town and then the fertilizer (feed).

My chicken business partner, Noah's daughter, also grows broccoli. I was impressed with that because we didn't know we could grow broccoli up here. So she's really in to help herself. Mum appreciated those kinds of people. I could have sold the waste from the chickens but since she was doing that I said she could have the waste to fertilize her garden; so she's got a bargain.

It's hard living in the village. You have your obligations to your extended family, like mum had, and Berni nowadays, trying to juggle everything at once. It doesn't seem fair. But I love it here and I love this house. I'm so proud of it.

During my first year at Divine Word, 2007, Mum decided to stand for elections. I was here for the semester break for two weeks. I drove her around during her campaign. I was always with her because it was such a cool time too. She had to give speeches. She was more humble than the other candidates. It was nice how she did it because it was so simple and people were eager to listen to what she had to say. At the time all the women were so proud; it really gave them a lift. It was a good time. She talked about a lot of things, but mostly about rights for women. That's what she wanted, a chance for women, instead of having a male-dominated parliament. She was a good speechmaker. She didn't have to have a written speech or anything. She just talked. This is unusual for a Hagen woman. Most women are nervous with men around; they can't really talk. They can't talk higher than themselves and they are worried that people will make fun of what they say. However, I am more like mum. I say what I think. I don't think I feel shy whether it's male or female. When we have our meetings at school, I'll speak up, because it really annoys me if you know something is wrong and it keeps on going.[2]

17
Weaving Threads: Women and Politics

I joined the National Council of Women (NCW) in 1979 after Agnes Kolta invited me to a meeting. The women felt they could relate to me and wanted me to be the President of the Western Highlands Provincial Council of Women. As it was my first time in such a role, I had no idea what to do or where to start.

I met two women from the Business Development office. Because they had the experience, I convinced them to become Secretary and Treasurer. They developed a structure for the Council. I made suggestions and we planned it on paper.

We managed to get together a very progressive program that appealed to a lot of people, especially Christian women. We started by doing projects like beautifying Hagen town, planting flowers and colorful shrubs along the streets. Elizabeth Pora worked with us in the Family Planning Department.

The male politicians at the time saw the organization as a threat to them so they did not support it financially. Nevertheless, out of goodwill, we organized their political conventions. They became big, popular events. It was a prime period in my life. I put a lot of energy into my work with the Council of Women.

After I came back from boarding school in Australia, I found it difficult to speak my language fluently. However, through my work with this women's association, going to the different villages and mixing with older and wiser women, I learned a lot. For me, it was equivalent to getting a university degree in traditional knowledge. I became very good at public speaking in *tok ples*.

However, there was tension among the women that led to our constantly arguing. Mostly it was over money. We did a lot of fundraising to finance the organization. We even bought a car, but because the office-bearers were driving it around, the village women got annoyed.

"The newly elected committee for the Western Highlands Women's Association." Left to right: (back row) Pamda Ross, Maggie Wilson, Lutheran Missionary; (front row) Mary Tengdui, Elizabeth Pora, 1979 (photograph by Lois Logan for *Hailans Nuis*. Reproduced with permission of Sir Raymond Thurecht, OBE).

After six years as president, I decided not to continue. There was always a minority group of women who didn't appreciate what was happening and continuously complained. As I didn't want to force my ideas on them, I asked Agnes Kolta if she wanted the presidency. I thought I could be a more constructive woman and help society without being in the organization.

REFLECTIONS
Rosita Henry

The years of Maggie's life when she was actively involved in politics were the same years I was busy giving birth to and raising my three children in Australia. Maggie's memoir is tantalizingly spare with regard to her experiences at this time of her life. As she also did not share much with me about it, to fill the gaps I have sought insight from other sources.

When Maggie was elected President of the Western Highlands Women's Council, she also became a member of the National Council of Women (NCW) in PNG. At the time it was a brand new non-government organization, established by the *National Council of Women Incorporation Act* of 1979. Under section 3 of the Act, the National Council of Women (NCW) consisted of one member from a principal Council of Women established in each province. There was much hope that the NCW, with its linked provincial councils, would provide a way for women to participate effectively in governance and development in PNG. Maggie was part of the first wave of women to take up the challenge, but she ended up completely frustrated at how little she was able to achieve from within this institutionalized framework. Maisonneuve (2006: 15) claims that the PNG "Councils of Women, tend to be donor-driven, lacking vision and efficient management practices, and characterized by internal politics, in-fighting, and personal political ambitions." Perhaps this is what drove Maggie away. I think Maggie came to the realization that "top-down," externally driven approaches were not an effective way to improve the lives of the majority of women in PNG.

Maggie resigned her position as President of the Western Highlands Provincial Council of Women in 1985, by which time the NCW was on its way to collapse. Many provincial councils had withdrawn from the national council and the NCP was effectively moribund, existing in name only.[1] The NCP was to find new life in later years, but Maggie preferred to work on other fronts.

I visited Lois Logan in Cairns to see what she knew. She did not remember a specific issue that might have led Maggie to resign as president, but she reflected upon the difficulties Maggie may have faced by providing an account of a minor event in which she herself was involved.

> There was trouble in the Women's association while Agnes Kolta was the president. The Deputy Prime Minister of New Zealand was coming, and the head of the Province asked me to arrange for some of the village women to dance but to tell them they would not be getting paid. I organized for a group to come and perform. They dressed up beautifully and put on a great *singsing*. But then one of the politicians put his hand in his pocket and took out some money and said, "Here's 250 kina for this women's group." That was the worst thing he could have done.[2]

The issue was that there were two different dance groups in the women's association. If the dance group that Lois chose had not been paid directly, all would have been fine, but because they were paid, and not the association as a whole, the women from the other dance group became jealous and angry.

> Some women from the different dance group got really pissed off with me. The women didn't come to me directly; they came to the office block next door and they said, "*Mipela like kilim* Lois," which means they wanted to fight me. They were armed with their umbrellas. I received a phone call saying, "These women are really mad with you and they want to fight you. They've got their umbrellas." This is how volatile it can be.

The tensions and conflicts that frustrated Maggie, but that she was adroitly able to field as president of the Council of Women, gave her the confidence to stand for the seat of Hagen Open in the national elections of 1982. This was the "second post–Independence election in Papua New Guinea for the unicameral National Parliament which resulted in the replacement of a five-party coalition led by Sir Julius Chan and his Peoples Progressive Party by a two-party coalition led by Michael Somare and his Pangu Party" (King 1989: 3).

Most candidates in 1982 ran under Party labels but Maggie bravely decided to stand as an Independent.[3] Three women were elected during the country's first post–Independence general election in 1977—Josephine Abaijah, Nahau Rooney and Waliyato Clowes. In 1982, seventeen women, including Maggie, contested, but only one woman (Nahau Rooney) won a place.

Although in an early draft of her memoir she included a chapter titled "Candidate 1982 General Elections," Maggie never wrote anything about her experiences during this election campaign nor did she write about the 2007 national elections for which she also stood. However, when I visited her in 2000, she proudly told me of a speech she had given at a rally during her first campaign. An orator at the rally had urged in *tok ples*, "You can give your vote to your own kind or else to the cross breed between the white pig and the wild cassowary." At first, Maggie did not understand what he meant but then it dawned on her that by "cross breed" he meant her. She insisted on responding and "used his *parable tok*[4] back at him," saying, "Those crossed animals are feeding from you and speaking your language. Are they therefore not one of you?" According to Maggie, many people were impressed with her speech and one old man expressed his admiration by putting his *omak* around her neck.

Maggie occasionally took her eldest daughter, Bernadine, with her around the electorate during her 1982 campaign. Bernadine was seven at the time. She remembers singing Maggie's campaign song through the loudspeaker while they drove through villages.

> *Votim Maggie, sanapim Maggie*
> Vote for Maggie, elect Maggie
> *Tingting nau, tingting nau*
> Think now, think now
> *Sapos yu no votim Maggie*
> If you don't vote for Maggie
> *Yumi meri nogat nem*
> We women have no standing
> *Yumi mas, yumi mas*
> We must, we must
> *Votim Maggie Wilson nau*
> Vote Maggie Wilson now
> *O yu mas, yu mas, votim Maggie Wilson*
> Oh you must, you must, vote Maggie Wilson
> *Maggie Wilson em i namba wa*n
> Maggie Wilson is the best
> *Long Mt. Hagen Open Electorate*
> In the Mt. Hagen Open Electorate
> *Maggie Wilson em i wanpela meri bilong yumi*
> Maggie Wilson is one of us
> *O yu mas, yu mas, votim Maggie Wilson*
> Oh you must, you must, vote for Maggie Wilson.

Maggie's commitment to representing women's issues and her growing disenchantment with male leaders she had greatly admired in the past played a significant part in her decision to stand for election. Lois Logan remembered that Maggie had been impressed with Paias Wingti[5] during his early political career.

> Paias wasn't in our scene but he was very charismatic. I was working for the local newspaper, *Hailans Nuis*. As soon as Paias was elected Maggie said, "Oh you need to interview this new member, Lois." He was only 26 when he was elected to Hagen Open.

> When she stood for election herself, Maggie asked me to support her but I said no. I felt there was a conflict of interest because I was working as the Premier's assistant at the time. Maggie lost the election quite badly. She put a lot of energy into it and didn't get anything for it really. Politicking in Papua New Guinea is not a good game.[6]

Maggie also faced disapproval from her Leahy kin. According to George Leahy, he and his father, Danny Leahy, fell out with Maggie because of her support for Paias Wingti.

> The only time I had a falling out with her was in the early days when she was very young and she was hanging out with people like Paias Wingti. Dad and I really, really got stuck into her and of course I didn't talk to her for quite a while. But we all have to do these things. You have got to make mistakes. Of course in later years she thought exactly like me in politics. She joined my party. We both were against Paias then, but it just took her a little bit longer. When I saw her following him around back then I was just so bloody angry. Anyway, she learned the hard way and in the end, she realized.[7]

Gerry Leahy, who traveled with Maggie everywhere on the trail during her first election campaign, said, "I guess it was a time when the role of the women was coming to the fore."

> Here in the Highlands there wasn't equal representation and participation. Politically Maggie had achieved a lot on a local level with women's groups, and was very successful and influential and very strong and she had grown her networks. It was probably through that experience that she thought, "Hang on, here's this vibrant, wonderful, rich nation and there's something wrong. Look at the role of women and how it's always been. Surely if we can manage the home and look after the nucleus or the basis of our society, shouldn't we also be able to do something at a national level?"
> She was a gifted speaker, very clear and concise, naturally because she spoke the language and understood the nuances as well. She could convey English concepts, the idea of politics and government. She was very skilled in *parable tok* too. She really had the gift of the language. Normally Hagen women don't speak like that but she could, and men would listen. I guess they broke away from the idea that she's a woman. It was like, non-gender. In English you say that you must earn respect, and she did. Men would often say, "She is equal to, or she's a man so it's ok, she can talk." She was a bit of a pioneer in the sense that she gave that to women in the Western Highlands and Hagen's culture.
> Of course, she had to go through struggles, but it never stopped her. She believed that regardless of culture, or whatever the situation, if you think it is right, then you should do it. Maggie would argue with people and they would

17. Weaving Threads

argue with her or talk about her behind her back for some reason, but Maggie would say, "If you're angry say it out and get over it and next day move on." She was not the sort that would carry a grudge. She might be hurt and upset but she would turn around the next day and be kind to the same person who might still hate her for the next ten years. She wasn't vindictive.

One thing with Maggie was that she had the ability to teach people that no one's perfect and nothing's ever going to be easy and a garden of roses but deal with the hand you've got, live within your means, do your best and treat people equally. Everyone is exactly the same at the end of the day, starts with the same and goes out the same way, so we are no better or no different to other people. All her life Maggie was an example of that.

Even though she didn't win that first election I felt she was successful in the messages that she conveyed. To a certain extent the system is not conducive and doesn't work for us. Here we are with the British system acquired from colonial masters in Australia. How appropriate is it for a nation of fragmented, segregated societies, with so many tribes and different languages, to follow a system like the Westminster system? Sure, it is inevitable and we do want a modern society and world but how do you move from a tribal system into this elected government system that's supposed to manage and run our resources? I have heard this country described as a mountain of gold, sitting on a sea of oil, surrounded by cash crops. It's so wealthy but it's the management of this wealth and these resources that is the problem. It doesn't happen under this system of government.

So there was Maggie, who to a certain degree felt the same way so wanted to get in there and try and do something. On a personal level and in terms of her connections and networking here in the Highlands, she succeeded. The system is not going to get the right person into parliament anyway. It doesn't work. You need money to get into politics, there is no platform; there is no loyalty to a party, no ideology. Sure we have had some good leaders, but working for what system?

Maggie was disappointed she did not win. On the other hand, it was not the be all and end all. She was one of those people who continued to do what she wanted to do. I see her as a person that always strived for the good of more than just [her]self. She was always concerned for righteousness and equality for all.

She had so many ideas that it would scare you sometimes. I was always happy to help her but I did get to a stage when I got a bit restless. So what I did at times was stop going round to visit Maggie because I'd go there and she'd want to get me working. It was me being selfish really, and not being honest enough with her to say, "Look, I don't want to work, I just want to spend time with you." We'd sit until all hours of the morning playing canasta and solving the problems of this country and oftentimes she'd then launch into some new scheme and want to do everything but it was like, "This is the great idea I've got, now you do it."[8]

When Maggie again stood for election in 2007, not all her family and friends were as enthusiastic or supportive of her decision to do so as they had been the first time she stood. During the early '80s there had still been an air of hope and excitement about the future possibilities of this new nation but by the time Maggie decided to stand again (25 years later), many Papua New Guineans were feeling deeply disillusioned with the political system and the electoral process. As Gerry Leahy admits,

> The second time she tried, for the 2007 national elections, I was not helpful. Had we had time to discuss the matter prior to her making a decision, I would have told her not to bother standing. I knew that she expected me to participate. I guess I was being selfish. I actually heard, but not directly, that some of her family and friends were upset with me for not being there for her, but I felt she should be focusing her energy on doing something better. She was already being productive and achieving things that don't require government. Under the parameters of how these last elections were operating, she did not have a chance. It was not something she should have bothered to try. My failure was that I never even gave her the time to say how I felt.[9]

When she decided to stand for election again in 2007, Maggie telephoned me in Australia to discuss her decision. She was fully aware that she faced an uphill battle but, as with everything she did, win or lose, she thought it was important to try. In PNG, like other Pacific countries, there had been very few women Members of Parliament. No women at all had won seats in the 1987 and 1992 elections. In 1997, two women were elected (Josephine Abaijah and Carol Kidu), while in 2002 Dame Carol Kidu was the only woman elected. Maggie wanted to stand up for women and give it a go. She was especially encouraged to stand again because of an increased national and international push to "address the massive under-representation of women as electoral candidates" (May 2006: 94). Under Prime Minister Morauta the government had introduced the *Organic Law on the Integrity of Political Parties and Candidates* (OLIPPC). "The OLIPPC provided that where a party-endorsed female candidate received at least 10 per cent of the votes cast in her electorate, the Central Fund would reimburse up to 75 per cent of the campaign expenses outlaid on her by the party" (May 2006: 97). In 2007, there were 101 women candidates (compared with 60 in the 2002 elections). Despite the increase in interest among women, they still only made up 3.7 percent of the total number of candidates who stood for election. The Highlands region recorded 26 women candidates of which Maggie was one. In the end, none of them won a seat. Only one woman was elected in the whole of the country, the incumbent MP Dame Carol Kidu (The Commonwealth-Pacific Islands Forum Election Assessment Team 2007: 11).

17. Weaving Threads

The literature on the struggle by women to attain political rights in PNG does not mention Maggie. Historical analyses usually only name winners. The transformative work of those who are not elected is rarely recognized. Maggie's groundbreaking effort was part of a struggle that "continues 38 years after PNG attained sovereignty in 1975," during which time women have "found it almost impossible to be elected to political office" (Dickson-Waiko 2013: 193).

Maggie had to work hard to garner the support and the financial means to run her election campaign in 2007. She turned to the strong network of kin and allies she had nurtured over the years in the Western Highlands and to her wider circle of friends elsewhere.

Although some of her kin disapproved of Maggie standing again, others encouraged and supported her, especially George Leahy.

Maggie was in my party—the New Generation Party. I support Bart Philemon.[10] Bart begged me to be President of his new party and because he is an old mate of mine I thought maybe I should do a bit. I told Bart that unless they are going to clean up the election process I am not going to waste my time. I spent about half a million of my own money on the election.

Maggie was standing for Hagen Open. Jim Leahy was our candidate for the Tambul Nebilyer electorate. Maggie was a good person and Bart Philemon of course is one of the few characters in parliament that is a person of good character. Sir Mekere Morauta,[11] Bart, a very small handful. They are very few and far between. And so she joined us, because they are of good character and they are the people she wanted to be involved with and be seen with.

But politics is so full of corruption in the country. Unless you have a huge source of money, you just can't get very far. If they could actually fix up the voting, people like Maggie would have a chance.

She would have made a wonderful member of parliament. But that didn't happen.... There was just too much money. There is so much manipulation of the whole process people are not given the right to choose their candidate.

MAGGIE WILSON

Candidate Mt. Hagen Open Seat
2007

VOTE 1 [21]

"RAIT MAMA"

Maggie Wilson, 2007 (National Election campaign pamphlet).

> She was mainly going from a woman's point of view because women are downtrodden in this country. We put a lot of accent on the younger generation of people; that we have to make a future for them. She was good, Maggie, but we are up against the corruption. We can't beat it. If you are trying to do the right thing, you can't go and be a corrupt person, can you?
>
> The politicians take the money and run. You think we are independent but we are not. Foreigners run this country by manipulating these politicians. It is a real travesty.
>
> It is only after someone leaves you, you think you should have spent more time with them. I thought that after she died. It took us all by surprise. We were expecting so much more of her, but it didn't happen that way. I killed a pig and called my brothers and sisters and we had a very nice evening in her memory. Joe distributed the pig. She had so much more to give and she would have given a lot more too, but it wasn't meant to be.[12]

After the 2007 national elections, Maggie and most of the other women who had stood for election were funded by the Australian Labor Party to attend a "Women in Politics" workshop in Cairns to debrief and discuss strategies to ensure a higher rate of success for women candidates in future elections. I took the opportunity to catch up with Maggie during her stay in Cairns. Maggie and the other women at the workshop agreed that they did not have any chance for election because of the bribery that other candidates had used to secure votes. The Commonwealth-Pacific Islands Forum Election Assessment Team (2007: 18) reported on "bribery," "intimidation" and "flawed processes" during the election. With regard to the Hagen Open electorate, the team observed "a clear absence of voter secrecy in several polling stations."[13]

> Two ballot boxes were hijacked by a candidate's supporters in the Hagen Open electorate of Western Highlands Province, and two further ballot boxes were damaged by supporters of a candidate. A number of arrests were made (we believe around 20), and two vehicles and a number of firearms were confiscated, in security operations around Mt. Hagen town. These were understood to be groups of supporters of particular candidates—one group was described as "terrorizing" voters at a polling station, while others were heavily armed and believed to be headed for another station [2007: 21].

Maggie told me that she was deeply disappointed that even some of her Penambi kin had sold their votes to other candidates. According to Margaret Duckworth some of these people are now regretful.

> Only now they are saying, "She is the one we should have given the vote to." On the one hand you have got people floating around with oodles and oodles of money, bags of money and on the other you have Maggie, straight up front. She said, "If you are coming to me and expecting me to give you money for

your vote, don't bother. You give your vote because you want me to action what I am saying. What I'm saying to you is what I am giving you. I am not going to give you money." Unfortunately, a lot of people let Maggie slip through. I know she gave it her best but unfortunately money talks in cases like elections.[14]

Maggie's brother, John Kawa, confirmed that Maggie did not have a chance of winning because she refused to buy votes. Many of her professed supporters, who respected her integrity and stand against corruption, fell prey to temptation and sold their votes to other candidates.

> In terms of politics, Maggie recognized positives from the Western world that were not in our country. She believed she could make some positive changes, but in Papua New Guinea and the Western Highlands politics is riddled with bribery. We gained a lot of supporters and had good numbers but we never gave them any money. We gathered over a *mumu* and that type of food to discuss policies. The supporters were happy but when we did not give them any money, they went to get it from other candidates. Money is immediate satisfaction. They can pay for alcohol, or gamble or buy food with it, and then it is gone. People don't think about this. Maggie ran a good clean campaign.[15]

While Maggie was in Cairns for the Australian Labor Party "Women in Politics" workshop, I spent an evening with her discussing her plans for the future. Maggie wanted me to work with her on some of the gender-based problems that she had been struggling to address in her own village and more widely in PNG. I suggested that since she knew so many of the women that had stood for the 2007 national election, we could write a book on the lives of some of these women. We could focus on at least one woman from each province, their experiences in the election, the reasons they had decided to stand and the reforms that they had hoped to make.

Excited by the idea, Maggie returned to Hagen, quickly drafted some questions and did a pilot interview with one of the women candidates from the highlands. We arranged to meet again early the following year when she was next scheduled to be in Cairns.

I was in Hawaii at a conference during most of Maggie's time in Cairns but I arranged to stop over upon my return before traveling on to Townsville, where I was scheduled to give a lecture the following day. Unfortunately, as my flight was delayed, I missed my connection to Cairns. I had a choice to make; fly directly to Townsville and teach my class or fly to Cairns to meet Maggie. I decided on the latter. I sat up all night guiltily preparing lecture notes to email to my students with an apology. It was unlike me to shirk my teaching responsibilities, but the urge to see Maggie was strong.

I will never regret that decision. Maggie and I spent the day together planning our research project, listening to the interview she had already done, and refining our interview questions. That was Wednesday, 1 April 2009. The next day I flew to Townsville and Maggie returned to Mount Hagen. On Monday, 6 April 2009, I received a phone call from Maggie's daughter Bernadine, who told me Maggie had passed away in the early hours of that morning.

I have not had the heart to continue research for the book that Maggie and I planned to write together on PNG women in politics. Nevertheless, in order to discover more about Maggie's political life and complete this chapter, I arranged to meet with one of the other women who had stood for election during 2007 and who would certainly have been a participant in our study had we been able to continue it. Maryanne Tokome-Amu stood for election in Enga Province, as an Independent in the Wapenamanda Open electorate. She met me at Rusty's Bazaar, the marketplace in Cairns where she had a stall selling *bilums* to raise money for women with HIV Aids. We cried together over the loss of Maggie and over the struggles both she and Maggie had faced during the elections.

> Maggie became something like a tower of strength for me. Maggie's experience was something that I could stand on, to go for my own.
>
> She was always talking about the few of us, the highlands girls that were going for election, forming a highlands block, and maybe on a fortnightly basis meeting and talking about the challenges we were going through and how we could strengthen each other. Maggie even invited all the girls to her hotel and said that when one of the candidates has her rally, all of us should get on the bus or get in our cars and go and stand with that girl for support.
>
> After the elections, Maggie rang me and said, "Now sis, how about we meet and talk about where things went wrong and what happened and share our experiences." We sat in her hotel in Hagen. I guess listening to the things that we talked about, I summed up that we had gone through the same thing. When one woman would start to talk and say something, another would say, "Yeah, me too!"
>
> Our banner was that we wanted to fight corruption from the grass roots. Maggie said that her people were thinking that she was going to buy the votes. She didn't want that to happen because that's eating away our country.
>
> Our kinship groups, our families, our brothers, and cousins, uncles, you would think that, because we feed them every day, we look after them every day, we pay for their kids' school fees, you would think that for what you stood for they would support you. But at that time, to sell their votes for money was more important to them than anything else. People were saying, "If you don't give me money I am going to vote for another. My first vote is for sale." They were giving Maggie and me lots of second votes. We tried to tell them that second votes would only mean something if we got enough first votes to count the second votes. Otherwise it's useless.
>
> The election was rigged. The people on some polling booths had already

written who to vote for. Most of our people cannot read. The person who doesn't read, they think they are ticking on Maggie but they are ticking on the second box, because the first has already gone to somebody else.

One of the things that we both wanted was that women had some sort of decision making power starting from the grass roots level, not necessarily in Parliament, but maybe to become a Councilor at the community level or somebody in peace mediation at the local village court; make their way up.

Both Maggie and I, we very quickly found out that we are both quite vocal, and we can stand up to talk and we wanted to impart that to our people who do not have that privilege. We wanted to be strong in talking, meaning that we wanted to talk in a crowd of men. It is about time that women can be allowed to express what they feel.

Another thing that we wanted was to give women financial freedom and financial power. We wanted to see women independent in managing or accessing money. We both agreed that we wanted to start with some kind of microfinancing thing to support them to do something at [a] community level.

We felt that women are not united. Women are their own enemies as well. We wanted to break that and we wanted to unite women so that together they will have one voice; together they can cry, like we are doing now; together they can be strong and travel safely if they have to go from one village to another, to spread the kind of information that needed to be spread.

Another thing that we both agreed was that in Papua New Guinea women will lose if we try to compete with men. Some girls were saying that we will break down men's power, and this and that, but we said, "No, that's not how we will work, because we want to work closely with our husbands. We want to work closely with our brothers and we cannot compete with them because when we start doing that we will lose."

We both felt that the government was not hearing the majority silent people and we wanted some change. We said, "We are now sowing something on the ground of politics and if we don't harvest it, our daughters will." We thought, "If we win it's good, if we don't win, we don't want to crucify ourselves either, because we feel happy all the same that we have given the people of the Western Highlands and of Enga province an opportunity for another perspective on politics," because they've always got this dirty rubbish kind of politics. We wanted to give them another side of politics—a clean politics with no violence, with truth and honesty.

Together, we had very powerful ideas. When we went to talk to people, I think we touched on what is really affecting people. They were crying. I saw tears, but the sad thing was that the tears were not reflected in the votes. I mean, people don't just cry; tears are not just something sitting up here that just blow off. They are emotions. They are beyond feelings. When people shed tears you've got something happening somewhere in you, but that was not reflected in the votes. When we sat down to talk about what happened we concluded that, "We shot their hearts but not their minds."[16]

18
Making Pictures

My interest in filmmaking started one evening when I was at Clem Leahy's house. Joe Leahy brought the filmmakers Bob Connelly and Robin Anderson to visit. They were making *First Contact* and were looking for a good local guide to do research for the film so I offered to do it.

During the research for the film, I learned a lot about my own family and my people. I introduced Bob and Robin to members of my Penambi Wia family who told them the stories that appear in the book they later wrote, *First Contact: New Guinea Highlanders Encounter the Outside World*.

Bob and Robin suggested that I do filmmaking myself so I got in touch with Chris Owen[1] at the Institute of PNG Studies and he suggested I go to the Skul Bilong Wokim Piksa at Goroka.[2] At that time, the Skul was organizing a six-month workshop in Goroka with the assistance of a film institute in Paris. I applied and was accepted. The workshop involved learning all aspects of filmmaking, including scripting, directing, camera, editing and sound, using Super 8 film. There were twelve of us in the workshop. To me it was exciting mixing with a new circle of people because I was only used to associating with the expatriate community and the Hagen village people.

The group of students was a mix of young Papua New Guineans from all over the country and each one had a different personality and a purpose for being there. I was the oldest in the group. What we had in common was the desire to communicate to other Papua New Guineans through film.

Reflections
Rosita Henry

Maggie embraced every opportunity that came her way. Filmmaking was no exception. In 1984, she jumped at the chance to attend the six-month video-making workshop at the Skul Bilong Wokim Piksa, delivered by Séverin Blanchet of the Ateliers Varan, the *cinéma vérité* school founded by Jean

18. Making Pictures

Rouch in Paris. After completing the course, she got a job as a stringer for EM-TV, a commercial free-to-air television station covering news items around the Highlands region. She then managed the EM-TV relay station in Mount Hagen.[3]

In 1986, Maggie won a scholarship to travel to France for an advanced workshop in 16mm filmmaking at the Ateliers Varan with teams from Papua New Guinea, Senegal, Brazil and Italy. I was at home nursing my second child when she excitedly called me to tell me about her experiences in Paris. She had made a film with two other Papua New Guineans entitled *Raiders of the Planet Mars*, which was a PNG perspective on French astronomers and their studies of the universe.

Maggie Wilson in her film-making days, c. 1986 (Wilson family collection).

Maggie worked for EM-TV for about four years, during which time she also established her own freelance filmmaking company, Tilkil Kuan Productions Pty. Ltd.,[4] named after herself (Tilkil,[5] daughter of Kuan). She made a wide range of documentaries. In 1984, she shot *Meri Hagen*, a film about subsistence farming from the perspective of a woman graduate in agricultural science who was married to the Premier of the Morobe Province, and *Papa Nindjipa*, a documentary about the important role of death and funerary exchanges in intertribal relations. In 1985, she made *Tenpela Krismas Behain* for the Western Highlands Provincial government, on the views of a broad cross-section of the population on PNG Independence. She shot *Praim Minista Long Souten Hailans*, covering the PNG Prime Minister's visit to the Southern Highlands prior to the 1987 general elections, and *Paias Wingti Long Ples*, contrasting Wingti's role as Prime Minister with his traditional tribal obligations concerning *moka* and other exchanges. In 1988, she made *Baiyer River Sanctuary*, about wildlife conservation, and *Kung Ou*, which was filmed in her own village of Kunguma while a dance group prepared for a cultural festival in Europe. That year she also made *Moki Men in Business*, on the establishment of a modern business company by two big men who maintain traditional obligations by paying off their debts through a *moka* ceremony. In 1990, she filmed *Bride Price in Hanuabada*, and *Kibung*, a film about the 10th National Urban Council conference in Mount Hagen and the problems faced by urban communities.

Maggie reveled in her work as a filmmaker. It gave her the creative outlet she craved and the opportunity not only to travel all over PNG but also overseas to workshops and conferences on filmmaking in the Pacific. These were heady days for her, when participating in the birth of an indigenous film industry in PNG allowed her to associate with people from many different walks of life, from grass roots subsistence farmers to a growing number of business and political elite.

As the first film director from the Western Highlands and the first woman film director in PNG, Maggie saw filmmaking as an opportunity to make a difference, to contribute to the development and healthy growth of post–Independence PNG, by encouraging people to value heritage in the face of rapid social and cultural change. While many of her films highlight frictions and contradictions between tradition and modernity, and she herself embraced and advocated change in several different areas of social life, particularly gender relations, she treasured the ways of her ancestors and was not in favor of thoughtlessly throwing out the old for the sake of the new. Through her work she sought to convey that what people thought of as modern or progressive could be "continuous with baseline traditional values" (Sullivan 2003: 379).

According to Gerry Leahy, who spent much time with Maggie during her filmmaking days,

> She was very good at it. She had a natural talent. It was the time that EM-TV was starting in the country. I was working for Maggie and helping her out while I didn't have a job, so there again for a long time she sustained me. It was good fun too because you were meeting people from all around the world.
>
> When she had the money, she never hesitated to give me what I might need. She was very generous that way. In the meantime, she still was bringing up her own young family. When I think back about it, they were struggling and finding their way but still, for her, it was only natural to give, unconditionally give. In the household, they had so many people to feed but I was always there to be fed as well. I was still single then.
>
> It was around that time that Maggie was getting into politics as well, so I'd help her out. I guess she was in her prime. It was just the time for her that everything was happening. She wanted to do so much.[6]

In addition to making documentaries for EM-TV and on a freelance basis, Maggie wrote and directed her own video drama, *Stolen Moments*

(1989). The film, which was billed as "a story of love and intrigue in contemporary Mt. Hagen," was co-produced and co-edited by anthropologist Nancy Sullivan. The budget of only about $10,000 was raised from local Mount Hagen businesses. According to Nancy Sullivan (2003: 379),

> The production mobilized old patterns of loyalty, work, patronage and exchange. Only two members of the cast were hired and the rest, like the crew, were associates and kin of Maggie's. All twenty-five participants coalesced around the projects as an enterprise in Maggie Wilson's name.

Sullivan argues that Maggie directed the film in a style typical of a Hagen leader. Its production required serious support from her clan members. The video-editing deck was purchased with clan monies and "crew members supported the project in some ways as they might the development of a cash-crop project or a political campaign" (2003: 379). Maggie's achievements, as Sullivan (2003: 379) continues, "rested on her ability to project her own idiosyncratic goals as clan-centric, both male and female, and traditional and progressive."

Maggie won a prize for her script *Ahh Great Coffee*, a documentary about the coffee industry. She was full of ideas and wrote many other scripts, but most of them did not make it into films for lack of funding. During this period of her life, Maggie also worked with other PNG filmmakers on their productions. One of these was the feature film *Tin Pis Run* (1991), "the first PNG entertainment film, the first PNG super-16-mm production, and the first big-screen PNG story" (Sullivan 2003: 381).

Maggie eventually deregistered Tilkil Kuan Productions to focus on her tourist lodge and other business concerns, but she still maintained a keen interest in film. For example, she applied to the PNG Prime Minister's Department for funding to make a video clip of a song she wrote about the war in Bougainville. Maggie conceived this project in collaboration with singer Nadya Golski, who performed the song "A Cry for Peace" during her tour of PNG in August 1998.

Perhaps the last time Maggie made a film for public screening was in June 2001, when she joined me in Australia for the Laura Aboriginal Dance and Cultural Festival. We pitched our tents and built a campfire on the embankment overlooking the Laura River, facing the dramatic escarpment from which the sounds of clapsticks and digeridoo echoed. While I conducted research on the festival, Maggie filmed the dance performances, focusing on the Mayi Wunba dance group from Kuranda. On our way back from the festival, we stopped at my sister's place in Kuranda, where Maggie sat up all night editing the footage into a short film, which we called *The Spirit of Mayi*

Wunba. Maggie took a copy back to PNG to see if EM-TV might be interested in airing it.

Given her interest and experience in filmmaking, Maggie was thrilled when I contacted her with a proposal to do research in the Western Highlands on the documentary films *Joe Leahy's Neighbors* and *Black Harvest*. I had won a small grant with a colleague, Christopher Morgan, to travel to Mount Hagen to interview Joe Leahy and members of the Ganiga clan who were featured in these internationally renowned films by Bob Connolly and Robin Anderson. Anthropologists all over the world had been using the films as an educational resource. I wanted to explore what members of the Leahy family and the Ganiga thought of the films.

Thus, in January 2000, Chris and I went to Kunguma Village to stay with Maggie while we conducted the research. Maggie carefully planned our visit to ensure our field trip was successful. She advised us on how we should approach people and how we might best convey our project to the Ganiga. Aware of expectations that Ganiga people might have because of their earlier experiences with filmmakers, Maggie recommended that we make it very clear that we were "just anthropologists." She wisely advised that if we wanted to use our video camera, we should explain up front that it was not to make a film like Bob and Robin but just to make a record of our research.

Maggie was happy to facilitate the project, accompanying us to Joe Leahy's Kilima Plantation in the Nebilyer Valley and arranging for her son Maki to act as a driver and translator. At the same time, she was keen for me to develop an interest in her projects with women in the Western Highlands. Maggie had seen women die in childbirth and witnessed the suffering of women who were victims of violence. Thus, for my visit she organized the construction of a traditional house so we could meet with the women of the village to discuss the problems they faced and their ideas for overcoming them. She jokingly called this women's meeting house "the anthropologist's house."

Maggie saw my research on the films as an opportunity to draw me into some of her own projects. Her passion and enthusiasm were inspiring. In the "anthropologist's house," Maggie laid plans with the women of her village to market their hand-woven *bilums* and garden produce to raise money for common projects.

There was a warm communal spirit in the house and while the women talked around the hearth, many of them continued to roll wool on their thighs to create the tight thread needed to make the *bilums*. We roasted sweet potatoes and mouth-watering pieces of pork in commensal ambience of the firelight.

The women's main goal was to build a birthing house in the village.

18. Making Pictures

Kunguma Women's Self-Help Group, Kunguma Village, 23 January 2000. Left to right: Naomi Mitti (back view), Piam Koa, Tress Kuipa, Kerowa Lex, Kerowa Patti, Tangpa Pint (photograph by Rosita Henry).

Maggie often helped in transporting women from the village down the mountain to the hospital in Hagen. She had assisted at difficult births and acted as a midwife in the village. She told me that on one occasion, the baby's umbilical cord was wrapped around its neck so she had to quickly improvise and unravel it using a banana.

Maggie was able to secure some funding for the Kunguma Women's Self-Help Group from AusAid to build a birthing house. The conditions of the grant required the women's group to contribute additional funds to complete the building.

During my visit in 2000, spirits were high as there was enough money to prepare the ground and start the building. The women planned to finish it off later with funds from the sale of their *bilums* at the Hagen market and to tourists at the lodge. Maggie set high standards, however, and would only stock the finest, most skillfully woven *bilums*. One day, when I came home from the market with one that I had bought merely because I found the design and color scheme attractive, Maggie expressed her disappointment by showing me what I needed to look for in a well-made *bilum*.

Tress Kuipa preparing the ground for building the birthing house, Kunguma Village, January 2001 (photograph by Rosita Henry).

Unfortunately, due to a range of factors, including jealousy and mistrust among the women about the financial arrangements of the women's group, the birthing house project eventually stalled. Nine years later, at the time of Maggie's death, it was still not complete—just one of a number of things that she was sad about when we last met. However, during my visit in 2000, there was still hope in the air and an expectation of success among the women. Together, around the fire, the women sang a song composed[7] for their group, which I recorded and Maggie later transcribed and translated for me poetically.

> *Na kuri gekantep*
> *Paraka gekantep*
> *Na Kunguma pene na wendoga*
> *Meglma nutl yampment*
> *Na mogl negamegl*
> *Nanga tondugl notugmol*
> *Wang wang tep*
> *Na tep knap*
> *Tep mep Gok pemporeng*
> *Kantekl pemponda*
> *Wang wang tep na tep knamp*
> I am crowned with the white bird of paradise plume
> Crowned with red bird of paradise
> Enhanced with possum fur, I proudly make my entrance
> On the Kunguma ceremonial ground
> Knowledgeable and wealthy people say
> I am a nobody
> But I have pride, strength and dignity
> Slowly but surely I will gain
> Knowledge and new skills
> I might pass this on to Gok
> And perhaps on to Kantekl
> That is my desire.

By building the women's meeting house especially for my visit, Maggie was clearly trying to steer my research in a direction that was more pressing and dear to her heart than Connolly and Anderson's films and how they represented the Ganiga. Joe Leahy, too, was not very interested in the problem of representation. As Joe told me,

> Because I was under pressure, I didn't give a shit whether Bob or Robin was there filming. Rhona did feel invaded but me I didn't give a shit. When I saw the film, it reminded me how hard things were for me and then I felt really sorry for myself. But good or bad, I don't care. They captured true actions. I'm happy with what they did.[8]

The Ganiga wanted more urgently to talk to me about the many years of war in the Nebilyer Valley that had continued long after the action captured in *Black Harvest*. They told me about what they considered the "root cause" of the war, and described the peacemaking process and series of compensation payments that were underway at the time (see Henry 2005).

Only Ganiga Korowa Tuga, who came up to Kunguma Village from his home in the Nebilyer Valley specially to see me, expressed reservations. Korowa worked with Joe Leahy at Korgua Plantation and was a key facilitator in the original land transaction with his Ganiga clansmen that allowed Joe to secure the lease for his coffee plantation. Korowa provided an account of the history of Kilima Plantation, filling in the parts that he thought Bob and Robin should have included in the films.

> My first reaction was that I'm the negotiator of the land and everything and I'm not included in the picture. I'm not happy about the way they just go and invite the young men and start the story from the middle and not the beginning. Otherwise, I am happy. Through the films, we've made a name for ourselves all over the world. Because of the films, you are talking to me and it's nice that the films help to open up relationships like that.[9]

In spite of other pressing demands on her time, Maggie translated interviews and generously helped me with the project, just as she had done years earlier for Connolly and Anderson, whom she sheltered during the tribal conflict in the Nebilyer Valley documented in *Black Harvest* (Connolly 2005).

When we were both at Maggie's house as guests of her family in September 2009 for a memorial event after her death, I asked Bob Connolly about his time with Maggie. Because of the escalation of tribal fighting in the Nebilyer during the filming of *Black Harvest*, Maggie had offered the filmmakers sanctuary at Haus Poroman Lodge. They stayed from June to November 1990, covering the tribal fighting from Kunguma Village. Their Ganiga translator came to work with them at the lodge to save them from traveling into the conflict zone, but one day when Bob went to the Hagen markets he was given a message by four Ganiga men. "They said that a group of women married into Kulga tribe had come across and told them that the Kulga had heard the story about guns bought with our money and they were going to kill both me and the translator and they were going to ambush us on the road. So that really shook me up." Bob consulted with Maggie, who quietly took care of everything. She appointed two of her clansmen, Noah and Noki to act as bodyguards. Bob reflected,

> The weird thing was that there was this incredible disjunction between going out there, where people were getting killed and there was terrible tragedy

18. Making Pictures

Maggie (left) and Rosita (right) working together, Kunguma Village, January 2000 (photograph by Chris Morgan).

going on, and coming back to this utterly idyllic, peaceful place up in the clouds. I would be shaking when I got home from filming. I'd go and have a wash and then go into the lodge and sit by the fire. There would be some new people to talk to, Maggie would come over, we'd sit there and chat, and I'd have a whisky.

According to Bob, watching what went on at the lodge was fascinating in itself. "You could have made a film about just that!" He remembered a busload of wealthy Italians arriving one day. Tara, the lodge manager, decided to make spaghetti with pineapple for them. She asked Bob if he'd cook the pasta and sent two huge pots of water for him to boil on his little two-burner stove. Bob laughed, "These Italians were sitting there looking at all this pasta with pineapple chunks through it. They probably didn't even eat pasta!" Another memorable incident for Bob during his stay at the lodge was when two of the roundhouses were burnt down. A French film group, who had been in China making a film on self decoration, were staying at the lodge. Their expensive camera gear and all of their exposed film stock from shooting in China was stored in one of the roundhouses. Maggie had arranged for them to film members of her *haus lain* [lineage] to dress in *bilas* [traditional finery]. While they were on the *singsing* ground dancing to the drums and being filmed, "about 20 guys went into the middle and started disrupting the performance." According to Bob, a leader from one of the other Penambi subclans, who was jealous of Maggie's success, had sent in his guys to stop the filming and Maggie "just hit the roof and went at him."[10]

In *Making Black Harvest,* Connolly (2005: 288) writes of Maggie's response,

> I'd known of Maggie's reputation but had never seen her performing in a standoff situation like this, and it was a joy to watch her reduce this overbearing gatecrasher to silence. Snarling at her, he beckoned his companions and they stalked off. Maggie shouted something after him, which brought a burst of laughter from her dancers, whom she now asked to take up where they'd left off.

That night, Connolly woke to find the houses where the French filmmakers were staying being consumed by "this huge roaring great fire." All their camera gear and film stock were destroyed in the flames. "Someone had poured kerosene all over the place. I was convinced it was the Kulga come up from the Nebilyer to knock me up, but it wasn't."[11] The suspected culprit, according to Bob, was the clansman Maggie had publicly berated at the *singsing* the previous day. It was thought that he had incited his men to "torch" the houses in revenge for his humiliation.

After hearing some of Bob's stories about the Haus Poroman Lodge, I could appreciate why he thought it would make for a great documentary film. I felt a stab of regret myself that I had not spent more time with Maggie during the heyday of the lodge. It would have made for a fascinating ethnographic case study on tensions arising from customary land tenure issues and the fledgling tourism industry in PNG.

That Maggie was able to build a business on customary land where few others had succeeded is mostly due to the quality of her relationship with her Penambi Wia clansmen but perhaps also partly due to their own identity and reputation. As Gerry Leahy told me, Maggie was a member of "a tribe that actually sheltered and took care of other tribes in their troubles. Being in the mountains, when there's fighting in the valleys, where do people flee? Into the mountains. They're still regarded as a different tribe in a sense, not mediators, but those that give shelter."[12]

19

Friendship Bonds: Haus Poroman[1]

Rosita Henry

Maggie was waiting at the airport, accompanied by Gerry Leahy, when our plane touched down in Mount Hagen in January 2000. Although Maggie had visited me several times in Australia, it had been over twenty-five years since I had visited her in the highlands at her uncle Dan Leahy's coffee plantation in the Nebilyer Valley.

My colleague, Chris Morgan, and I disembarked to the wonderment of a colorful crush of Hageners jostling to meet the plane from Port Moresby. After excited greetings, Maggie led us through the crowd to the Haus Poroman Lodge vehicle. The lodge driver shook our hands vigorously, introducing himself as "Tari Thomas." He drove us through Hagen town and then expertly up the slippery mountain road to Kunguma Village. I held my breath as deep, muddy furrows in the road threatened to slide us over the edge into the valley below. On the way, Maggie pointed out the houses that Gerry and Annette Leahy had built on the clan land of their father, Clem Leahy.

Maggie asked the staff at the lodge to prepare a small *mumu* to welcome us—pieces of succulent pork meat and fat, *kaukau* (sweet potato), edible ferns, *kumu* (green leaves), cabbage, *pitpit*, peanuts, and slices of fresh ginger, all laid out on the table on a bed of leaves. Maggie was clearly thrilled to welcome me for the first time to the tourist lodge she had built in her village among her clan and to show me all she had achieved since we were at school together.

After dinner, Maggie directed us to the well-appointed roundhouses she had set aside for our use. The lodge consisted of ten such houses built two by two, in keeping with the Western Highlands practice of pairing. Carefully tended garden paths separated each pair. The roofs, constructed of six beams

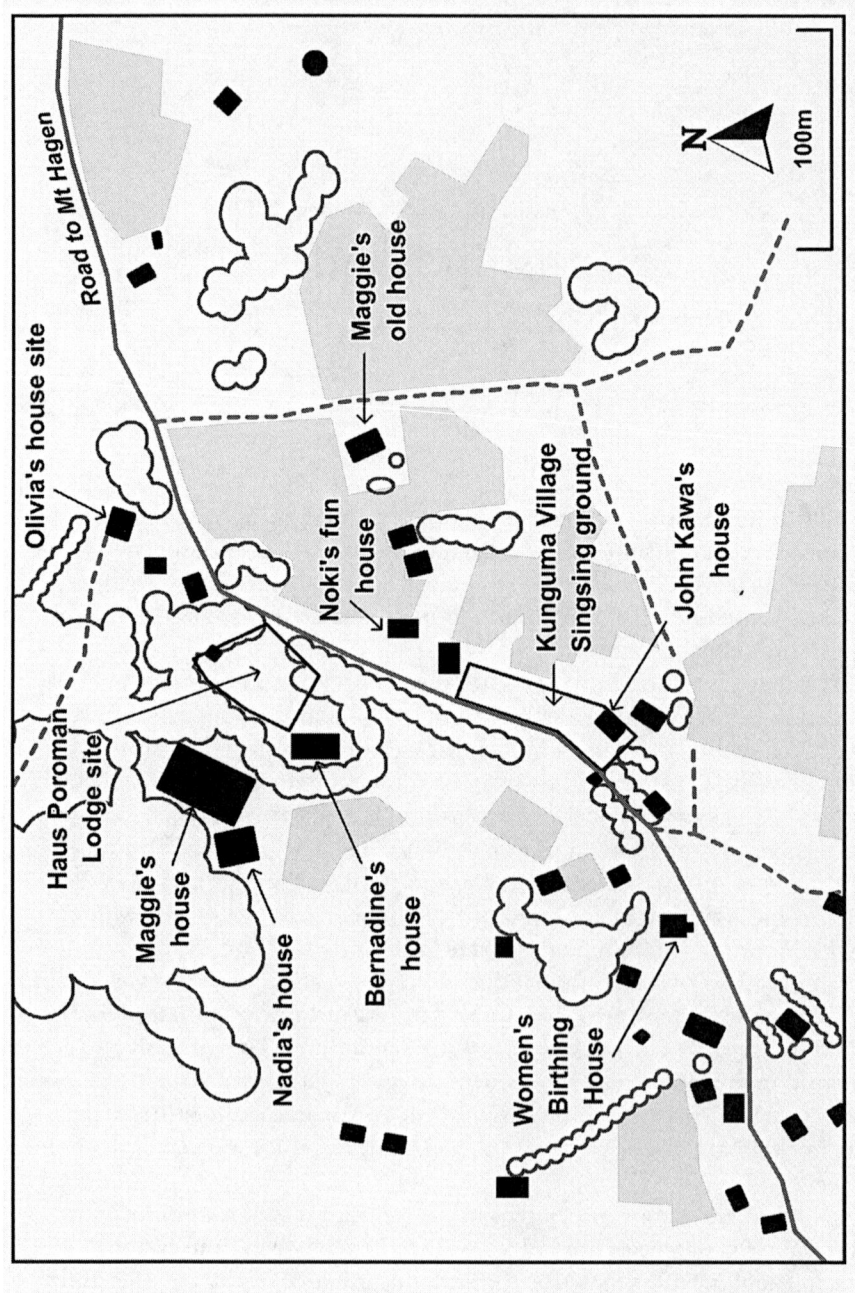

Map of Kunguma Village showing Maggie's house, the Haus Poroman Lodge site and the village *singsing* ground (drafted by cartographer Jennifer Vetali. Reproduced with permission of Terra Search Pty. Ltd., Townsville).

19. Friendship Bonds

Roundhouse at Haus Poroman Lodge, Kunguma Village, January 2000 (photograph by Rosita Henry).

joined conically, were thatched with *kunai* grass. I admired the expertly woven *pitpit* blinds that served for walls, the polished wooden floorboards, double French doors and little balconies. Each roundhouse consisted of a large room furnished with beds, a desk and an en-suite bathroom. Lodge staff primed the generator each night for electric lighting and lit a fire outside under a 44-gallon drum to provide hot water for showers.

Meals were served in a longhouse made from the same natural materials. This building housed a kitchen, dining room, bar and lounge room. Guests were served meals around a long dining table set on tree stumps and covered with painted bark cloth. There was a small cozy nook in one corner with a television set. The trilogy *First Contact*, *Joe Leahy's Neighbors* and *Black Harvest* were favorites among the guests. I noticed the lodge staff watching from behind the bar, laughingly reciting some of the dialogue by heart. In the center of the building was a huge round fireplace around which guests could gather before and after dinner, and where I soon relaxed, soaking up the ambience.

In addition to the main communal building and the roundhouses, there was a sharehouse for families, backpackers' quarters, and a conference room. Here Maggie regularly ran Tok Pisin courses for volunteers who had come to work in PNG under the auspices of the Japanese International Cooperation Agency (JICA).

Although Maggie did not manage to write anything about Haus Poroman for her memoir, among her papers I came across an undated draft of a speech she wrote for a tourist industry event at which she won an award for twenty-five years of outstanding service to tourism. Her speech concluded with an account of her experiences with the lodge.

> Back to the old haus of friends, my family and I were lucky being in the right place and the right time, living in the village, interacting with people from both the village and individual foreign travelers who were recommended by friends who lived in Cairns to visit me when in PNG. Those visitors helped me to appreciate the beauty of everyday village life style and I was eager to share it with them. Thus the idea of a village guest *haus* was born.
>
> We started a small backpacker's hut where visitors brought their own food, bedding and looked after themselves. We only provided a contact point in town and transport. Telephone communication and reliable transport system is a must. We were fortunate to operate a retail business in town, which provided both of these requirements.
>
> We wanted to build a larger lodge—just one building that had the bedrooms and all facilities together. We were lucky that one of our visitors took an interest in the next step in our plans. With her investment, we built the next stage and installed facilities, such as refrigerator, kitchen stove, beds and mattresses, blankets, tables and chairs, TV and video and a small bar.
>
> Later we built individual round houses in the grounds near the main lodge building. This was a gradual process with my village men working on a contract basis to erect each building, as and when we had money available. When six rooms (roundhouses) were built, the bedrooms were removed from the main lodge building.
>
> Today we have ten round houses with private bathrooms. We also constructed another building with four rooms all sharing one bathroom at a lower price range. All the time we also kept a hut for the backpackers.
>
> We knew nothing of marketing; we tried a little advertising by way of a brochure. The best advertising was by word of mouth, which eventually led to a write up in the *Lonely Planet* guidebook.
>
> As the lodge was on my customary land, it was not easy to get finance from the banks. We may have had some small loans over the years but nothing of a significant amount. This made the construction of the lodge a long and slow process as new rooms and equipment could only be purchased as the lodge made its own money.
>
> Looking back, it was probably a good thing that the banks did not grant a big loan to set the project up. At times, we would have next to no guests at the lodge and the bank would have required regular monthly payments whether we had guests or not.

19. Friendship Bonds

Maggie with a group of tourists outside Maggie's house with the guest house to the right. Left to right: Maggie, Dianna Russell, Judy Watson and Carol Ruff (front), Kunguma Village, 1984 (photograph by Christine Mitchell).

When Maggie and Keith moved from Hagen to live in Kunguma Village during the late 1970s, they first lived in a small house next to the *singsing* ground, with the agreement of Maggie's clansmen. After a couple of years in that house, Maggie asked them for permission to build a new house on a ridge nearby that was still bushland and not being used. They agreed and, after an exchange of pigs, Maggie had the land cleared and a house built. She then added a guest house next door.

Maggie's daughter Bernadine remembers an idyllic childhood, meeting and getting to know the many interesting characters that Maggie gathered around her.

> After we first built the new house, mum kept the old house near the *singsing* ground for backpackers. One night these two white guys came running up without their shirts on and knocked on the door; they had been robbed. I think mum and dad managed to get all their stuff back but after that incident mum built an extension on to our house and had the guests staying there. They had their own cooking facilities but sometimes mum would say, "Come and have dinner with us," so it was always quite full and quite close.

There were always people around. That was nice. Some people really make an impact on your life. Don was one. He built the lodge. He was an American, an arty kind of guy. He'd find bits of wood that looked a certain way and then make a snake out of it. When he first came, he had long, long hair. I thought he looked like Tarzan and Olivia and Maki thought he looked like Superman. He stayed on. He just became part of the family. He walked upstream collecting rocks and bits of wood and he found a waterfall with a swimming hole and showed us, so we started going swimming there. I think he ended up getting deported because he overstayed his Visa.

Then there was an artist from Kainantu, Charlie Devine. He came up with an arts teacher. Then the tour guides that came with all the groups, they ended up being close to mum, people like Grant Trewenack, Raz Cherbelis, David Cholai. Mum just had all these people that she collected.

Tara was another one. She was eccentric. She was an amazing woman. I have a memory of her before her car accident. She was a stunning woman, thin, beautiful figure. It was Christmas or something. She wore a tuxedo, black tights, a little jacket, and a red bow tie. She was just absolutely gorgeous. Then she had her car accident, but even after that she would get dressed up in all this fancy gear. She lived up here and died when I was 16. She had a hemorrhage and died in the lodge.

Liz[2] was part of our lives. She was a single mother with a daughter, Sara, the same age as Olly. Sara was about five or six when she came and they left when she was about eleven. Liz was running the lodge with mum when she met Seba Miyoni who was from Milne Bay. She married him, went to Milne Bay, and later returned to Australia.[3]

At the time of my visits in 2000 and 2001, most of the staff at the lodge was Maggie's kin, both paternal and maternal, who were living in Kunguma Village and the nearby village of Knep, but there was also some staff from neighboring clans.

Maggie and Keith also employed their daughter Olivia and her boyfriend Denis Doyle. Maggie could see that he was a lost young man finding his way in the world and in need of some loving care, so she and Keith took him in and treated him like one of their own children. Denis shared with me some of his experiences working at the lodge and his reflections on Maggie.

> I felt content after I got up here. How the lodge was run, it's more like a family atmosphere. I didn't know much so I had a lot to learn and just tried to do what I was asked. Maggie was definitely like a mother to me and I looked up to Keith. He was so different and I saw how he treated his kids. He is a decent guy and he is very principled. I never had much in my life.
>
> Olly and I were together and then we split up for a few years. Olly decided to go back to England but Maggie kept me on. She made it known that I had a job regardless, so I decided to stay.

19. Friendship Bonds

Arolyn Ai Kawa (Maggie's brother, Kawa's daughter) at work in the lodge, January 2000 (photograph by Rosita Henry).

I had a car accident when I was working at the lodge. This was when Olly and I broke up. After that for a few weeks, I went out drinking. I flipped the car and ended up in the hospital. I think Keith was annoyed but Maggie was very worried. She wasn't angry.

I felt a lot of guilt about the accident and abusing their trust—the fact that they trusted me with the business vehicle and I crashed it. I started feeling that I have to try better. They never said I had to pay back anything. I still had a job; I never lost it. Then I felt a lot more loyalty, a bit more like family and love.

That for me sticks out about Maggie. I never had many people like that in my life. I thought, "Why would she do that? She doesn't know me or have to do that for me." She always cared. It was never a negative thing with Maggie. It was always a positive thing—you can do it and you just have to believe in yourself. Just the trust, you know. Even when you made a mistake there was always the trust.

But she was very tough also. If I made errors on the job she would tell me straight out. She would have a go at me if I did not do the right thing. I think that was good because you need to know.[4]

Establishing and running the lodge was not an easy task for Maggie, although she took it all in her stride, bolstered by the love and support of

Keith. Although she had built the lodge on land freely granted to her by her clansmen for her own use, she soon learned that to run a privately-owned business on customary land created jealousy. Maggie had to constantly walk a precarious tightrope in keeping her wider clan group happy.

As the business grew, Maggie decided that she needed better security of land tenure in order to ensure its continuing success. In 1980, she applied to the then Department of Lands, Surveys and Environment for a lease on the 4.72 hectares around her house. As it was customary land, the State first had to acquire the title from the customary landowners in order to allocate the lease to Maggie. A survey of the land conducted in 1983 was the first step and, in 1987, the lease was finally registered. Yet, jealousies among her clansmen over the business continued to haunt Maggie.

In 1994, Maggie applied for a freehold title to the land (Portion 1203C at Kunguma) under the *Land (Tenure Conversion) Act* of 1963. One of her clansmen submitted an objection and the case went to the Land Mediators Board in Mount Hagen. The Board ordered Maggie to pay K2000 to the complainant. While she agreed to the sum, she wrote to the Land Mediators Board in a letter, dated 4 February 1994,

> I am willing to make this payment, NOT to purchase the land as it is rightfully mine and confirmed by your decision made 3 February 1994, but as stated by you for the goodwill and understanding between myself and the disputing parties and other members of the clan.... I understand ... that there will be no harassment or damage done to myself, my family, my property or to tourists who will be staying at the lodge that I have constructed on the land and also that there will be no further action to prevent me obtaining the state lease title over the land.

Maggie finally secured a freehold title to the land in 1996. Nevertheless, now and again over the years, disgruntled members of neighboring subclans, jealous about the success of the lodge and the riches they imagined flowed from it, continued to make demands.

Another issue that affected the smooth running of the lodge business was the road from Hagen to the village. Apart from its poor condition, although it is a public road, the customary landowners along the way consider themselves the rightful owners. On occasion, certain landowners would get fractious and block the road to demand compensation from passersby, including Maggie. For example, an undated letter in Tok Pisin that I found among her papers reads as follows (my translation),

> Mipela laik blokim rot long hap graun bilong mipela.
> We want to block the road along the land that belongs to us.
> Sapos yu laik usim rot long hap graun bilong mipela orait, mipela laikim yu

mas baim mipela long (K40,000) forty thousand kina pastaim yu ken usim rot bilong mipela.
If you want to use the road that goes past our land, then you have to pay us 40,000 kina.
Sapos nogat, yu no inap usim dispel rot.
If not, you cannot use this road.
Mipela I laik long toktok wantaim you long dispel week Friday.
We want to talk to you about this on Friday.

Maggie built her lodge on the traditional land of the Penambi Wia, her own clan, unlike her cousin Joe Leahy, who established his coffee plantation on the land of another tribe, the Ganiga. Joe was not a Ganiga and therefore had to grow his relationship with the Ganiga over time in order to legitimate his title to the plantation land (Henry 2013). Nevertheless, like Joe, it is clear that Maggie dealt with simmering tensions over her use of the land for a business. She worked hard to maintain convivial relationships not just with her own lineage, the Wia Ulgamp Komp, but also with the other lineages and subclans of the Penambi Wia and with the neighboring clans of the Kopi and Mogei tribes. Still, the tensions she confronted were never of the magnitude that Joe had to face (Connolly and Anderson, 1989, 1992; Connolly 2005). According to Gerry Leahy,

> Maggie was always closely connected to her tribe and family. Joe Leahy's situation with his plantation is totally different to Maggie's lodge. He is not dealing with his own tribe and his own tribal ground. Where Maggie built her lodge was her place. That's her identity. So it was never a question of can I do this on your land. It was her land, her tribe. She grew in that relationship. It's not that you are actually taking from anyone. She'd always lived up there and, as you see, her children live up there. Maggie didn't marry someone from another tribe so, as a woman, she didn't have to go to her husband's place.
>
> The situation with land is that, whilst it may be passed on through the male side, if it's not used then it is really not yours. So if there is a piece of clan land you claim to own territorially, and if there is vacant land to be used for gardening and you have a need to feed your family, you take this land and it becomes yours. But if you don't use it then it's really not yours. It should be then for the next clansperson who actually needs it. So I guess, in a way it's like the land is transient, it's not forever yours.

During my visit in 2000, Maggie was in the process of building a new family home. Although Keith was initially reluctant, Maggie had convinced him that it was time they replaced their old house. Maggie designed the floor plan of the new house. She purchased wood for the building harvested from trees that Joe Leahy had planted many years earlier on his coffee plantation.

Morning view from Maggie's house, Kunguma Village, 2009 (photograph by Kanawi Danomira).

The house was finished by the time I returned a year later, so Maggie invited me to stay with her there, rather than at the lodge. I recall falling asleep each night to the soothing fragrance of freshly curing wood. In the cool mornings, we would have breakfast on the front verandah as the mist rose from the valley below. As I drank in the spectacular view, I could see why Maggie had chosen to build on that spot, her little piece of paradise. I could not imagine her ever leaving.

Yet, less than four years later Maggie moved to Hagen. She had decided to expand and diversify her business interests by managing, and later purchasing, an old rundown hotel, the Hagen Park, with her friend Elizabeth Pora. I met Elizabeth at the hotel in April 2010 to find out more about this business venture that they had decided to name "Hotel Poroman."

> We shared almost everything. We would talk about everything. She was like a sister. One day, she called me and said, "We have to get together, I have an idea." I contributed some money and we leased the hotel as a business from David Yak. He is from my husband's people, one of his tribesmen, a Yamka. The place was actually owned by Malaysian Chinese and David was just acting for them. They had bought it and couldn't run it so he was running it for them. He asked Maggie to come in and manage it and I helped her and we paid the rent to him.
>
> Then Maggie and I went to Lae to see the Asian owner. We told him we wanted him to come and see what we had done with the place. He couldn't believe what we had done. He told David, "These girls have done a fine job. I think for the place to run properly, I am going to sell it but these girls have to be in it." So then, David, Maggie and I became partners. That's how it started.
>
> The hotel employs a lot of workers. The good thing is that the family at

19. Friendship Bonds

least are employed and we have something in life that will keep us going. Maggie wanted her people to see that if you work you can get something.

Maggie took great pleasure in renovating the hotel, landscaping the grounds and planting colorful shrubs and flowers. She employed Oliva and Denis there, training them in hotel management so they could eventually take over the reins. The hotel did better than the lodge because it attracted a different clientele. According to Denis,

> At Hotel Poroman, the people we rely on are the locals and the regulars for accommodation and stuff; they are not tourists. Being up at the lodge is a lot different; you can offer a lot more. I'd love to do it down here at the hotel, showing *First Contact* and all that kind of thing, but that is not our business. We have to look in a different direction with the hotel.
>
> Three years ago, we struggled a bit with the hotel financially but it has slowly been getting better. Now it's a lot more comfortable, a lot easier, but it doesn't mean it's okay; we still have to work hard. With this LNG[5] thing, there is a lot of potential. There is a lot of talk about the spin-off business coming to Hagen. I think there is a future now in the service industry with this LNG, which will hopefully benefit us.
>
> With the hotel side of things, definitely you can see the way it has progressed and all the opportunities Maggie gave to people. If people came and asked Maggie for money and they had a need, she wouldn't say no to them. She would find a way to help them. She always had trust and faith in people.

In the meantime, Bernadine managed Haus Poroman Lodge and continued to live in Kunguma Village with her husband Kanawi and their children. It was difficult to make ends meet as the tourist industry had slumped drastically in PNG. Fewer and fewer tourists booked to stay at the lodge. Often the place was completely empty, yet the staff still needed to be paid and the buildings and grounds required maintenance. Finally, in April 2007, the family decided to close the lodge and focus on the hotel. When I returned in 2009, only the concrete fireplace of the main lodge building still stood— a lonely cenotaph in the carefully tended gardens.

To learn more about Maggie's move to Hagen town in 2005 and her decision not to return to her home in Kunguma Village, I turned to some of her family and friends. Her brother Thomas went right back to the first slash of the machete and chop of the axe used to clear the land for her house.

> Maggie got her uncles and her people to cut down the bush. There was nothing here. It was all thick bush, and she got women to cut down the bush area and we were making gardens and all that.
>
> She built a house here and she gave our mother, Jara, and me her old house that was next to the *singsing* ground. I was single then. I was running a little

trade store in there. From the trade store, I was paying for school fees and for my lunch and all that. Maggie helped me a lot, showed me how to do it.

She built a little hut on the side of her house, and she was putting up backpackers there and I was up there helping the backpackers and guiding them and my English developed from the tourists.

Then she wanted to do something bigger than the guesthouse. She had a dream of building a lodge. There was a time when there was an American tourist here. His name was Don, I remember, and he agreed to build the lodge house. They talked about it and decided it was going to be like a traditional men's house, but extra-large. So they cut down a big, big forest tree and they stood the big central pole and all the rafters going down and made a giant men's house.

When the old man, Tugl, saw the house, he got up and said, "You can't build that house. It will fall down. It's too big," but somehow they got it built and from there they started to call it "Haus Poroman Lodge."

The people were happy that there were white people popping up in the village. They were getting photographs. They were buying things. Young people were getting jobs. Laundry work, clean-around work, little jobs. No one from this village had a job in town so when people were getting jobs they were uplifted; they were so proud and they were happy.

On the other hand, there were conflicts. There were differences in the village. People were talking about the lodge, and they wanted something more.

During the election times in 2007, these guys got dressed up in traditional fighting gear. When I heard that, I came up there, to the lodge gate, but I saw that I was outnumbered. Oh, there was a whole tribe up there. If I tried to do something, I would have been murdered. I came, saw them and just sat there. They were trying to put up a tribal fight with us. They had weapons, knives. They had on traditional dress. They had feathers in their hair. That's tribal fight dress. The village was empty. I was the only guy there.

After that, we had a big talk up at the *singsing* ground. All our guys got up and said, "Look we should give them something," but Maggie said, "I will not give them anything."

My brothers Kawa and Pora said, "No, we should give them something so they will cool down." So they contributed about a grand and my cousin-brother Noah put in a pig worth about 700 kina. Maggie said, "No don't give it to them. If you guys want to give it to them, you give it to me too, because they disturbed me at the lodge gate."

When my brothers gave the pig and money to these guys she was so cross that she just left. She closed down the place completely, because it is not good for the tourists. They were having a hard time getting tourists up here. So that's how she went to town and she stayed in town for a while. Maggie was probably thinking, "How could my own brothers and their families turn their back on me? After all this time that I've built a home, I've looked after them, paid school fees and everything." She was heartbroken.[6]

19. Friendship Bonds

After hearing Thomas's account, I wondered how Maggie's relations on the Leahy side might have understood her reasons for moving to Hagen, so I asked Margaret Duckworth. We reminisced over a coffee in her house in Hagen. Margaret did not mention any specific incidents that Maggie had to deal with, but her views on why she decided to leave the village generally corresponded to those of Thomas.

> I think that Maggie left Kunguma because of the struggles up there, for years and years. When you are actually living in the village, it's a constant, 24/7, and it's every day. You know, what your cousins want or your uncles want, or your brother wants, your sister wants, in order for you to stay there. It's a constant thing that you always have to juggle.
>
> Thank goodness, I live in town so I don't have to go to the extent that Maggie had to. I am lucky, every bride price, every compensation I don't have to take part. Whereas when you are actually living in the village, you know village people like everyone else, all talk, "Maggie didn't come to this one." Because Maggie was Maggie, and who she was, there was that extra pressure on her, which is unfair. I feel she did enough up there in her time.
>
> Take the whole road situation. The road caves in; everyone looks at Maggie to get it fixed. Half the time Maggie was forking out for it from her own pocket. Maggie was the one who was instrumental in getting government people up there, someone with a bulldozer, electricity, getting community work happening.
>
> You need someone who is strong, who can lead, motivate people. She was basically up there on her own doing it. To do that constantly is wearing and I suppose she thought, "I can't have all my eggs is one basket, us relying totally on *Haus Poroman*."
>
> I thought it was very sad that Maggie ended up back in town because she loved it up the top. That was home for her, to be more involved with the village, especially the women and the kids up there, trying to get them all motivated. She had the women up there making *bilums*. "You got to make good *bilums*. You make good *bilums* you can sell them at a good price and in return people will buy them"; trying to encourage them to do those sorts of finer things; that was a big thing for Maggie.
>
> It was also very challenging because, you get a lot of village politics. If you help one woman more than another there's trouble even if you didn't do it on purpose. All those sorts of challenges are constant and then at the end of the day they are also your relatives and you want to do the right thing by everyone, but there is a lot of pressure on you as well.
>
> And another factor was being a woman, living up here in what is still to this day very much a man's territory.
>
> The saddest, saddest part is that people are only appreciating what Maggie did now. That is the saddest part—absolutely sad. I am sure a lot of that all built up. I think over time it just drained her.

> She would have loved to have stayed up there right to the end, but it just got too challenging and again health problems on top of it. I'm glad she did leave because being in town gave her a different outlook and a different start. It was exciting, trying new things to see what worked, getting out of the village scene and totally focusing on what was here in town.[7]

While staying at Maggie's house on the mountain, I sat with Bernadine many an evening discussing what life had been like for her mother and father during the years Haus Poroman was open for business.

> When I was in high school, I remember more of the trials of living up here. It seemed that mum and dad just took it in their stride. Like that big tribal fight between the Ulgas and the Kulgas. They fought in town, when I was about 13, and then they all ran over our way to get back to the Nebilyer. We could hear gunshots and we were all at home.
>
> Mum and dad locked up their shop in Hagen and came home early that day and we were so excited that they had come home early, not realizing that a fight had just happened in town and they had to close their business. Now I know that running a business in town and dealing with that kind of stuff is not easy; the stresses of not having business for one day and still having to pay your staff, you are thinking about where your income is going to come from and thinking about being safe and getting home safely. But Mum and dad didn't seem to stress out that much. They were happy when they got home.[8]

Bernadine's memories of her childhood were of an idyllic time, when she felt safe and protected by her parents and her clanspeople on the mountain. It was only later, when she moved back to Kunguma Village with her husband and family, after finishing her law degree in Australia, that she began to fully appreciate the complex social world in which her mother was embedded and the problems that she had to field on a daily basis.

I told Bernadine about the day Maggie and I spent driving around Cairns looking for a house and asked her why she thought Maggie had wanted to live in Cairns. "I think part of the reason was an incident on the road as a result of conflict that erupted between neighboring tribes over factional voting during the 2008 council elections," Bernadine recollected.

> In the lead up to the election, they cut down a tree across the road, so we couldn't get to town. Denis couldn't get to work. Kanawi and I couldn't get to work. So we rang mum and she said, "Are you all right?" and we said, "Yeah, don't worry about us. We're all right. We're fine up here." The next day the same thing. We couldn't get into town. Then mum started to get worried. She didn't want her family to be on one side and her on the other, because we were all up here with our kids. She said, "You lot come down the road and I'll

come from town and we'll meet these people and find out what's going on." So we thought, "All right, let's do that." We wanted to talk to them and say to them, "We do not have any political affiliations so we don't see why you are blocking us from coming and going. We didn't tell our councilor to go with a certain faction. He does what he wants to do. It's not up to us."

Mum only had Kawa's daughter, Arolyn, and another woman, Rose, with her. When we got there, one of the men got up and said in *tok ples* to mum, "Do you know what is going on here?" and mum said, "No, that's why we are here. We are here to find out what's going on." He had a knife and by this stage some young blokes had come up with knives as well. They held their knives and made it obvious that they all had knives, young boys of 15 or 16, they weren't men. They were really harsh and threatening to mum. When one of the women told them to have some respect for mum, they all started screaming at her and almost wanted to kick her because she was sticking up for mum. One of the armed guys said to mum, "You can leave your car here and you can go and when you get your brother, Councilor Kawa, to come, then you can have the car back," and he took her car keys off her. It was just me, Olivia, Kanawi and Denis, nobody else, no Penambis, nothing, so we said, "Ok, we'll go home," because we had left all our kids up there in Kunguma Village. On the way home, I rang dad in town to go and pick mum up because I did not want her to walk back to town on her own.

That was the first time I had ever seen my mother disrespected. Every other time people went out of their way to listen to mum and everybody was silent when mum talked. It was heartbreaking because here is just an elderly woman and her children. We were unarmed and we did not have our *haus lain* behind us. We were just going in to say that we had nothing to do with these council elections.

Later we found out the reason why they did that was because they thought mum had supported Apa Kawa and told him to join another faction and there were rumors that this faction was using mum's hotel as a meeting ground. They accused mum of something she didn't even do. Because Kawa helped mum during her national election campaign in 2007, as one of her campaign managers, they thought she had reciprocated and sponsored him. But Kawa said that at every council election he had paid his own nomination fee. He had never received any money from mum.

Mum was angry about her car being taken. She never told me how she felt personally about what happened but I think that was partly why she thought about leaving Hagen. Her home, filled with a deep richness of culture and tradition, was slowly disintegrating around her. It was the lack of respect for good leadership that I think deeply disappointed her.[9]

Immersed in the memories of Maggie that her family shared with me, I wandered around the grounds of her home, trying to find the site of the roundhouse where I stayed in 2000. Flowering shrubs still graced the narrow garden paths leading to each site. The roundhouses were gone, but the big sharehouse, now the home of Oliva and Denis and children, was still standing, as was the backpacker house next to Maggie's, which Nadia had made her own. Bernadine and Kanawi had built their own two-story house on the other side of the family compound, just below Maggie's house.

As the mountain breeze caught my hair, whispering of Maggie's hopes and dreams, I wondered what the future would bring for her children. On my way back to her house, I turned towards Olivia and Denis's place, where I later arranged to meet Denis. "It was easier with Maggie here," he said. "She would know what to do and things would be under control. Maggie used to walk around with me and she'd have her dreams about this and about that. I'd like to see some of her dreams come true."

20

Mending Breaks: Haus Krai

Rosita Henry

Shattered, I put down the phone and sank into the nearest chair. How can this be? Bernadine had just called to say her mother had passed away in the early hours of that morning in her apartment at Hotel Poroman. I had spent time with Maggie in Cairns just four days earlier. She seemed healthy and strong, eagerly looking toward the future.

We spent most of the day planning our book on PNG women in politics and I had promised that I would join her in Hagen later in the year to conduct interviews with women who, like her, had stood for the 2007 national elections. That day she also told me of her trials over the past few years regarding Haus Poroman and Hotel Poroman, but she was more peaceful and relaxed than I had ever seen her.

In the late afternoon, we happily drove around the foothills of Cairns looking at houses. Maggie dreamt of having a home in Australia where she could stay whenever she visited. It had to be on top of a hill with enough land for a garden and big enough for all her children and grandchildren.

I phoned my parents and my sister Rosemarie to break the devastating news to them and tell them I was going to fly to Mount Hagen. Rosemarie decided to join me and, although we just missed the funeral itself, we were able to attend the last few days of Maggie's *haus krai*.

Bernadine gave me an account of the events leading up to our arrival, which she later recorded in a letter to Audrey McCollum in the USA. Audrey had stayed regularly at Haus Poroman while she was researching and writing a book about her friendship with Pirip Kuru, a Kuma woman, and her struggles to build a women's center. In the process, she became friends with Maggie.[1] Below are selections from Bernadine's letter to Audrey (28 April 2009):

Bernadine daubed in white mourning clay at Maggie's *haus krai*, 6 April 2009 (photograph by Kanawi Danomira).

Mum passed away at her hotel in the early hours of the morning. Monday 06 April 2009. We believe she had a heart attack. She had been suffering from high blood pressure, high cholesterol and an enlarged heart first diagnosed after she had a stroke approximately 4–5 years earlier.

Four days prior to her passing mum returned from Cairns after spending 3 weeks with Maki. She looked refreshed and energized; lost a bit of weight and was just beaming with happiness, giving each of us an extra-long hug. I doubt I'll ever forget how happy she was; she seemed almost content.

We got to the hotel [at] roughly the same time, had the doctor visit and made the easy decision of not having mum autopsied or embalmed, both things she wouldn't have wanted. Dressed mum, made the necessary phone calls to Maki (in Cairns) and Nadia (studying at Divine Word University Madang) and took mum home to the mountain after a short procession through town.

As soon as mum was home, Dad and I walked up to the village *singsing* ground to cry a little with our apas and start our house cry. People arrived that afternoon, showing just how quickly word gets around. Mum had always said to me that if she passed away she was never to be left alone and one of us always had to be present at the *haus krai*, because people were coming to cry with us.

Nadia arrived home in the afternoon. Having Nadia home was great. She

20. Mending Breaks

set photos, rocks, shells and candles out on a table near mum. It was beautiful and made it a happy, peaceful place to sit with mum.

We were back at the *haus krai* the next morning at about 8 a.m., all the women and men from the village were covered in white clay. Mum's sisters arrived and so did guests. There is not a lot I remember about the *haus krai*; despite being there every day, it all seems a blur.

You need to know that our road is s**t, it is really bad, there are a couple of spots where the road is just wide enough for vehicles to get over. So we knew that all the people that came to the *haus krai* wanted to be there. Schools came, starting with our own Kuta Community School, primary, secondary and tertiary institutions. It was truly a portrayal of who mum was and her commitment to education at all levels.

The most powerful of these images was Kuta Community School, children aged between 7–13 years old. When they started up the little hill on to the *singsing* ground, you could hear the crying and upon first glance you saw 4 to 5 teachers in front to the side; behind the teachers were rows of log pieces pointing to the sky coming up the hill. Step by step the log pieces progressed up the hill. As they started to reach the flat of the *singsing* ground, you saw the tiny little bodies that carried these log pieces twice their size. It was beautiful. All the boys had these big pieces of firewood and all the girls had bags of *kaukau* and *kumu*. They came and placed them down in front of us and then went and sat down. I will never forget that image.

Mum had also been specific about not being viewed. She wanted everyone to remember her the way she was when she was alive and not at her death. I thought this was going to be one of the hardest things I would have to convince her sisters and brothers about, let alone the rest of the village, but they all respected mum's wishes.

Despite *haus krais* usually going for 5 days, the burial and then the feast, mum wanted to be buried after 3 days. Most people in the village had no objection to this because in the last couple of years with deaths in the village mum would convince everyone to lay the body to rest around the 3rd or 4th day.

So Monday–Wednesday our days were spent up at the *haus krai* and our evenings at home, organizing the funeral, printing programs, and of course discussing the day's events, ensuring our lists of donations corresponded with that of our apas. Thursday was the funeral and it was a beautiful day; got a little bit too hot towards the end but this meant that all the umbrellas came out to keep the sun off people and it was just magnificent color. In our newspaper notice on mum's passing, we asked that everyone wear bright colors in celebration of her life. We also decided that it was going to be a celebration of her life, *not a funeral*. Olivia read a poem in the beginning of the service, Jim Leahy did the eulogy, each of the *haus man* representatives said their little goodbyes, and both Nadia and I said something. We were all happy. After the service, we took mum home to her view and laid her to rest.

That afternoon mum's best friend Rosita Henry arrived with her sister Rosemarie. Despite the funeral being over, we still wanted her to be with us because our mourning doesn't end until after the feast. I knew that mum would have wanted Rosita there. Rosita and her sister stayed with us for the weekend and left the following Sunday. It was bittersweet—having them there and then having to say goodbye.

The Saturday following her Thursday funeral we paid "bus fare"[2] to mum's mum's people. We also let everyone know that we would do the pig kill the following Saturday. We killed 37 pigs in total and hoped that everyone was satisfied.

Mum's whole *haus krai* was beautiful with no rain and just sunshine. Everyone in the village said this meant mum was happy. The celebration of mum's life continues…

Maggie was laid to rest not in the village cemetery, but in a little garden pocket right next to her house. My sister and I arrived in the afternoon and went straight to Maggie's grave to grieve with her family. They had buried her in the bare earth, wrapped in a *bilum* blanket, as she would have wanted, not a concrete tomb of the style that had recently become fashionable among the well-to-do in PNG. We cried together around the pile of fresh cut flowers that blanketed the soft red earth of her grave.

Rosemarie and I stayed with Maggie's husband and children at the house during the four days of our visit. Each dawn and dusk, we sat with the family beside the grave. At nightfall, an armed party of her clansmen from the village took over to guard the grave from *sanguma* (sorcerers) that they feared might come during the night to consume her body. The men set up lights and torches and kept vigil in shifts all night long. They warned Denis to lock up his dog overnight as *sanguma* can appear in animal form and the dog might be mistaken for one.

In the morning, we walked to the village *singsing* ground to spend the day at the *haus krai*, sitting in mourning with Maggie's kin while they accepted the condolences of group after group of people who had made their way up the mountain to present mortuary gifts. I watched with interest the diverse ways that people expressed their grief. Some people came up sorrowfully, gently hugging Maggie's husband and children (and Rosemarie and me, too), shedding just a few quiet tears; others keened loudly. Men pulled at their beards or, if they were clean shaven, at imaginary beards. Some people's faces were covered with white clay. Expressions like these are highly valued. There is a cultural expectation of reciprocation for such intangible "gifts of grief," as much as there is for the gifts of money, pigs and food crops that people customarily present at a *haus krai* (Henry 2012).

20. Mending Breaks

While grieving myself, I felt too tense and worried by the proceedings to give in to my sorrow. My attention was on Maggie's daughters and how they were feeling as well as on the nature of their relationships with Maggie's *haus lain* and the other Penambi Wia subclans. I felt a motherly concern for Maggie's children, particularly her two older daughters who had settled with their husbands in Kunguma and built houses on their mother's land. Their security of tenure partly rested on Maggie's lifework of relationship building within her own clan and with neighboring groups. I decided to take copious notes during the *haus krai*, thinking this might help Maggie's daughters keep track of who came and what they gave as funerary gifts. I knew that Maggie's family would have to distribute the gifts according to custom on the final day of the *haus krai*. Later, they would also need to distribute pork at the feast, or "pig kill," customarily held after a *haus krai*.

I could see Maggie's children trying hard to keep track of the intricate web of relationships into which their mother had linked them, not only for the sake of ensuring everyone was happy with her *haus krai*, but also for the longer term. They would have to pick up some of the threads that Maggie had dropped in death and manage the future expectations of people with whom Maggie had woven an intricate pattern of exchange relations during her lifetime, including during her election campaigns.

Displaying their oratorical skills, mostly men, but also some women, presented gifts on behalf of their clan groups and other kinds of social entities—schools, clubs, and women's groups. One day, a man stood up and made a point of inviting women to speak because "Maggie had paved the way" for them. A woman stood up and spoke on behalf of the widowed and unmarried women of the village, who had pooled earnings from their garden produce and sale of *bilums* to present as a funerary gift.

After the long day in the sun, we wearily returned to Maggie's house to a tasty curry that my sister Rosemarie had cooked for dinner. Joe Leahy's son Jim and his wife Rita arrived from Hagen with their family to spend the evening, armed with more pots of food. After dinner, we watched a slide show on Maggie's life and of her funeral the previous day, to the background music of her favorite song (Paul Simon's *Graceland*). The close-up expressions of grief in the faces captured by Bernadine's husband Kanawi in his amazing photographs brought me to tears again. After the long, emotionally charged day, I thought it would be impossible to sleep, but that was not so. As soon as my head touched the pillow, I fell into a deep and dreamless sleep. If any *sanguma* had tried to get to Maggie's grave, I would not have heard a thing.

The next day, we drove down the mountain to the apartment at Hotel Poroman in Hagen, where Maggie had spent her final years. It was the first time I had been there, as on my previous visit she was still living at Kunguma. Maggie's bed was still unmade, bedside table covered with her little treasures. Flowers drooped in a vase, food was starting to spoil in the fridge, shallots and a cabbage wilted on the kitchen counter. Children's clothes and toys were scattered in two other bedrooms, where Maggie's young children, Malt and Magdalena, and her brother's teenage daughter Jaralyn slept.

Although Maggie had told me that she had taken two more children into her care, Malt from her own Wia Ulgamp Komp lineage and Magdalena from its lineage pair, the Wia Ulgamp Angimp, the effect of her death on these children did not hit me until that moment in her bedroom. Their respective parents had offered Malt and Magdalena to Maggie as a way to build ties with her and to ensure that their children received a good education. Maggie undertook the tasks of feeding and clothing them, along with Jaralyn, and sending them to private schools in Hagen. Malt was eight years old and Magdalena was seven.

"What a terrible shock it must be for them," I thought aloud, wondering what would become of them. Bernadine, Rosemarie and I sat on Maggie's bed discussing the issue. Bernadine revealed that she had tried to dissuade her mother from accepting the children, because her other children were already grown up with families of their own. Keith, too, had expressed concern, but Maggie was nothing if not determined. The family had already met to try to resolve what to do about the children. Should they go back to their parents in the village or should Maggie's husband and adult children accept responsibility for them? Nadia was too young, Maki was returning to live in Australia, and Bernadine and Olivia had husbands and children of their own to consider. They had not yet come to a resolution.

As soon as we got back to Kunguma, we returned to the *haus krai*. It seemed to be bigger than the day before, with many more people attending, perhaps because it was Saturday. Fourteen pigs tied to stakes on the *singsing* ground were on display. Several good orators got up one by one, parading up and down. Before they presented their pigs and money donations, they talked about Maggie, the relationships she had forged, how widely she was admired, and her strength in business and politics. Speakers reiterated how Maggie's husband Keith and their children belonged among the Penambi Wia. While Maggie herself had passed, her children were her legacy. Twaima, the Wia Ulgamp Angimp leader from the neighboring village of Knep, gave a long speech before presenting gifts on behalf of his group. Koim Kip spoke on behalf of the Maramp subclan of the Penambi Wia. He said that Maggie and he had often argued, but they had always resolved matters. He declared that although Maggie was a woman, she could "talk like a man."

20. Mending Breaks

Maggie with Jaralyn (back), Magdalena (front) and Malt, Hotel Poroman, Mt. Hagen, 7 March 2009 (photograph by Kanawi Danomira).

After quietly taking in the proceedings, I requested permission to make a speech of my own. Through Maggie's brother Thomas Las, who translated for me into *tok ples*, I made a contribution of 300 kina towards the *haus krai* pool and gave another 180 kina to Maggie's siblings. I said something like, "I have been Maggie's friend for nearly 40 years. She first told me about her home in Kunguma Village when we were at school together in Australia, two lonely girls missing our families. She told me stories about her *haus lain*, her parents and you, her brothers and sisters. Knowing Maggie has made me the person I am today and because you contributed to making her the person she was, I am thankful. Therefore, I would like to present each of you with a small gift to comfort you in your loss." I called out the names of each of Maggie's siblings, her sisters, Prul, Poning, Tali, Lauie and Rita, and her brothers, Kawa, Kuipa, Pora, and Thomas. To each I gave 20 kina through an intermediary, as is the custom.

Lastly, Joe Leahy stood up to speak, first in Tok Pisin and then *tok ples*. He used the chance to lecture everyone about needing to look to the global market. He chided people for worrying about their little local battles when they should be thinking about making business in the outside world. He said, "PNG has coffee factories but no money factories." Pointing to a small green chimney on the roof of a toilet nearby, he exclaimed, "That's your money factory!" He urged people to think of themselves not in terms of clans but as Papua New Guineans, and to work for the good of the country as a whole. He finished by presenting a large, fat pig and some cash.

We were just about to take a break and retire to Maggie's house when suddenly someone, I am not sure who it was, decided to thank me for having come all the way from Australia. Spontaneously people started a collection to help me pay my fare back. Some gave as much as 20 kina, some gave 10 kina, some 5 kina, and several old women gifted 2 kina each, so that the final tally came to 106 kina. Deeply touched, I marveled at the generosity of these people, for whom money is so hard to come by.

After a coffee break and some hot cross buns, we walked back to the *singsing* ground to complete the *haus krai* events. A huge crowd was waiting. It was time to pay Maggie's mother's clan, the Melka Kopiamp people. Customarily among Hageners, the paternal kin of a deceased make mortuary payments to the maternal kin. In addition, all the mourners attending a *haus krai* are given a small sum for their fare home and all those who help in one way or another are recompensed, including those who bring clay to rub on the mourners.

We were ushered into a house at the top of the *singsing* ground. It was Maggie's brother John Kawa's place. The house was full of men counting the cash given during the *haus krai* and discussing how to redistribute it to the crowd waiting outside. After agreement, everyone clapped once in unison and we went outside to gathering rain clouds and impending darkness.

In total, there was 17,934 kina to be distributed. I could see Oliva trying to keep record of what was given, and to whom, so I decided to help by keeping a record as well. Fortunately, a woman next to me, Barbara Kauga, was able to translate and explain who was who.

I would have normally stood back from such a large crowd, but here I was in the middle of it, people pressing close to receive their share or just to witness the distribution as the night closed in around us. It was intensely communal and I felt completely safe, enveloped in the embrace of the *haus krai*. Little did I know then that not everyone felt as safe as I did. Some people from neighboring groups were afraid to attend Maggie's *haus krai* due to unresolved conflict among the clans.

We walked back to Maggie's house by torchlight, picking our way through the settling fog. Unfortunately, Rosemarie and I were booked on a flight back to Australia the next day. Although I had teaching responsibilities that beckoned, I was loath to leave. So much was unfolding in the wake of Maggie's death.

I wanted to be there for the pig-kill the following weekend and I wished I had more time to explore the concerns some of Maggie's clanspeople had revealed to me about the sudden and unexpected nature of her death. There were whisperings of treachery towards Maggie due to jealousy of her success in business. Someone even suggested that she was a victim of *poison* (sorcery)[3] in revenge for an incident that occurred at Hotel Poroman. Maggie's brother told me it was not appropriate to air such suspicions publically at a *haus krai* but that, in order to ensure their continued well-being, Maggie's *haus lain* would call a meeting soon, where they would *outim* (confess) any actions anyone may have taken against Maggie's interests.[4]

Although I was at Maggie's *haus krai* as her friend, I could not help but also experience the events from an anthropological perspective with an appreciation for the fragility of the damaged web of social relations that her sudden death had left (Henry 2012). For example, after a *guria* (earth tremor) that sent dogs running around the house barking one night, a woman came from the village to inform us that one of her nephews had tried to contact Maggie's spirit by calling a special number on his mobile phone. The woman interpreted the *guria* as a sign that Maggie was unhappy.

I noted with keen interest the interpretations people gave for certain individuals becoming sick after Maggie's death. Among Hageners, people believe that betrayal can cause the death of a person betrayed. The victim's ghost is then likely to wreak sickness and other misfortune on the betrayer and members of his or her group.[5]

    I spent the last hours before our flight on the verandah of Maggie's house, immersed in the copy of her unfinished memoir her children had given me. It was obvious that Maggie had been too busy to add much more to the draft I had read nine years ago. Having missed the chance to work on the manuscript with Maggie when she was alive, I decided to offer to finish it. The book would be my way of reciprocating the gift of Maggie's long and steadfast friendship. Research for it would also afford me an excuse to return to her mountain and the family I had grown to love.

21

Reflections: Tying Up Loose Ends

Rosita Henry

Maggie grew up feisty and headstrong, with all the qualities that people admire in a leader in the highlands. She lived life joyfully and with the expectation that she could achieve anything that she set her mind to. Although her dreams did not always come to fruition as planned, and there were times when she felt deep disappointment, she was committed to weaving a strong and lasting legacy for her children. This book is part of that legacy.

In beginning to write her memoir, Maggie set out to record what she saw as an amazingly transformative time in the lives of her people. She felt that she was incredibly lucky to have been born at this particular turning point in history. She was grateful for the exciting opportunities she had to participate in the birth of Papua New Guinea as a nation and she embraced every chance given to her with contagious excitement and passion.

Maggie's memoir paints a picture of an idyllic childhood. Feeling secure in her father Kuan's loving care and the love of her Penambi Wia clanspeople provided her with a firm foundation for all that she later went on to achieve. Like her clanspeople, Maggie worked hard throughout her life to plant and cultivate relationships by growing up children. In addition to her two biological daughters, she adopted one son and a third daughter and later in life began to care for two more children. Her story and those of her children reveal much about concepts of personhood and belonging in the Highlands of Papua New Guinea. The word adoption is inappropriate in this cultural context. In fact, although Maggie herself used the term adoption for the sake of her Western readers, adoption is not a word or a relationship that her children are comfortable with. Penambi people rarely openly discuss adoption. While most adults are fully aware of the "circulation of children"[1] within the clan, and it is obvious to all in the village when a child is transferred from the birth mother to another woman, it is not considered appropriate to talk about this openly. The circulation of children among highlanders and the "public secret"[2] about it can be understood in terms of a concept of personhood that is performative. That is, a person is made through active care work, including feeding, clothing, educating, and contributing to life-cycle payments such as brideprice and so on. Just as Maggie saw Kuan as her father in substance, because it was he who fed her and grew her from the produce of the land on which he had also grown, so also do all of Maggie's children see themselves as being a part of her and part of one another. Open announcement of the secret of adoption threatens ontological security by putting in jeopardy the relationships of substance (sameness) that parents work hard to create with their children through nurturance. For many Papua New Guineans, as Demian (2004: 106) writes, "the conditions for distinguishing between parents and non-parents are not solely couched in terms of 'blood,' and because multiple parenthood is perfectly acceptable, the index of parent-child relationship is the work performed by parent for their children and by children for their parents." Breaking the secret devalues the work that has gone into creating sameness. Making differentiation explicit through revelation puts love's labor at risk of being lost.

I started working on Maggie's memoir five months after her funeral, in September 2009, invited by her family to stay with them at her house in Kunguma Village. In memory of her, they had decided to host a special gathering of some of her old friends from Australia for the PNG Independence Day Ball at Hotel Poroman. It was a fitting celebration for Maggie, because staging a ball each year had been her idea. She called it the "Reflections Ball" because she wanted people to reflect upon the things that Papua New Guinea had achieved since Independence. This year was to be the fifth such ball. Among the invited friends staying at Maggie's house were filmmaker Bob Connolly and his new partner Sophie from Sydney, and Maggie's old friend Lois Logan, who had flown up from Cairns. Maggie's husband Keith, kind and easygoing, proved to be a gracious host.

Maggie's daughter Olivia was in charge of the kitchen at Hotel Poroman. She wanted a different menu for the ball from the everyday fare they usually served, so she asked me to bring some of my sister Rozana's Sri Lankan spices to make a curry feast. Unlike my sister, who is a talented chef, I am not particularly at ease with cooking, especially for large crowds. Nevertheless, armed with Rozana's recipes and instructions, I rose to the challenge. I spent the day before the ball in the hotel kitchen making several huge pots of chicken curry, a beef curry and a mixed vegetable curry finished with coconut milk, which we stored in the fridge overnight. I was worried that the coconut milk would spoil by the next day and regretted adding it so soon. It should have been left until just before serving the food. On the morning of the ball, Olivia and I returned to put the final touches on the dishes. I prepared some Sri Lankan coconut sambol and a *mallung*, spiced green leaves fried with grated coconut.

A photographic exhibition of Maggie's life covered the walls of a room adjoining the dining room. Here, memorabilia and examples of her creative work were also displayed—*bilum* designs, fabrics based on traditional Hagen motifs which she had created for the bedspreads and curtains of the lodge and the hotel, and images of her landscape garden designs. Many expatriates and members of well-to-do Hagen families attended, in addition to Maggie's cousins from the Leahy side and her sister Rita and brother Councilor John Kawa. Nadia honored her mother by wearing the unique *bilum* dress that Maggie had designed for Olivia for the Miss PNG pageant.

Gerry Leahy, Bob Connolly, Lois Logan and I were invited to give speeches. Addressing a room full of Hageners, who have a discerning appreciation for

At the reflections ball. Lois Logan (left), Nadia (center) wearing the *bilum* outfit designed by Maggie for Olivia (right) for the Miss PNG pageant in 2001, 13 September 2009 (photograph by Kanawi Danomira).

good oratory, was intimidating to say the least. Luckily, attention soon shifted to Sophie, a talented musician who offered to sing a song in Maggie's memory, and then the band started to play.

I met anthropologist Polly Wiesner on the dance floor. She said she was in the highlands for the opening of the new cultural center in Enga Province on Independence Day, and to return over thirty years of her field research. She invited me to attend the opening. "It will be a great ethnographic experience," she urged, introducing me to someone who could give me a lift to Wabag. I gladly accepted before the music danced us apart.

Everyone was keen to be on the floor so no one lingered too long over dinner. If anyone had noticed the slightly off taste of the coconut milk in the vegetable curry, it did not seem to stop them from enjoying the night. We drove back up the mountain in the early hours of the morning, tired but satisfied that the ball had been a great success.

The next day, we rose early to help prepare for a memorial *mumu* for Maggie. Her *haus lain* from Kunguma and members from her mother's *haus lain*, who lived nearby and had worked for Maggie in the lodge and hotel, attended and helped prepare the feast. I noticed that Malt and Magdalena were also there with their parents. The children had returned to live with their birth families, but with continued support from Maggie's husband and children.

One of Maggie's brothers killed the pig with a single blow to the head. Councilor John Kawa expertly butchered it, first cutting off small pieces for roasting over the open fire in which stones for the *mumu* were heating. Joe, Clem, Gerry, Jim, and Bryan Leahy arrived with their families in time to cook their pieces of *mit kont* (pork). We all stood around the fire communally cooking the ribs and other small pieces of pork on long wooden skewers, soaking up the mouthwatering fat on bundles of edible green leaves.

Later in the day, when Maggie's brothers opened the *mumu* pit and distributed the cooked meat, Bernadine presented the pig head, which customarily goes to someone of importance, to her grandfather Wia Kut. After we all ate our fill, Bernadine, Bryan Leahy, Bob Connolly, and Joe Leahy all gave speeches.

I missed most of the speeches as I was inside the house with Thomas Las, who wanted to share with me what had been happening in the five months since his sister's death.

> So when Maggie died, one of our clansmen died a week later and something went wrong with the joints of another guy; he couldn't walk straight. In the local understanding it's like you come from one mother's womb or something. So one guy died and the other guy is ill. Things happen like that.

21. Reflections

Joe Leahy (left) and Bob Connolly (right), Kunguma Village, 14 September 2009 (photograph by Kanawi Danomira).

People said, "Look Maggie's a good woman. She died and there's one of you guys going to die soon," and so a week later, one died and now the other is sick, can't walk.

Maggie had a heart for the old people. Every time old people died in the village she would arrange for a coffin box and the clothes that they would wear. Everybody who died, their spirits were with Maggie, so if anybody did anything wrong to Maggie, they would get a harsh punishment. It's a local thing but it happens. People believe that. I believe that. There is always jealousy in the village. There is always jealousy in the families and when you get to do something better than someone else there is always jealousy.

The *mumu* proved to be a perfect opportunity for me to arrange meetings with Maggie's family and friends, to learn more of Maggie's lifeworld. While the other houseguests from Australia left the next day, I stayed on for the rest of the week. Bernadine shared with me some of the events that unfolded in the aftermath of the roadblock, when Maggie was threatened and her vehicle stolen.

Following the roadblock, tensions escalated over the outcome of the council elections and a tribal fight erupted. The fighting stopped after a few days but before the peace process was completed, Maggie died. I was oblivious to this when I attended Maggie's *haus krai*, but the danger of attack meant that some people from the enemy side who would otherwise have come were too afraid to attend. Bernadine explained,

> One guy got shot and he died in the tribal fight. They had bows and arrows, and spears but they also had a few guns. Eventually it calmed down and *bel kol* money was paid, about 8,000 kina. *Bel kol* is a little bit of initial compensation just to quell the fighting. It buys the tribe that's doing the compensation time to go and organize stuff. By doing that you are opening up your movements. When you pay *bel kol* you know that peace is being negotiated so you can wander freely. If you don't pay *bel kol* it's like the tribal fight is still going on so at any point you can be attacked. When you are angry you are *bel hat*, which means "hot stomach," and *bel kol* is to cool your temper.
>
> Mum's funeral was after the *bel kol* but before the main compensation, so they were still scared; only some women came and a couple of men who are married to women in our line came to her *haus krai*.
>
> At the compensation, the Penambi and our allies gave the tribe of the man who was killed in the fight about 20,000 kina, plus two horses, a cow, two snakes (pythons), two cassowaries, two or three possums, and 60 something pigs. But before this Apa Kawa gave compensation to his own Penambi people. Our family was given a pig at the compensation to say sorry for the inconvenience and for what had happened to mum on the road.
>
> We gave some money towards the compensation for the man who was killed. At the time, I wanted to be able to say that they had disrespected mum. I was all fired up, but when I got there, everybody kind of covers it up a bit; they are not direct about what they are upset about. I also felt that I shouldn't get fired up and upset about it because I might incite other people to get angry as well. As it was a peace process, I should speak in a way that encourages the process to happen.
>
> Prior to me speaking some prominent people spoke and they said there's laws in place and that nobody should die over council elections. So I said that I agreed that there were different laws in place that we could look to instead of tribal fighting and that when we stopped on the road we did so because we felt it had nothing to do with us and that mum was an elderly woman with us kids. We had no tribe behind us; we had no weapons. I wanted to say that they should pay for the car because it was the hotel car and the car ended up being destroyed, but I didn't say that. I just said that she was an elderly woman and that she had ended up forgiving them.
>
> After the incident at the road block, when they took her car, Mum got really upset. She was all fired up and wanted me to write statements to the police. She wanted to charge them and she was all ready to go, which kind of annoyed me because deep down I knew that she was not going to follow through with it. But I did it anyway. I wrote statements for her. Then she changed her mind and she said, "It's all right, I'm not going to worry about it. I am going to leave it up to God. I am not going to take revenge into

my own hands, God can deal with it the way he wants to and I'll forgive them."

So at the compensation time, I said to them all, "You know the quality of a leader my mother was. She led by example and she showed the way and that's the kind of leadership we want to follow. I know that she forgave you and for that reason we are here and we also forgive you."

Later, at the return compensation, the tribe responsible for the road block gave us a really big pig probably valued between three and four thousand kina to apologize to mum, and we accepted on her behalf.

I thought I could complete Maggie's memoir and get it published in just a couple of years, but it has taken me almost ten years. Each year, I traveled to Kunguma for a few weeks to conduct further research. In the process, I was able to document some of the telling events that unfolded after her death. The threads of Maggie's life continue to be woven through the lives of her children, her Wia Ulgamp Komp *haus lain*, the other subclans of the Penambi Wia, the Melka people from her mother's side, and the wider web of relationships that she created during her lifetime. The echoes of her presence will long resonate around her mountain home and wherever those who knew and loved her travel.

In April 2010, I returned to Hagen to spend two months in Maggie's village working on her memoir. My eldest daughter, Lani, who was then a medical student, took the chance to accompany me. She had arranged a placement at the Hagen Hospital. We met Bernadine and Maggie's sister Rita in Port Moresby on our way through. Bernadine was in Moresby to give birth. She had been sure she was going to have a girl, as the baby was due on the first anniversary of her mother's death, one year to the day, but the ultrasound test showed that she was going to have a boy. Her Penambi Wia kin were overjoyed when they heard it was to be a boy. Rita said, "Between you and Oliva, you will have enough boys to establish your own *haus man* among the Penambi."

After Maggie's death, Olivia and Denis took over full responsibility for running the hotel. They lived with their three sons in an apartment in the hotel complex during the week and on weekends returned to their house in Kunguma. Maki returned to work in Australia and Nadia went back to her studies at Divine Word University in Madang.

Lani and I shared a room in Maggie's house for the two months we were there. For the first week, while she was on holiday from university, Nadia also shared the room with us. Originally, she had made up a bed in Maggie's room, but she became frightened there during the night after a dream.

In Nadia's dream, I was sitting with her on the couch in Maggie's house.

Maggie came in angry and upset, crying, "Everyone thought I was dead, but I wasn't. I was buried alive!" As Maggie's sister Rita had also dreamt of Maggie while staying at the house and I had woken up during my last visit to a strange buzzing noise and a pain in my heart, it was a comfort to us all to sleep together in the same room.

During my years of research among Maggie's kin, I was to hear many more dream narratives involving the appearance of Maggie. People usually call upon men or women in the village credited with a special talent in dream interpretation to help determine what their dreams might mean. Recently dead relatives commonly appear in dreams among Hageners. "They do not appear for nothing, but to convey comments on the current situation" (A. Strathern 1989: 304). In one of Bernadine's many dreams about Maggie, her mother came to her and said, "It is hard for me to watch you guys from the outside," after seeing Bernadine's struggle to field the expectations of her Penambi Wia kin regarding contributions to brideprice and funerary payments.[3]

While Lani was working at the hospital, I spent my days in the village. Maggie's brother Thomas proved to be an excellent research assistant, guide and translator. We walked to Noki Kut's fun *haus* next to the village *singsing* ground. Noki sells cigarettes, *buai* (betel nut) and a few groceries. Mostly men, but also some women, go to the fun *haus* to socialize, watch videos and play pool or cards. Pinned to the wall was an old election poster of Maggie's from 2007 and a couple of laminated photos I had taken during my visit to her in 2001.

When Thomas told Noki that I was there to research Maggie's book, he declared that preachers from all across the country were using Maggie as a role model for others because, although she was "mixed-race" and a "business woman," she had refused a fancy concrete grave and tombstone, such as had become the trend among the elite. It seems the story had become part of local mythology, with people coming from far and wide to see her simple "grass roots" grave with their own eyes.

One day Thomas took my daughter and me for a long walk to the site of the original village where Maggie's *haus lain* had lived before they moved to Kunguma and Knep. The place, Kugulwe, was partway down the mountain on the Nebilyer Valley side towards Korgua. Most Penambi Wia people still keep gardens in Kugulwe and regularly walk the distance each day. I found walking down the steep and slippery rainforest track strenuous going. Thomas pointed out the old house and garden sites of Maggie's father Kuan and his brothers Tugle, Penepel, Wai and Kut. We located the sites of Kuan's men's house, Jara's house where Maggie was born and the *tanim het* house where Maggie had attended courtship parties.

21. Reflections

Noki Kut in his trade store and *fun haus*, with Maggie's 2007 election poster on the wall, Kunguma Village, September 2017 (photograph by Bridie Egan).

It was easy to picture Maggie as a happy young girl flourishing in that place. I could imagine her also on that fateful day, when she took Bernadine and others for a walk there, skipping like a child through the gardens eating cucumbers, only to return home and sick and with no memory of her visit until she appeased her father's spirit with the sacrifice of a pig.

Thomas Las (left) at Kugulwe pointing out to Rosita Henry (right) Joe Leahy's Kilima Plantation in the Nebilyer Valley below, April 2010 (photograph by Roselani Henry).

The view from Kugulwe over the Nebilyer Valley was breathtaking. Thomas pointed out Joe Leahy's Kilima coffee plantation in the far distance, a grey square in the checkerboard of darker green and brown plots. On our way back to Kunguma, we met two young boys with slingshots. They had been trying to catch birds for their dinner. They ran ahead of us and Thomas would have followed just as nimbly if he had not been solicitously helping me to negotiate the slippery track.

Bernadine arrived back from Port Moresby with her baby son on 1 April 2010. She had decided to name him Musje. The next morning, Maria Kuk, married to Councilor John Kawa, came to see the baby. She sat at Berni's feet, sobbing and crying for nearly half an hour, while Bernadine breastfed Musje. She declared that all of Maggie's Penambi kin were happy she had a boy because they had been worried that Berni and Olly would leave Papua New Guinea after Maggie's death. Now that the girls had five boys between them, they were sure to stay on and their sons could form a *haus man* to "hold" the land.

21. Reflections

As it was already a year since Maggie died, it was time to hold a memorial pig kill for her. Thus, during the final weeks of my visit in 2010, there was much activity as her kin prepared for the event. First, they had to decide whether to do it on the village *singsing* ground or on the smaller *singsing* ground that Maggie had built for the lodge.

Councilor John Kawa called a meeting at his house to discuss the matter. The family members agreed to do it on the village *singsing* ground where it would be more open to the public. Next, there was much discussion regarding the number of pigs required to honor Maggie and to ensure a substantial amount of cooked meat, enough for distribution among all the Penambi Wia subclans as well as to her mother's Melka subclan.

In anticipation of the *mumu*, Maggie's husband and children had bought five piglets the year before to fatten. On the eve of the pig kill, Maggie's friend and business partner Elizabeth Pora contributed three more pigs, and Bernadine and Olivia went with their Uncle Kawa to purchase some extra ones. They did this by driving along the highway until they spotted a tall stake with flowers tied to the top. This was a sign that someone had a pig for sale.

In the meantime, I took the opportunity to go with Thomas to meet his brother Pora, who, after a long account of his relationship with Maggie, concluded,

> Now we are here organizing her funeral feast, or a year after the funeral feast. We are not doing much; it's just paying honor to the dead, doing that part, to get the pigs and clear the spirits. All of us brothers we have just contributed one pig each and so we are helping to get the *mumu* done and helping to give food to the friends and relatives around. So the story comes to an end here and I have nothing more to say, but I thank you for hearing me.[4]

The next morning my daughter and I rose before five to watch the pig kill and *mumu* preparation on the village *singsing* ground. I was enthralled to see how Pora shared out the *mit kont* to all present. He went around to each person present, including the children, melodiously calling out their names, even mine ("Rosita-o! Rosita-o!"), before handing each of us a pork rib or other small piece of pork to roast over the open fire where the *mumu* stones were heating. Malt's father, Dos, had cut down a tree he had planted many years ago to contribute the firewood.

Some of the offal was given to a group of women who sat preparing parcels of food wrapped in leaves for adding to the three *mumu* pits with the hot stones and layers of *kaukau*, taro, cabbages, bananas, *kumu*, and the butchered pigs—legs, heads, bellies, backs, flanks.

As an introduced root crop, carrots had recently come into fashion and I noticed some of the women decoratively adding chopped carrot pieces to

Pora distributing *mit kont* (pork pieces) to women making their bundles at the one-year memorial "pig kill" and *mumu* feast for Maggie, April 2010 (photograph by Rosita Henry).

21. Reflections

their arrangements of peanuts, pig meat and *kumu* (green leaves) soaked in pig blood. Each woman prepared her parcel according to her own aesthetic pleasure, knotting the bundle with lengths of plant fiber in such a way that she could recognize it when it later came from the *mumu* pit.

Suddenly, there was a commotion near the butchered pig. Two women were shouting and pushing each another. There was a gasp from the crowd and the men shouted a warning as one woman nearly fell into a bloody pile of pig meat. Interveners quickly herded the women away and activities continued as if nothing had happened. Later someone told me that the women were the co-wives of one of Maggie's brothers and that the altercation was not a big deal as "co-wives always fight."

In the afternoon, the *mumu* pits were opened and the steaming food carefully removed. The cooked meat and vegetables were publically distributed by Councilor John Kawa among each subclan of the Penambi Wia, to Maggie's maternal kin—the Melka—and among her friends and allies in neighboring clans. Even I was presented with a share, much to my surprise.

Clem Leahy commented that the family could feel proud of what they had achieved. He was particularly impressed with the large number of fat

Maggie's brother Councilor John Kawa presenting gifts of cooked pork at the one-year memorial "pig kill" for Maggie, April 2010 (photograph by Kanawi Danomira).

pigs they had managed to assemble for killing, cooking and distributing in Maggie's name.

That evening, we retired to Maggie's house to prepare for a visit from her nine siblings. They were to receive a share of Maggie's clothes and other effects. Such a distribution usually happens sooner after a death, and some of Maggie's siblings were unhappy about the delay, but Maggie's children had not been able to bring themselves to do it sooner. Bernadine said she felt giving away Maggie's things would mean that her mother was gone for good.

I sat with Maggie's daughters in their mother's bedroom as they forlornly went through her clothes, dividing them up into nine equal bundles. After Maggie's siblings arrived, Bernadine explained and apologized for the delay before handing to each a plastic bag of clothes and 300 kina from Maggie's last pay at the hotel. In contrast to the large public *mumu*, this was a quiet event, with Maggie's closest family huddling sorrowfully around the fireplace. My heart broke for them all, especially for her sister Poning, with whom Maggie and I had spent a lot of time during my visit in 2001, and who had helped compose the song for the Kunguma Women's Self-Help Group.

I thought that the memorial *mumu* one year after her death might be the last that I would hear Maggie mentioned in public, but my subsequent field trips to Kunguma were to prove otherwise. Each year, I found the memory of her as alive and as strong as ever. Orators continued to bring up her

Poning (left) and Maggie (right), January 2001 (photograph by Rosita Henry).

name in their public speeches on the *singsing* ground, at brideprice exchanges, funerals, and other such events. As Stewart and Strathern (2005: 46) write, "The past is neither fixed nor complete, and in death the question of 'What is lost?' is inseparable from 'What remains?' What remains in effect is a sense of agency of the dead, and that perceived agency is the source of the ongoing relationship between them and the living."

This ongoing relationship was made evident to me by Bernadine when she provided me with an account of the confessional[5] that was held after Maggie's *haus krai*. I asked Bernadine what had happened when her *haus lain* had met to "*outim wrong sin*, so that *behain behain* we will be okay as a family." According to Bernadine, Maggie's brothers were worried that they had angered Maggie when they offered to pay the neighboring subclan compensation to cool them down after they had blocked the lodge gate. Prior to the *outim wari* meeting, Bernadine had not considered the significance of this incident, but after hearing everyone talk, it occurred to her that her mother may still have been harboring resentment about it at the time of her death.

> Mum never said anything to me, but then at this meeting that we had when *mipela outim all wari*, when we all spoke up about our concerns, I got this feeling that mum was hurt because they never said sorry to her for going ahead and giving those people compensation. By doing that, without realizing, they might have made mum feel like she was an outsider. They might have made her feel that she wasn't one of their sisters, because they didn't say, "She's our sister and you shouldn't do that." I felt that was what happened, so I said, "You didn't say sorry to mum and mum was hurt by that." When I said that to Apa Kawa and them they said, "Yeah true you could be right; we will say sorry to her and do a *mumu*."[6]

Before Maggie died, her brothers had accused one of their own *haus lain* of inciting a neighboring subclan to come and claim compensation from her. The accused swore on his father's grave, insisting, "I didn't do it. If I did then I'll die." Not long afterwards, he developed a blood disorder and went to Port Moresby for treatment. He came to the airport to see Maggie when she was passing through Port Moresby on her way home from her last trip to Cairns. She gave him some money and told him to get better and come home, but he died just two weeks after Maggie died. As Bernadine recounted,

> Apparently, he found out she died and then he lost all hope and just died as well. Because he said he was going to contribute the pig for compensation to the neighboring subclan, everyone in the village thought that was an admission of guilt.
> Mum said, "Maybe he said it without thinking about the consequences of his talking." Mum was the only one who was nice to him in the village and

when they were growing up she really looked up to him, so I don't think it was intentional on his part.

When he got sick, of all places he got sick in his mouth. That was the first place he was bleeding from, so everybody said that because it came from his mouth, that was the place he got sick.

Towards the end, mum kept saying, "I want to go to Australia and I want to live there." So I think she was hurt, not just hurt by everything that was happening here regarding the lodge but hurt by the election thing because a lot of people really let her down. She expected people to vote for her and they didn't.

I think I let her down, too, at that election time. She wanted me to be her campaign person, type up everything, and I just didn't want to do it, because mum's the kind of person who works all night. She doesn't stop; she just works and works and works, and you would feel guilty because you would think, "Here's my mother who's so much older and she's just go, go, go, work, work, work; and how come I can't do it?"[7]

The belief that the dead can cause sickness and death of their own kin is well documented among Hageners. However, as Marilyn Strathern (1972: 126) notes, after the death of an older woman, her kin "only fear vengeance ... if there was some specific grievance at issue. Female clan ghosts act because of a wrong done to their children or to them in their lifetime." Otherwise, the ghosts of sisters "care for the overall prosperity of their living clansmen."

The continuing agency of Maggie among her clanspeople also came to the fore at her daughter Nadia's brideprice. In 2012, Nadia decided to get married to her partner Hebrew Maipson, a Mogei Nambuga man. Although neither of her sisters, Bernadine and Olivia, nor her mother Maggie, had married according to the tradition of accepting brideprice from the groom, Nadia wanted to be married in this way. The family invited me to attend the event, which was to take place on 28 December 2012 on the *singsing* ground of the groom's village. This would be followed a week later by the customary return of wealth by the bride's group to the groom's group, referred to as the *bekim* in Tok Pisin. At the *bekim* in the bride's village of Kunguma, there was also going to be a marriage service performed by the Catholic priest, Father Garrett Roche.

I eagerly accepted the invitation, arming myself with a video camera to record the events for the bride and groom. At the same time, the wedding was a good opportunity for further research to tie up some loose ends in Maggie's memoir.

The significance of the dead among the living and the past in the present was evident in the speeches at the brideprice exchange. Maggie's name came up often. She was clearly present in spite of her absence. As the mother of

21. Reflections

Olivia (left) and Bernadine (right) representing their mother, Maggie, at their sister Nadia's bride price exchange, 29 December 2012 (photograph by Rosita Henry).

the bride, Maggie would have received a big pig (*mam peng kng* in *tok ples*), but Bernadine and Olivia were given the pig in her place.

Interestingly, the Mogei Nambuga acknowledged not only Maggie in their speeches, but also her paternal grandmother, the mother of Maggie's fathers,[8] the five Wia Ulgamp Komp brothers—Kuan, Tugl, Penapil, Wai and Kut. This woman, named Kopenamp, was killed during a tribal war that took place in the late 1920s, just prior to the arrival of the first white men, the Leahy brothers, on Penambi Wia territory. During that war, the Penambi and the Mogei were enemies, so the Mogei accepted responsibility for the death of Kopenamp. Since her killing, all marriages between the two groups had been either infertile or resulted in "only girls." More than seventy years after her death, the agency of Kopenamp is still active in the relationship between the Mogei and the Penambi. So much so that before going ahead with the brideprice exchange, the Mogei Nambuga saw fit to present the bride's group with a pig and 300 kina to "break her curse" so that Nadia and Hebrew, who already had two daughters, might have a boy.[9]

I imagine that like old Kopenamp, Maggie will play a role in relations among the living well into the future. There is no doubt that the seeds she

Evening view from Maggie's house, Kunguma Village, 2009 (photograph by Kanawi Danomira).

planted and grew during her lifetime will bear fruit for many generations to come. While they feel her loss deeply, Maggie lives on in the dreams, hopes and achievements of her children and her wider kingroup. Memories of Maggie will long continue to inspire their endeavors, animate their dreams, rouse the speeches they make, and move the songs they compose.

Weldo we, ya weldo we:	Chorus
Knep ya morgup kantmegl:	Looking from Knep I can see
Kunguma kapa lo penem:	The Kunguma house with the tin roof all locked up
Ina werel tigi pont:	I am so lost
Mogpe nenba ampbegl agimp:	The only person I could talk to
Kunguma mey rawa ngump:	Is buried at Kunguma
Klanda mana ora kilt penem:	Tears run over my pillow
Pep ropeldop pelepent:	I cannot sleep at night, thinking of you
Weldo we, ya weldo we	Chorus[10]

Chapter Notes

Editor's Introduction

1. Gerry Leahy, personal communication, 17 September 2009.

Chapter 1

1. Running water is associated with life and fertility among Hagen people (Strathern 1972: 168).
2. According to the Catholic mission records held at Rebiamul, Mount Hagen, Maggie was baptized on 30 April 1950. Her date of birth is given as 28 February 1950. On her marriage certificate, her date of birth is recorded as 28 December 1952.
3. Father William Anthony Ross (1895–1973) was a missionary of the Society of the Divine Word (S.V.D.). He was ordained a priest on 10 June 1922 and made an expedition in 1934 to set up the first Catholic mission in the Western Highlands, initially at Wilya, near the Leahy station at Kuta. The mission station was moved from Wilya to Rebiamul in 1938. Father Ross died on 20 May 1973 at Rebiamul and is buried in the mission cemetery. See Mennis (1982).
4. Many anthropologists prefer to use the term "bridewealth" because "brideprice" carries with it the connotation that the payment is for the woman or bride, whereas the exchange actually marks the beginning of an alliance and continuing exchanges between the clans of the bride and groom. However, I use the term "brideprice," as this is the term that Maggie used and that is commonly used in Papua New Guinea.

Chapter 2

1. In terms of the kinship terminology, a person's father's brothers are also referred to as "father." After Kuan died, Maggie's mother Jara married his brother Tugl, so he became Maggie's father in this sense.
2. Connolly and Anderson (2005: 157–159, 226) recorded Tugl's account of the outbreak of tribal warfare that Maggie describes here in their book *First Contact*. It was Maggie who introduced them to her father Tugl. This particular tribal war took place at the threshold of European colonization; Tugl would have been about eleven or twelve at the time he escaped with his brothers into the protection of the Melka people.
3. According to custom, individuals are referred to by their clan name followed by their given name. A woman's name is also usually prefaced with the word for "woman"—*amp*.
4. Thomas Las, personal communication, 9 April 2010.
5. Wia Kut sadly passed away in February 2015, aged at least 90 years old.

6. Wilya is where the Leahy brothers first set up camp and built an airstrip. In January 1934, the Divine Word Order, led by Father William Ross, set up a mission station at Wilya. In late 1938, the main mission station was transferred to Rebiamul (Kruczek 2007: 45). According to Mennis (1982: 84), Rebiamul was at the time a battle ground and "a no-man's land, between the Mogei Kominigas and the Mogei Nampagas."
7. Kangelt means "young man."
8. Wia Kut, personal communication, 31 March 2010, as translated by Thomas Las.

Chapter 3

1. "Hunta mull" is the way Maggie spelled the name of the original creation being who is believed to live up at Mount Mugl (Mt. Bul) and to have provided people with "spiritual guidance." Thomas Las spelled his name to me as "Aundige Mugl Timbil." Aundige (Hunta) is the name of the mountain range and Mugl (Mull) is the name of the particular mountain in that range where the creation being lives. Here the women were singing about digging up and carrying away Aundige Mugl Timbil's rock (i.e., the gold at the Leahy mine at Kuta), Thomas Las, personal communication, 9 April 2010.
2. Andrew Strathern (1979: xv) defines *moka* as "a major integrative preoccupation of the Hagen people. It is a form of exchange…by which individuals and groups are both bound together and compete for prestige and influence." For a detailed ethnographic account of this ceremonial exchange system, see A. Strathern (1971).
3. *Omak* are made of small bamboo sticks linked together to form a neck piece. They are worn around the neck with the bamboo sticks resting on the chest. Each bamboo stick is said to represent eight exchange transactions, thus the *omak* would grow in length over a man's lifetime in accordance with his success in ceremonial exchanges. The *omak* does not represent a man's personal accumulated wealth, but his strength and power in exchange transactions. As Marilyn Strathern (1972: 136) notes, "It is the ability to draw valuables to oneself which makes one wealthy, and these include shells as well as pigs."
4. Spellings for tribal names are not fixed. Moki is often spelled "Mogei" and "Penambi" is sometimes found as "Penambe" in both popular and anthropological sources.

Chapter 4

1. Wia Wai worked as a carrier for thirteen months on a large Administration Patrol led by James Taylor in 1938 (Connolly and Anderson 1987: 172).
2. A slightly different version of this song is included in Connolly and Anderson (1987: 173). The filmmakers were introduced to Wai by Maggie and recorded his story for their film *First Contact*.
3. Koina attended Maggie's funeral and shared with me some of her memories of Maggie. She lived long enough to attend the wedding of Maggie's daughter Nadia in January 2013 before passing away later that year.
4. Joe Leahy, personal communication, 14 April 2010.
5. Joe Leahy, personal communication, 14 April 2010.

Chapter 5

1. According to O'Hanlon (1989: 67), in the Western Highlands people refer to "that which is concealed (whether betrayal, anger or grudges) as being twisted, narrow knotted. Twisting and knotting are more generally associated with death-dealing powers.... In contrast, the revelation of a grievance, the bringing of it into public, may be spoken of as an unknotting."

2. Kundul translates as "white" or "light-skinned."

3. While *omak* are worn by men, in the past a girl might be adorned with an *omak* made by the groom upon marriage to signify how many valuables he gave for her in bridewealth (M. Strathern 1972: 150, citing Vicedom & Tischner 1943). Later, a woman might wear her husband's *omak* to signify the transactions he has made with her kin through her (M. Strathern 1972: 150).

4. "White woman" (*amp* means "woman"; *kundul* means "white")

5. Tali, personal communication, 17 September 2009 at Palimbri Village. Tali spoke in Temboka and my taped interview was later translated into English by Maggie's brother Thomas Las. What I have included here is a summary based on Thomas's translation of Tali's account.

Chapter 6

1. Vunapope Catholic Mission was established near Kokopo, East New Britain Province, by French Missionaries of the Sacred Heart (MSC) during the late 1880s. The first sisters of our Lady of the Sacred Heart arrived in 1885. In 1898, the Vunapope Catholic Mission opened a school especially for "mixed-race" children (Volker 2017: 174).

2. During the Australian administration of the then Territory of Papua New Guinea, there were two types of schools in the country—"A" schools (following the Australian curriculum and standards) and "T" schools (territory schools).

3. Rita Tul, pers.comm., 15 September 2009.

Chapter 7

1. Thomas Las, personal communication, 13 September 2009.
2. Kuipa, personal communication, 7 April 2010, as translated by Thomas Las.

Chapter 8

1 George Elmer Bernarding, SVD (Society of the Devine Word), was born on 5 February 1912 in Carrick, PA, USA. He was appointed Vicar Apostolic of Mount Hagen in 1959. In 1966 he was appointed Bishop of Mount Hagen and in 1982 he was appointed Archbishop. He died on 21 December 1987.

2. Joe Leahy, pers. comm, 14 April 2010.

3. Sir Julius Chan was Prime Minister of Papua New Guinea from 1980 to 1982 and 1994 to 1997. He won the seat for New Ireland Province in the 2007 national election.

4. Clem Leahy, personal communication, 15 September 2009.
5. Gerry Leahy, personal communication, 17 September 2009.
6. Nancy Leahy, personal communication, 14 September 2009.
7. Margaret Duckworth, personal communication, 17 January 2011.
8. George Leahy, personal communication, 17 January 2011.

Chapter 10

1. Nancy Leahy, personal communication, September 2009.
2. Joe Leahy, personal communication, 14 April 2010.
3. Rhona Leahy, personal communication, 30 April 2010.
4. Lois Logan, personal communication, 6 October 2009.

Chapter 11

1. The Australia and New Zealand Banking Group.
2. Bernadine Danomira, personal communication, 9 January 2011.
3. Joe Mek Tiene later became the member for the Kundiawa-Gembogl District in the Simbu Province of Papua New Guinea. He passed away on 25 April 2011. Enga Governor and leader of the People's Party Hon. Peter Ipatas described him as "a visionary leader" who "lived for his people" and was "widely respected in the Highlands" (http://www.peoplesparty.org.pg, accessed 22 December 2012).
4. Australian Agency for International Development.

Chapter 12

1. Public Motor Vehicle
2. Thomas Pora, personal communication, 16 April 2010, as translated by Thomas Las.

Chapter 13

1. CUSO (Canadian University Service Overseas) is a development organization that works through volunteers. It was founded at McGill University in Montreal in 1961. In 2011 it merged with several other organizations to become CUSO International.
2. Meg Taylor is the daughter of Yerima, a Hagen woman, and Jim Taylor, one of the first white men to explore the highlands with Maggie's uncles—the Leahy brothers. She received her Law degree from Melbourne University and practiced law in PNG. From 1989 to 1994, she was Ambassador of PNG to the United States, Mexico and Canada in Washington, D.C. She was made a Dame Commander of the Order of the British Empire in 2002. She served as Vice President, Compliance Adviser Ombudsman for the International Finance Corporation (IFC) and the Multilateral Investment Guarantee Agency (MIGA), World Bank Group. In 2014 she was appointed Secretary General to the Pacific Islands Forum based in Suva Fiji.
3. Keith Wilson, personal communication, 19 September 2009.
4. Bernadine Danomira, personal communication, 10 January 2011.

Chapter 14

1. Scientific name: *coix lacryma-jobi.*
2. Scientific name: *goura victoria.*

Chapter 15

1. Proper names, or autonyms, stress individuality and imply a distinction between "self" and "other," as Levi-Strauss (1966: 192) pointed out in *The Savage Mind*. In contrast, the adoption of reciprocal food names downplays such distinctions. Food names are "relational" terms that erase the boundary between self and other.
2. *Kewa* means "foreign."
3. Maki Wilson, personal communication, 7 August 2009.

Chapter 16

1. Tara Monahan, born Joyce Higginbotham, came to Papua New Guinea from Australia as a child with her parents. She spent over forty years in PNG and was well known and

respected for the contributions she made to the country as an explorer, mountain climber, interpreter, pilot, naturalist, wildlife advocate, museum curator and collector. She was the first white woman to climb Mt. Wilhelm and the first ever to climb Mt. Otto. With just two carriers and her two Australian terriers named Tosca and Nini, she was the first person to make an expedition between the Fly and the Sepik Rivers, walking 400 miles. She was one of the founding directors of the J.K. McCarthy Museum in Goroka. After she suffered a serious car accident in 1987, Maggie invited her to recover in Kunguma Village and employed her as a tour organizer and manager at Haus Poroman Lodge, where she oversaw the creation of the gardens and constructed and maintained a wildlife sanctuary. Tara died on 2 December 1990 at Haus Poroman Lodge.

2. Nadia Wilson, personal communication, 20 March 2010.

Chapter 17

1. See Fungke Samana (1987) for an account of the rise and decline of the NCW (http://nzetc.victoria.ac.nz/tm/scholarly/tei-GriWom2-c2-6.html).

2. Lois Logan, personal communication, 6 October 2009.

3. The general elections of 1982 were only the second since PNG Independence but the fifth since universal adult suffrage was introduced in 1964. According to Premdas and Steeves (1983: 992), "There has been a steady and progressive increase in the number of candidates contending for public office. While only 298 candidates contested in the 54-member 1964 colonial house, in the 1982 contest for the 109-member independent Parliament, an astounding 1,125 candidates entered the electoral fray."

4. *Parabel tok* (also called *tok bokis* in Tok Pisin) refers to a style of speech where the orator uses particular metaphors that are generally familiar to cultural insiders, but may also disguise meaning. For this reason it has also been called "veiled speech" (A. Strathern 1975).

5. Paias Wingti is a member of the Jiga tribe from the Western Highlands of PNG. He served as the third Prime Minister of Papua New Guinea between 1985 and 1988 and became Prime Minister again from 1992 to 1994. Wingti served as the governor of Western Highlands Province from 1995 to 1997, when he was defeated for re-election by Father Robert Lak. He defeated Lak in 2002, regaining the governorship. He was defeated in the 2007 election but was elected again in 2012 and then subsequently served as elected Governor of the Western Highlands.

6. Lois Logan, personal communication, 6 October 2009.

7. Lois Logan, personal communication, 6 October 2009.

8. Gerry Leahy, personal communication, 17 September 2009.

9. Gerry Leahy, personal communication, 17 September 2009.

10. Bartholomew Philemon (b. 16 April 1945) was elected to PNG National Parliament in the 1992 general election and held his seat for twenty years. In 2007 Philemon founded his own New Generation Party and became a leading figure of the Opposition. In August 2011, when Peter O'Neill formed a majority in Parliament and took power from Sir Michael Somare, Philemon was appointed Minister for Public Service and Sport. However, he lost his seat in the 2012 general election.

11. Sir Mekere Morauta (b. 12 June 1946) served as the sixth Prime Minister of PNG (1999–2002) and then as leader of the Opposition. He left the Parliament in June 2012.

12. George Leahy, personal communication, 17 January 2011.

13. See May et. al. (2013) for further analysis of the 2007 election. See Rumsey (1999) for an analysis of earlier election voting and violence.

14. Margaret Duckworth, personal communication, 17 January 2011.

15. Councilor John Kawa, personal communication, 16 September 2009.

16. Maryanne Tokeme-Amu, personal communication, 8 May 2010.

Chapter 18

1. Filmmaker Chris Owen was the Director of the PNG National Film Institute. He spent nearly forty years in Papua New Guinea making films, including such ethnographic films as *Man without Pigs* (1990), *Bridewealth for a Goddess* (2000), *The Red Bowmen* (1978), *Malangan Labadama* (1980), *Gogodala: A Cultural Revival?* (1976) and *Betelnut Bisnis* (2004). Owen was made an "Officer of the Order of Logohu" (OL) by the PNG government for "service to the community through his significant contribution over 37 years in the documentation in films of PNG's rich cultural diversity and the social participation in the different levels of the country's traditional and modern values."

2. Goroka architect Paul Frame established the Skul Bilong Wokim Piksa in 1980 (Sullivan 2003: 381).

3. Until 2008, EM-TV was PNG's only free-to-air television station. The station commenced broadcasting in July 1987 in Port Moresby, opening a relay station in Mount Hagen in 1988.

4. Tilkil Kuan Productions Pty. Ltd. was established in 1987. It was deregistered on 21 November 1996.

5. Maggie spells her name Tilgil elsewhere; phonologically there is no distinction between /k/ and /g/ in her language, Temboka.

6. Gerry Leahy, personal communication, 17 September 2009.

7. The song was composed by Maggie, Poning, Pen and Tress with input from Maggie's cousin Noah.

8. Joe Leahy, personal communication, 30 January 2000.

9. Ganiga Korowa Tuga, personal communication, 26 January 2000, as translated by Maggie Wilson.

10. Bob Connolly, personal communication, 13 September 2009.

11. Bob Connolly, personal communication, 13 September 2009. For a more detailed written account of these events, see Connolly (2005: 130–234; 284–292).

12. Gerry Leahy, personal communication, 17 September 2009.

Chapter 19

1. Maggie's manuscript for this book included a chapter headed "Haus Poroman Lodge." She clearly planned to write something about the lodge, but she never managed to do so. I have based this chapter on my visits to Kunguma Village in 2000 and 2001, while the lodge was still in operation, and on later interviews with Maggie's family and friends.

2. Liz Wright was a partner in lodge business.

3. Bernadine Danomira, personal communication, 10 January 2011.

4. Denis Doyle, personal communication, 10 January 2011.

5. The PNG LNG (Liquefied Natural Gas) Project is an Exxon Mobil development in the Southern Highlands, Hela, Western, Gulf and Central Provinces of Papua New Guinea, involving over 700 kilometers of pipelines connecting the facilities, including a gas conditioning plant in Hides and liquefaction and storage facilities near Port Moresby.

6. Thomas Las, personal communication, 13 September 2009.

7. Margaret Duckworth, personal communication, 17 January 2011.

8. Bernadine Danomira, personal communication, 10 January 2011.

9. Bernadine Danomira, personal communication, 13 January 2011.

Chapter 20

1. McCollum (1999: 168–171) includes reference to Maggie in her book.

2. It is customary to give a gift to the mourners on the deceased mother's side. Today

people call it "bus fare" in recognition that people leave their homes, jobs and gardens to travel to the *haus krai*.

    3. See M. Strathern (1972: 173–182) for an account of beliefs about "poison" among Hageners.

    4. See O'Hanlon (1989) on the concept of betrayal in the Western Highlands, Rumsey (2008) and Strathern and Stewart (1998) on the practice of confession, and Rumsey (2013) on deception.

    5. O'Hanlon (1989: 63–64) discusses beliefs in the Western Highlands about the causes of illness following betrayal. He writes, "The damage caused is not in Whagi thinking restricted to the deaths of those betrayed. Instead, a whole series of misfortunes—sickness, stunted appearance, infertility, death—within the group of which the victim's said betrayer(s) are members, may be attributed to a single betrayal. The moving force here is generally thought to be the ghost of the betrayed."

Chapter 21

    1. Bowie (2004).
    2. Taussig (1999).
    3. Bernadine Danomira, personal communication, 17 June 2010, via telephone.
    4. Thomas Pora, personal communication, 16 April 2010, as translated by Thomas Las.
    5. See Rumsey (2008) and Strathern and Stewart (1998) on this practice.
    6. Bernadine Danomira, personal communication, 13 January 2011.
    7. Bernadine Danomira, personal communication, 13 January 2011.
    8. Hageners refer to their father's brothers as father.
    9. For an account of the brideprice and wedding, see Henry and Vávrová (2016).
    10. Mawa Pil, an Ulga woman married into Maggie's subclan, the Wia Ulgamp Komp, composed this song. I first heard it at a performance by women from Kunguma and Knep villages seven years after Maggie died. The women had dressed a group of Australian students I took there on a field trip, funded under the Australian Department of Foreign Affairs and Trade (DFAT) New Colombo Plan, in *bilas* (traditional body decoration). When the women danced to this song, it visibly reduced many of the spectators to tears.

References

Ashton, Christopher (1978). "The Leahy Family." In J. Griffin (Ed.), *Papua New Guinea Portraits: The Expatriate Experience* (169–193). Canberra, Australia: ANU Press.
Bowie, Fiona (2004). "Adoption and the Circulation of Children: A Comparative Perspective." In F. Bowie (Ed.), *Cross Cultural Approaches to Adoption* (3–20). London: Routledge.
Commonwealth-Pacific Islands Forum Election Assessment Team (2007). *Papua New Guinea National Election, June–August 2007.* Report.
Connolly, Bob (2005). *Making "Black Harvest": Warfare, Film-Making and Living Dangerously in the Highlands of Papua New Guinea.* Sydney, Australia: ABC Books.
Connolly, Bob, and Robin Anderson (1987). *First Contact.* New York: Viking Penguin.
Demian, Melissa (2004). "Transactions in Rights, Transactions in Children: A View of Adoption from Papua New Guinea." In F. Bowie (Ed.), *Cross Cultural Approaches to Adoption* (97–110). London: Routledge.
Dickson-Waiko, Anne (2013). "Women, Nation and Decolonisation in Papua New Guinea." *The Journal of Pacific History, 48*(2): 177–193. doi: 10.1080/00223344.2013.802844
Fowke, John (1995). *Kundi Dan: Dan Leahy's Life Among the Highlanders of Papua New Guinea.* St. Lucia, Australia: Queensland University Press.
Fungke, Samana (1987). "Establishing a National Machinery for Women's Development in Papua New Guinea." In V. Griffin (Ed.), *Development and Empowerment: A Pacific Feminist Perspective: Report of a Pacific Women's Workshop. Naboutini, Fiji. 23–26 March 1987* 45–50). Kuala Lumpur, Malaysia: Asia and Pacific Development Centre.
Gubrium, Jaber F., and James Holstein (2008). "Narrative Ethnography." In S. N. Hesse-Biber, and P. Leavy (Eds.), *Handbook of Emergent Methods* (241–64). New York: The Guilford Press.
Hays, Terence E. (1994). "The Mi-Culture of the Mount Hagen People, Papua New Guinea / Book Review." *American Ethnologist, 21*(4): 1020–21.
Henry, Rosita (2005). "'Smoke in the Hills, Gunfire in the Valley': War and Peace in the Western Highlands, Papua New Guinea." *Oceania, 75*(4): 431–443.
Henry, Rosita (2012). "Gifts of Grief: Performative Ethnography and the Revelatory Potential of Emotion." *Qualitative Research, 12*(5): 528–39.
Henry, Rosita (2012). *Performing Place, Practicing Memory: Indigenous Australians, Hippies and the State.* Oxford, England: Berghahn Books.
Henry, Rosita (2013). "Being and Belonging: Exchange, Value, and Land Ownership in the Western Highlands of Papua New Guinea." In A. Aikhenvald, and R. M. W. Dixon (Eds.), *Possession and Ownership* (274–290). Oxford, England: Oxford University Press.
Henry, Rosita, and Daniela Vávrová (2016). "An Extraordinary Wedding." *Anthrovision, 4*(1). doi: 10.4000/anthrovision.2237
Herzfeld, Michael (1997). *Portrait of a Greek Imagination: An Ethnographic Biography of Andreas Nenedakis.* Chicago, IL: The University of Chicago Press.

References

King, Peter (1989). "Parties and Outcomes in the 1982 Elections." In P. King (Ed.), "Pangu Returns to Power: The 1982 Elections in Papua New Guinea," *Political and Social Change Monograph 9*: 1–26. Canberra, Australia: Australian National University.

Kruczek, Zdzislaw (2007). "Abridged Description of Mt. Hagen Archdiocese in Papua New Guinea." *Melanesian Journal of Theology*, 23(2): 43–56.

Leahy, Michael J., and Maurice Crain (1937). *The Land That Time Forgot: Adventures and Discoveries in New Guinea*. London, England: Hurst & Blackett.

Maisonneuve, Gisele (2006). "The Women's Movement in Papua New Guinea as a Vehicle to Enhance Women's Participation in Development." *Contemporary PNG Studies: DWU Research Journal*, 4: 10–30.

May, R. J., Ray Anere, Nicole Haley, and Katherine Wheen (Eds.) (2013). *Election 2007: The Shift to Limited Preferential Voting in Papua New Guinea*. Canberra, Australia: ANU Press. Retrieved from: http://press.anu.edu.au?p=241561.

May, Ron (2006). "Political Parties in Papua New Guinea." In R. Rich, L. Hambly, and M. G. Morgan (Eds.), *Political Parties in the Pacific Islands* (83–103). Canberra, Australia: Pandanus Books.

McCollum, Audrey (1999). *Two Women, Two Worlds: Friendship Swept by the Winds of Change*. Etna, NH: Hillwinds Press.

Mennis, Mary R. (1982). *Hagen Saga: The Story of Father William Ross, First American Missionary to Papua New Guinea, with Notes and Articles by Father Ross*. Port Moresby, Papua New Guinea: Institute of Papua New Guinea Studies.

Merlan, Francesca, and Alan Rumsey (1991). *Ku Waru: Language and Segmentary Politics in the Western Nebilyer Valley, Papua New Guinea*. Cambridge, England: Cambridge University Press.

Mount Hagen Town Authority (n.d., c. 1990). *People and Places of Mount Hagen*. Mount Hagen, Papua New Guinea: Mount Hagen Town Authority.

O'Hanlon, Michael (1989). *Reading the Skin: Adornment, Display and Society Among the Wahgi*. London, England: The Trustees of the British Museum.

Premdas, Ralph R., and Jeffrey S. Steeves (1983). "National Elections in Papua New Guinea: The Return of Pangu to Power." *Asian Survey*, 23(8): 991–1006.

Rumsey, Alan (1999). "Social Segmentation, Voting, and Violence in Papua New Guinea." *The Contemporary Pacific*, 11(2): 305–333.

Rumsey, Alan (2008). "Confession, Anger and Cross-Cultural Articulation in Papua New Guinea." *Anthropological Quarterly*, 81(2): 455–472.

Rumsey, Alan (2013). "Intersubjectivity, Deception and the 'Opacity of Other Minds': Perspectives from Highland New Guinea and Beyond." *Language and Communication*, 33(3): 326–343.

Simpson, Colin (1962). *Plumes and Arrows: Inside New Guinea*. Sydney, Australia: Angus and Robertson.

Strathern, A., and P. J. Steward (1998). "The Embodiment of Responsibility: 'Confession' and 'Compensation' in Mount Hagen, Papua New Guinea." *Pacific Studies*, 21: 43–64.

Strathern, Andrew (1971). *The Rope of Moka: Big-men and Ceremonial Exchange in Mount Hagen, New Guinea*. Cambridge, England: Cambridge University Press.

Strathern, Andrew (1972). *One Father, One Blood: Descent and Group Structure Among the Melpa People*. Canberra: Australian National University Press.

Strathern, Andrew (1975). "Veiled Speech in Mount Hagen." In M. Bloch (Ed.), *Political Language and Oratory in Traditional Societies* (185–203). London, England: Academic Press.

Strathern, Andrew (1989). "Melpa Dream Interpretation and the Concept of Hidden Truth." *Ethnology*, 28(4): 301–315.

Strathern, Marilyn (1972). *Women in Between: Female Roles in a Male World, Mt. Hagen, New Guinea*. London, England: Seminar Press.

References

Strauss, Hermann (1990). "The Mi-Culture of the Mount Hagen People." *Ethnology Monographs*, 13. Pittsburgh, PA: University of Pittsburgh.

Sullivan, Nancy (2003). "Television and Video Production in Papua New Guinea: How Media Become the Message." In T. Miller (Ed.), *Television: Critical Concepts in Media and Cultural Studies*, Vol. 1, Part 3 (369–391). London, England: Routledge.

Taussig, Michael T. (1999). *Defacement: Public Secrecy and the Labor of the Negative*. Stanford, CA: Stanford University Press.

Volker, Craig Alan (2017). "The Legacy of the German Language in Papua New Guinea." In M. Klaus (Ed.), *The Cultural Legacy of German Colonial Rule* (167–191). Berlin, Germany: De Gruyter.

Wilson, Maggie (1987). "Beer and Shotguns—Is This Development?" In S. Stratigos, and P. J. Hughes (Eds.), *The Ethics of Development: Women as Unequal Partners in Development* (173–177). Port Moresby, Papua New Guinea: University of Papua New Guinea.

Index

Abaijah, Josephine 132, 136
adoption 81, 83, 113, 119, 122, 123–124, 179–180
Anderson, Robin 36, 142, 146, 149, 150, 197*ch2n2*
Aripe, Thomas ix, 153
Ateliers Varan 142, 143
Australian International Aid Agency (AusAid) 91, 92, 147
Australian Labor Party 138, 139
Australian National University 5, 13, 77

Bernarding, Bishop, 54, 63, 68, 83, 84, 85, 97, 199*ch8n1*
bilas (body decoration) 58, 151
bilum (net bag) 9, 10, 11, 41, 49, 79, 86, 108, 140, 146, 147, 165, 172, 173
Black Harvest 3, 146, 150, 155
body decoration see *bilas*
bosboi (white man's offsider) 26, 36, 37
brideprice 10, 14, 21, 43, 45–46, 47, 78, 97, 100, 180, 186, 193, 194–195, 197*ch1n4*, 203*ch21n9*

Cairns 51, 66, 70, 71, 72, 74, 76, 77, 78, 93, 94, 115, 131, 138, 139, 140, 156, 166, 169, 170, 180, 193
cassowary 19, 34
Cherbelis, Raz 126, 158
Chimbu 7, 33, 49, 50, 64, 65, 95
Cholai, David 158
compensation 23, 25, 28, 48, 150, 160, 165, 184–185, 193
conception 13
confession 177, 193, 203*ch20n4*
Connolly, Bob ix, 36, 146, 149, 150–152, 161, 180, 181, 182, 183, 197*ch2n2*, 190*ch4n2*

Danomira, Bernadine ix, 3, 44, 81, 82, 83–92, 93, 97, 100–102, 107, 108, 110, 113, 122, 124, 125, 126, 127, 133, 157–158, 163, 166, 169– 170, 174, 182, 183, 184–185, 186, 187, 188, 192, 193–194, 195
Danomira, Kanawi ix, 2, 53, 63, 84, 91, 92, 162, 163, 166, 167, 168, 170, 173, 175, 181, 183, 191, 196
Divine Word University 122, 123, 126
Doyle, Denis ix, 102, 103, 110, 158–159, 163, 167, 168, 172
dreams 185–186
Duckworth, Margaret 65, 66, 67–68, 71, 138–139, 165–166

elections 112, 127–128, 132–141, 164, 166, 167, 169, 173, 183, 184, 186, 187, 194, 199*ch8n3*, 201*ch17n3*, 201*ch17n5*, 201*ch17n10*, 201*ch17n13*
Elti Penambi 15–16, 19, 20, 27, 31
EM-TV (television station) 143, 144, 146, 202*ch18n3*
Enga Province 34, 49, 126, 140, 141, 182
ethnographic biography 7–8

filmmaking 120, 142–146, 149–152
First Contact (film) 36, 119, 142, 155, 163, 198*ch4n2*
Foley, Kerry 82, 85, 93, 97
funeral 3, 15, 16, 40, 42, 48, 84, 85, 169, 171, 172, 173, 180, 184, 189, 193, 198*ch4n3*

Ganiga (tribe) 114, 146, 149, 150, 161
Ganiga Korowa Tuga 150
Golski, Nadya 108, 145
grass skirt see *purpur*

Hagen see Mount Hagen
Hagen Open (electorate) 132, 133, 137, 138
Hageners (Hagen people) 7, 14, 22–23, 25, 134, 153, 176, 177, 181, 186, 197*ch1n1*, 198*ch3n2*, 203*ch20n3*
Hailans Nuis (Newspaper) 95, 130, 133

Index

haus krai (mourning) 169–177, 183, 184, 193, 203*ch*20*n*2
haus lain (patrilineage) 10, 151, 167, 171, 173, 176, 177, 182, 185, 186, 188, 193
haus man see *haus lain*
Haus Poroman Lodge 6, 12, 14, 40, 96, 102, 111, 125–126, 150–152, 153–169, 201*ch*16*n*1, 202*ch*19*n*1
Herberton 3, 70, 74
Hertzfeld, Michael 7–8
Hotel Poroman 62, 95, 110–111, 162–163, 169, 173, 175, 177, 180

James Cook University ix, 91–92
Japanese International Cooperation Agency (JICA) 14, 125, 156
Jara, Melka Amp 9–12, 14, 16, 37, 41, 43, 46, 57, 83, 86, 87, 163, 186, 197*ch*2*n*1
Jara Clothing (shop) 89, 94, 99
Jiga (tribe) 16, 31, 36, 69, 88, 201*ch*17*n*5
Joe Leahy's Neighbours 3, 80, 146, 155

Kailge (place) 114, 116, 117
Kauga, Barbara ix, 177
kaukau (sweet potato) 17, 21, 87, 120, 153, 189
Kawa, Councilor John x, 43, 53, 104, 127, 139, 159, 164, 167, 176, 181, 182, 184, 188, 189, 191, 193
kiap (colonial government officer) 26, 27, 35, 82
Kidu, Dame Carol 136
Kilima Plantation 38, 146, 150, 188
kina (money) 47, 61, 78, 84, 97, 108, 132, 161, 164, 176, 177, 184, 185, 192, 195
kina (shell) 26, 34, 41, 78
Knep (place) 5, 14, 59, 88, 104, 158, 174, 186, 196, 203*ch*21*n*10
Kolta, Agnes 129, 131, 132
Kopi (tribe) 16, 31, 55, 116, 118, 161
Korgua (place) 5, 37, 54, 55, 56, 59, 60, 61, 62, 63, 65, 66, 67, 68, 79, 90, 150, 186
Kuan, Wia 9–14, 16, 17, 24, 37, 41, 42, 44, 90, 143, 179, 180, 186, 195, 197*ch*2*n*1
Kugulwe (place) 5, 20, 90, 186, 188
Kuipa, Wia x, 43, 54, 55, 57, 58, 59, 90, 95, 104, 119, 122, 123, 124, 176
kukboi (white man's cook) 36–37
Kulga (tribe) 150, 152, 166
kumu (edible green leaves) 39, 42, 153, 171, 189, 191
kunai grass 14, 54, 155
Kunguma Village 3, 5, 6, 14, 53, 56, 57, 59, 63, 86, 115, 119, 122, 146, 150, 158, 166
Kunguma Women's Self-Help Group 147, 192
Kut, Noki 150, 186, 187
Kut, Wia 16, 17, 18, 19–21, 22, 41, 182, 186, 195, 197*ch*2*n*5

Kuta (place) 5, 7, 9, 17, 18, 22, 24, 25, 27, 30, 31, 32–37, 46, 55, 57, 60, 63, 69, 79, 97, 118, 119, 197*ch*1*n*3, 198*ch*3*n*1
Kuta Community School 113, 171

Las, Thomas ix, 16, 17, 18, 19–22, 43, 56–57, 58, 105, 119, 163–165, 176, 182–183, 186, 188, 189, 198*ch*3*n*1, 199*ch*5*n*5
Leahy, Agnes 55, 61–62, 81, 87, 98
Leahy, Annette 97, 119, 125, 153
Leahy, Bernie 67, 97
Leahy, Bryan 65, 71, 182
Leahy, Clem x, 36, 55, 61, 63–65, 81, 85, 87, 98, 112, 115, 116, 142, 153, 182, 191
Leahy, Daniel 9, 13, 25, 27, 32, 36–37, 44–45, 51, 54, 55, 56, 60–61, 62–65, 66, 68–69, 70, 71, 72, 79, 80, 81, 83, 134, 153
Leahy, George x, 62, 68–69, 102, 134, 137–138
Leahy, Gerry x, 8, 55, 61, 65–66, 89, 119, 134–135, 136, 144, 152, 153, 161, 181
Leahy, James, Jr. 81, 137, 171, 173, 182
Leahy, James, Sr. 33, 69
Leahy, Joe x, 3, 30, 36–38, 55, 62–63, 64, 65, 80, 81, 82, 83, 87, 98, 100, 138, 142, 146, 149, 150, 161, 173, 176, 182, 183, 188
Leahy, Michael 9, 27, 32, 33, 34, 36–37, 55, 64
Leahy, Nancy x, 65, 66–68, 71, 81, 87, 119
Leahy, Patrick 9, 12, 32, 36–37, 60, 61, 62, 63, 69, 79, 81
Leahy, Rhona x, 81, 93, 87, 149
Logan, Lois ix, 82, 94–95, 130, 131, 133–134, 180, 181

Marauta, Sir Mekere 137
Marianville College 51, 52
marita (variety of *pandanus*) 39, 40
McCollum, Audrey 169–170
Mel, Michael 31
Melka 16, 17, 18, 32, 41, 176, 185, 189, 191, 197*ch*2*n*2
Melpa 7
Merlan, Francesca 19, 114, 116
mi (divinatory substance) 22–23
mit kont (pieces of pork) 182, 189, 190
Mogei (tribe) 15–16, 18, 22, 31, 45, 48, 50, 78, 143, 161
moka (ceremonial exchange) 27, 31, 89, 143, 198*ch*3*n*2
Moki see Mogei
Monahan, Tara 125, 151, 158, 200*ch*16*n*1
Morgan, Christopher 38, 146, 153
Mount Hagen (town) 2, 3, 4, 5, 6, 7, 13, 14, 20, 22, 30, 31, 34, 35, 36, 44, 45, 47, 48, 52, 54, 68, 98, 99, 125, 138, 145, 175
Mount St. Bernard College 3, 62, 70–72, 74, 91, 93

208

Index

mourning ritual see *haus krai*
Mugl Timbil (ancestral hero) 17, 30–31
mumu (earth oven; food cooked in earth oven) 17, 18, 39, 56, 59, 66, 81, 89, 104, 118, 139, 153, 182, 183, 189, 190, 191, 192, 193
muruk see cassowary

narrative ethnography 8
narrative practices 8
National Council of Women 129, 131
national elections see election
Nebilyer Valley 7, 13, 16, 22, 37, 40, 63, 79, 89, 90, 112, 114, 115, 137, 146, 150, 152, 153, 166, 186, 188
net bag see *bilum*
New Generation Party (political party) 137, 201*ch*17*n*10

omak 27, 41, 42, 108, 133, 198*ch*3*n*3
Organic Law on the Integrity of Political Parties and Candidates (OLIPPC) 136
outim sin see confession
Owen, Chris 142, 202*ch*18*n*1

paired groups 19, 20, 31, 174
Palimbri Village 44, 45, 46, 199*ch*5*n*5
patrilineage see *haus lain*
patrilineal descent 18
Penambi Wia (tribe) 3, 6, 10, 14, 15, 19, 31, 37, 46, 50, 55, 79–80, 114, 138, 142, 152, 161, 167, 173, 174, 179, 184, 185, 186, 188, 189, 191, 195, 198*ch*3*n*4; Wia Kundulamp 21, 22; Wia Maramp 21, 22, 174; Wia Penambimp 21, 22; Wia Ulgamp 20, 21, 22, 124, 161, 174, 185, 195
Penapil, Wia 16, 41, 195
Philemon, Bart 137
Pil, Mawa 203*ch*21*n*10
pitpit 12, 26, 42, 58, 153, 155
Pius, Tali x, 42, 43, 44–46, 47, 52, 60, 88, 93, 98, 100, 176
politics *see* women in politics
Pora, Elizabeth ix, 129, 130, 162–163, 189
Pora, Thomas x, 43, 88, 95, 164, 176, 189, 190
purpur (grass skirt) 48, 55, 108

Rebiamul Catholic Mission 12, 22, 46, 47, 54, 58, 59, 61, 85, 97, 98, 197*ch*1*n*2, 197*ch*1*n*3, 198*ch*2*n*6
reciprocal naming 115
Roche, Father Garrett ix, 22, 194
Rooney, Nahau 132
Ross, Father William 12, 46, 47, 48, 54, 197*ch*1*n*3, 198*ch*2*n*6
Rumsey, Alan x, 19, 114, 116, 117, 203*ch*20*n*4
Rusch, Rosemarie x, 169, 172, 173, 174, 175

sanguma 172, 173
Schneider, Almut x
singsing (public ceremonial ground; dance) 12, 18, 33, 55, 89, 107, 116, 132, 152, 154, 157, 163, 164, 170, 171, 172, 174, 176, 186, 189, 193, 194
Skul Bilong Wokim Piksa 142, 202*ch*18*n*2
sorcery see *sanguma*
Strathern, Andrew 7, 19, 22, 193, 198*ch*3*n*2, 201*ch*17*n*4
Strathern, Marilyn 14, 38, 194, 198*ch*3*n*3
Strauss, Hermann 19, 22–23
Sullivan, Nancy 144, 145
sweet potato see *kaukau*

tanim het (courtship ceremony) 38, 43–44, 45–46, 58, 80, 186
Tara see Monahan, Tara
Taylor, Meg 97, 200*ch*13*n*2
Temboka (language) 7, 19, 38, 57, 113, 199*ch*5*n*5, 202*ch*18*n*5
Tiene, Joe Mek 89, 200*ch*11*n*3
Tilkil Kuan Productions 143, 145, 202*ch*18*n*4
Tok Pisin 7, 14, 19, 38, 57, 113, 125, 155, 160, 176, 194, 201*ch*17*n*4
tok ples (the vernacular) 7, 17, 58, 60, 86, 90, 125, 129, 132, 167, 176, 195; see also Temboka
Tokeme-Amu, Maryanne x, 140–141
Trewenack, Grant 158
tribal fight 15–16, 27, 34, 126, 150, 164, 166, 183, 184
Tugl, Pora x, 95–96
Tugl, Wia 11, 15, 16, 41, 42–43, 44–45, 46, 47, 48, 54, 55, 57, 58, 78, 83, 88, 90, 97, 99, 164, 186, 195, 197*ch*2*n*1, 197*ch*2*n*2
Tul, Rita x, 16, 43, 52–53, 55, 56, 86, 88, 93–94, 100, 107, 123, 176, 181, 185, 186

Ulga (tribe) 16, 31, 166
University of Papua New Guinea 91

Vunapope 49–50, 51, 54, 56, 62, 64, 66, 199*ch*6*n*1

Wahgi Valley 16, 26
Wai, Wia 16, 34–35, 39, 59, 186, 195, 198*ch*4*n*1, 198*ch*4*n*2
wantok 95
Western Highlands Council of Women 30, 95, 129, 130, 131, 132
Wilson, Keith ix, 93, 96, 97–101, 102, 113, 117, 118, 122, 123, 157, 158, 159, 160, 161, 174, 180
Wilson, Maki ix, 101, 104, 106, 112–121, 122, 123, 124, 125, 146, 158, 170, 174, 185
Wilson, Nadia ix, 101, 104–105, 106, 107, 119,

209

122–128, 168, 170, 171, 174, 181, 185, 194, 195, 198*ch4n*3
Wilson, Olivia ix, 101, 102–111, 113, 122, 124, 158, 167, 168, 171, 174, 180, 181, 185, 189, 194, 195
Wilya (place) 20, 22
Wingti, Paias 133, 134

women in politics 138, 139, 140
Women's Association *see* Western Highlands Council of Women
Wright, Liz 158, 202*ch19n*2

Yak, David 162